D1326834

A MANIA FOR SENTENCES

A MANIA
FOR SENTENCES

D. J. Enright

DAVID R. GODINE · PUBLISHER · BOSTON

First U.S. edition published in 1985 by
DAVID R. GODINE, PUBLISHER, INC.
306 Dartmouth Street, Boston, Massachusetts 02116

LC 84-48300
ISBN 0-87923-549-7

First printing

Printed in the United States of America

Contents

Author's note

The essays collected here began life (they have grown or changed slightly since) as reviews of new publications or reprints. Hence as criticism, which is what reviews can be, they belong to the time-honoured genre (more recently dishonoured, it seems) which might be called 'practical'. That word, I assume, implies that, when it comes off, such criticism is of practical use to readers by describing, drawing out, comparing, concurring or quarrelling with the work it is discussing. (No one who reads can be called 'common', so we must now forgo that otherwise handy adjective; nor, for other reasons, dare we use it of critics.) Criticism of this kind does not seek to erect itself into a science or to pursue some solely autonomous business, but relates itself in an ancillary way to the grander functions of creative literature. If this suggests a narrow view of the critic's role – the nose firmly down to 'the words on the page' – we should remind ourselves that words are not lifeless black marks impressed on paper like squashed flies. (Of course all enterprising writing avails itself of a degree of what looks like independence from its subject, straying not away from it but around it.) Lawrence was not being all that humble when he remarked that 'literary criticism can be no more than a reasoned account of the feeling pro-duced upon the critic by the book he is criticizing.' The practical critic, the reviewer, may be a handmaiden (*ancilla*) or a cup-bearer, but he or she serves in a family of gods. Or sometimes of demons, and more often of clowns and cranks, from all of whom something can still be learnt.

As for language, it is a bad workman who blames his tools. And I would not be too prompt to talk about 'weasel words', their shiftiness and promiscuity. Words, it is true, are 'almost human': which is not surprising in view of the intimate relationship we sustain with them. At times they seem to do our thinking and feeling for us. But if there is trickery around, it is we who are the weasels as much as the victims, for the final power of choice rests with us. Words stand ever ready to inspire or deceive, but they do not force themselves upon our helpless tongues or pens.

It may be that the present writer suffers from the well-attested British cowardice in the face of literary theory, even in the face of what might modestly be reckoned one's own. And yet we expect literature to enact or intimate rather than declare, since only thus can nuance and reality be achieved, so shouldn't we allow a critic's 'principles' to reveal or half-reveal themselves in passing, in action, rather than have to be stated? To state something is to be stuck with it, with what Lawrence called the 'ugly imperialism' of absolutes, which at their extremes lead to liking virtually anything or disliking virtually everything: *un*critical, either way. Whether on literature or on linguistic phenomena, critical commentary ought surely to be more accessible, at any rate not (as it often is) less accessible, than what it is commenting on. It might also think of giving pleasure now and again – otherwise it is a poor advertisement for what it admires and an impotent antagonist of what it deplores.

My grateful acknowledgements are due to the editors of the journals in which much of the material appeared in its original form: *Encounter, The Listener, The London Review of Books, The New York Review of Books, The Observer, The Sunday Times* and *The Times Literary Supplement.*

– I –

DEMOCRACY OF GODS
A Life of Heine

We continue to hear that biography is the most esteemed, indeed the most popular, of literary forms nowadays. If this is true, then, first of all, it is a pity, since the novel – the form of literature which can wield the widest and strongest influence – ought to occupy that position. (Poetry may cut sharper, but one doesn't use a razor to chop down trees.) Secondly, if it is true, it is incredible. For biography is a highly dubious enterprise. Its author is concerned with, concerned to re-create, another person, a real (even if dead) one, of whom he is bound to know less than all and whom, with insufficient sure evidence to go on, he is bound to keep judging whether or not he intends or desires to. Dissatisfaction with the pious memorial class of biography, Great Sexless Lives and so forth, led (once the world was made safe) to all sorts of imaginative reconstructions or 'imitations' (a word suggested by Robert Lowell's 'free translations' of verse), sometimes entertaining, often impertinent. Girls Galore, and latterly Boys too. Perhaps one comforting thing about 'the truth' in this sense of the word is that you can only tell it when it doesn't matter, it can't do any harm: 'revelations' even turn out to be a latter-day form of piety. As for it bearing witness to a new, liberated and vivid interest in the ways of humanity – tell that to the vexed ghosts!

It was perhaps the suspicion that God alone knew the whole truth about a man and He was too busy to write it out which provoked the theory that biography should and would aspire towards the condition of fiction or poetry. Some years ago Richard Ellmann (whom we have to take seriously) asserted that we now 'ask of our biographers the same candour that our novelists have taught us to accept from them'. One hardly dare object to candour. But the candour of a novelist is something different in nature from the candour of a biographer. The novelist tells us frankly (this seems the sense of 'candour' intended here) about his

3

own inventions. And so he should: it is up to us to decide whether or not we want to listen. The biographer however is being candid about objective verities. Naturally the novelist's candour is intended to serve some general truth about mankind, but the biographer is talking about a specific, actual human being. The biographer is a historian, and we still expect historians to get things right, or at least aspire to: the real deserves a special respect. No doubt this respect is difficult to ensure – the historian wasn't there, whereas the novelist *is* there, in the middle of his creation – but difficulty is no excuse for confusing genres. One extreme to which the ostensibly liberalizing theory of biography has led is 'psychobiography', a practice which bears much the same relation to truth-telling as necrophilia does to love.

These remarks are not intended for Jeffrey L. Sammons's full and painstaking biography of Heine. Though he subtitles it 'A Modern Biography', he intends, he tells us at the outset, to avoid 'the derring-do of psychobiography', and he ventures the hope that the reader 'will accept more or less on faith my conviction that it is the works that make the life important, and that the purpose of literary biography is to be a handmaiden to a more informed and alert apprehension of the works'. That 'more or less on faith', though it follows on from Sammons's announcement that he will be 'characterizing' rather than interpreting Heine's writings, betrays a nervous recognition of the state of opinion on biography as outlined above. Taking it for granted that only men and women who have *done* something qualify for biographical treatment and that therefore a better understanding of the things done will be of the essence, an earlier generation of readers would not have needed such a plea for acceptance.

But Heine himself calls up another general thought about biography: the inclination in some biographers to grow ratty with their subjects. This, I take it, is a separate phenomenon from the mounting impatience often to be observed in doctoral theses, where the candidate simply wants to get away and lead his or her own life at last. Here, it appears as a resentment provoked by the subject's inconsistencies or irrationalities, his recalcitrance to pigeon-holing. What makes the subject interesting turns out to make him exasperating: he is dead but he won't lie pinned

4

down. It might be felt that such biographers ought to approach the condition of fiction sufficiently closely to read some of it – and then ask themselves this question: if in major novels a fictional character, made up freely by its unconstrained author, can be so complex, why should they expect a real person to be straightforward, transparent, comfortable to cope with? Reality is stranger – and untidier – than fiction can afford to be.

It is not always realized – or if realized, not sufficiently allowed for – just how 'unscrupulous' a writer can be in the pursuit of his vocation and obsession. I don't mean in the sense of listening at keyholes, turning friends into figures of fun, burning the baby's fingers to see exactly how it will react. Nor the sharp practices he may consider necessary to promote his own survival: those shabbinesses referred to by Heine on one occasion as 'often praiseworthy when they put us in a position to serve the great idea of our life the more worthily', but which Sammons describes as 'disconcerting to the biographer'. Rather, I have in mind the cool remorselessness with which the writer exploits everything in himself and everything that comes his way, by 'acting it out', sucking whatever can be sucked from it. After all, this is an aspect of the respectable faculty we call 'imagination'; and it is related to Keats's shrewd professional depiction of the chameleon poet who has no identity because he is 'continually filling some other body', who 'has no character' and is 'everything and nothing'. The process is less deliberate, less willed, than a general account must make it seem; less a conscious matter than Sammons's term 'the fictive persona' may suggest. One might say that, at such moments, the writer needs to be deceiving himself first of all. Deliberateness vitiates the process, and the individual who courts some grand personal distress in order to enhance his art through suffering is likely to procure nothing but personal distress. The protean capacities of every writer have their limits, narrow or broad: he can only make use of what touches on a nerve maybe hidden from his awareness but alive in him. To class him as an actor is less than apt, though to his biographers he may seem, alas, exactly that: in serious eyes, a hypocrite. The best biography of an artist, I incline to think, would take the form of a critical commentary on his work plus a *Who's Who* entry.

Heine is a prime irritant in this connection. Not only do his biographers regard him askance, or else askew, but they come close to hating one another as well. A maker of trouble for himself and his contemporaries, now he makes trouble for them. To confine oneself to the more manifest externalities of the man: he was a German who spent the greater part of his adult life in France; he was a Jew, a baptized Christian, and a free-thinker; 'a brilliant soldier in the war of liberation of humanity' (Matthew Arnold) and 'a modern Tannhäuser' loitering in the salons of the Venusberg (Engels); an egalitarian and an intellectual aristocrat ('we are all brothers, but I am the big brother, and you are the little brothers, and I am entitled to a more substantial portion'); a lyricist and a satirist; highflown and piercingly raw; egregiously active and enormously invalid . . . In short, it has been suggested, a schizophrenic: for what the diagnosis is worth. True, if poetry comes out of the quarrel with ourselves, Heine was abnormally well endowed with selves to quarrel with.

But what hair-raising contradictions, what incongruities, what shabbinesses, will the biographer uncover once he penetrates below the surface? What hope can he entertain of establishing – the natural ambition of all who lay pen to paper – a 'pattern'? There is undeniably 'something peculiar' about the case of Heine. 'In moments of exhaustion,' Sammons confides, 'I sometimes wonder if there is not a strange curse lying on the topic.' It is not merely that Heine is surrounded by 'rough debate' (would it be fit and proper to name a new university in his home town of Düsseldorf after him?) or that he engages 'allegiances, prejudices, antipathies, and ideological commitments of all kinds'. It is worse than that, for he attracts extremists and crackpots and 'can generate the most eccentric styles, not only of public altercation, but sometimes of scholarly discourse'. It doesn't seem quite fair to visit the sins of the children upon the father, but all the same, in this case . . . Sammons then cites some unseemly incidents that have marred the calm and civility of scholarly conferences – one of them involving a Düsseldorf policeman of an artistic bent who took the platform by storm: quite Grassian, that – which may not produce the shock horror effect he anticipates.

Heine was an awkward cuss, given to saying a lot, and also given to saying nothing; and the latter habit has created greater hardships for the biographer even than the former. 'Over large and important areas his silence is downright deafening.' And hence, one supposes, his deafened biographers have been forced to shout loudly, and possibly incautiously, in their attempts to say 'what he would have said if he could have said what he meant'. (The proposal suggests that he was an unusual subject for biography: an inarticulate illiterate.) Stage-managing reality to suit himself, Heine created one 'Heine', and from Heine's 'Heine' the biographer must make 'yet another "Heine" devised for our own purposes and to suit our own notions of what we would like him to have been'. This process, Sammons remarks with immoderate temperateness, has shown signs of getting out of control, and he warns or assures us that 'my own purpose cannot be to present the "true Heine", for I do not know what that is'. In the event we perceive that behind this declaration of non-intent lies a decent and apposite modesty rather than an abject admission of incompetence. Happily, the adjective in Sammons's subtitle means nothing – or only that the book was published in 1979.

Heine's troublesomeness starts very early, with his date of birth. 1797 (as is generally accepted)? 1798? 1799? 1800? 1779? – no, obviously a slip of Heine's pen in applying for admission to the doctoral examination . . . 'If we were to recapitulate the problem in all its details, it would take him almost as long to get born as Tristram Shandy.' But why did he give different dates on different occasions? Was he concealing the fact that he was born out of wedlock? Did he deceive in order to dodge the draft? Seemingly no in both cases: he was born in wedlock, and he was too young anyway for the Napoleonic wars. Sammons thinks it possible that Heine actually didn't know when he was born: 'one's birthdate is not, after all, a datum of experience.' We shall have to rest content with the knowledge, beyond dispute, that he *was* born.

However, Sammons views the matter as an omen of wider import, presaging Heine's carelessness with the truth. 'He did not strike his contemporaries as a person of integrity, and it must be said in frankness that he cannot always appear so to his biographer today.' Integrity is a

7

point a biographer may properly concern himself with. One curious implication is that only those bodies interested to make a hero of revolutionary morality out of Heine have managed to find him a man of integrity – and this doesn't say much for either the ingenuity or the devotion of campaigners on the side of reactionary morality.

When we look into the question of Heine's Jewishness we encounter a similar disorderliness. As a young man, Sammons suggests, he 'did not feel very uncomfortable about his Jewishness'. (Ought he to have done? No, Sammons doesn't mean that.) Later he was to feel uncomfortable – uncomfort was his forte – but uncomfortable in his Heineishness rather than his Jewishness. I suspect he felt Jewish when he felt like feeling Jewish, or when it suited his purpose and, for instance, he could use Jewishness as a stick to beat something else with. His interest in the subject seems to have constituted one form of self-exploration and explanation (he was fascinated by himself) and, in the manner of all creative writers and particularly poets who more than others spin out of their own guts, of self-exploitation. He upheld Jews against brands of nationalism that discriminated against them, but when it came to denouncing bourgeois commercialism and philistinism he did not discriminate between Christians and Jews. In any case his inability to take religious sentiment seriously for long at a stretch would have inhibited any very profound Hebraism.

In politics also, for all his socialistic beliefs and busyness, he is equivocal, more obviously so than Brecht, evincing that final scepticism towards ideologies to be detected in the majority of intelligent people, poets or otherwise. His most effective satire is directed less at wealth or privilege or capitalism than at puritanical elements in the party of progress and the 'universal kitchen-equality' (as he put it in a letter of 1840) of grey, grudging proletarianism. Nor are such shafts discharged wholly in the spirit of 'whom the Lord loveth he chasteneth'. For him, the purpose of revolution was to bring about the lineaments of gratified desire. He spoke of fighting for 'the divine rights of humans' (*not* 'the human rights of the people'), for a democracy of equally blissful gods – a levelling-up of some magnitude – and answered the 'censorious reproaches' of the 'virtuous republicans' with Sir Toby's tag: so 'there shall be no more cakes and ale'? Though he became a notorious dissident and the object of Metternich's special attention, he insisted that 'the true poet is the true hero' while 'the true democrat writes like the people, sincerely, simply and badly'. Interestingly enough, in *Atta Troll* ('A Midsummer Night's Dream'), 1841, the bear personifying the radical poets is summed up in a phrase reminiscent in a contrary sense of Keats's passage on the chameleon poet: 'Kein Talent, doch ein Charakter!'

Sammons reports Heine's political skirmishing in slightly suffocating detail, possibly in order to avoid any hint of tendentious selectiveness. True, he was a great fighter – that is, bellicose by nature – and 'a brilliant soldier in the war of liberation of humanity', but he fought for a republic not of this world. He ran into that 'very modern dilemma' (as S. S. Prawer termed it some time ago) whereby intellectuals come to realize the likely effects on *them* and the things they hold dear of the cause they have been championing. While Marx seems to have preserved a degree of fondness for the 'old dog' (from whom he derived the famous analogy between religion and opium), after his death in 1856 Engels likened him – not altogether felicitously – to an earlier poet who incurred the tyrant's frown and then 'crawled up Augustus's rear'. The redoubtable radical journalist Ludwig Börne had earlier held much the same view, while expressing it more genteelly: Heine kept a set of mouseholes in his opinions, and if you tried to pin him down, he escaped through one hole and peeped out of another. To compound the offence, Heine has proved the cause of mouseholes in others, and it is typical of him and his phenomenon that since the Nazis could not possibly exclude his famous early poem 'Die Loreley' (so Germanic!) from their songbooks, they attributed it to 'author unknown'.

Professor Sammons may not know what the 'true Heine' is, but he knows what it isn't, and he comes out firmly against the 'scripting of soap-opera' that has afflicted much writing on the theme. He comments, amusedly rather than aggrievedly, that 'Heine's erotic life has been a great deal more frustrating to his critics and biographers than it probably was to him.' While one would have liked him to develop and support his summary verdict that Heine was 'a complex but not really a

profound writer' (cf. Günter Grass: 'In a devious way I'm uncomplicated'), he brings out well the element of 'play', as for instance in the
'camel problem' propounded by the poet. If the rich had more hope of
passing through that needle's eye, perhaps they would be less grasping
and hard of heart while on earth? Heine lent a helping hand towards this
desirable outcome by lampooning the friendly Rothschilds and simultaneously (as a deserving man of letters) extracting financial aid from
them. The protean are bound to want it at least both ways.

'Play' is not the right word, of course, hardly more so than 'devious-
ness' or 'duplicity'. Sammons uses the word 'multiplicity', implying an
honest acknowledgement of the real difficulty of his task, and he certainly adduces a multiplicity of evidence. Heine made poetry out of
politics – where others made poetry into politics. That proposition could
be repeated in other fields. His 'return' to religion following his physical
collapse in 1848 hardly took the edge off his tongue, since he could ask
God for the pleasure of seeing a few of his enemies dangling from the
trees outside his window. 'Yes, one must forgive one's enemies, but not
before they are hanged . . .' Earlier, and proteanly, he had written, 'I am
accused of having no religion. No, I have them all.' To observers not
wholly committed to a party line of one sort or another, it must be
reasonably clear what Heine's priorities were. 'Ultimately,' Sammons
concludes, 'Heine was of his own party.' Yes, and his party was poetry.

What we now need is some good criticism of Heine, a cogent exposition of what in Heine's work is worth knowing and why. And, if possible,
some translations more convincing than we have seen so far, and not
only of the romantic and lyrical verse.* Outside the scholarly conference
hall and the political arena ('Wherever books are burnt, in the end
people are burnt too') Heine must be one of the most misconstrued of
famous writers, taken in small arbitrary doses, and outside Germany
surely the most shadowy. Now that we know so much about his life,
perhaps we could get to know something about the works which make
that life important to us.

---

*A desideration admirably met by Alistair Elliot in *The Lazarus Poems* (1979), while a
respectful bow is due to Hal Draper for *The Complete Poems of Heinrich Heine* (1982), an
immensely brave undertaking, unequal in its execution.

THE STORY OF TWO SOULS
Goethe and the Manns

By Way of Goethe

This introductory note is an indulgence on the part of the author, who has already made one attempt to account for (and naturally to weaken) British resistance to German literary classics, to that 'qualité d'Allemand; I mean – how shall I put it? – a certain four-squareness, rhythmical heaviness, immobility, grossièreté', as the impresario Fitelberg manages to ·put it in *Doctor Faustus*.* Ostensibly an introduction to Thomas Mann, it may (besides marking the 150th anniversary of Goethe's death) even serve, indirectly, as such. That seeming four-squareness and immobility, at times even that *grossièreté*, is common to Goethe and Mann, and so is the 'boldness and esprit' which Fitelberg (who was actually talking about music) acknowledged, and so is much else.

As the eighty-two-year-old poet was dying, those present saw him tracing on his blanket a large W. Was it for his middle name, Wolfgang? Or was it, as others have surmised, for *Welt*, World? It could well have been for both, since Goethe was himself a world.

During his long and unceasingly working life he produced lyrics (apparently untranslatable in their simplicity), philosophical poems, plays, satires, travel books, novels, autobiographies, criticism and scientific treatises. He was not so much a man of letters as a literature; and later generations of German writers must have felt there was little for them to add beyond footnotes. More than that, it was he who by an unparalleled one-man effort dragged Germany into the intellectual forefront of the nineteenth century.

In our century and in this country his reputation has fallen sadly into

*See 'Aimez-vous Goethe?': an Enquiry into English Attitudes of Non-liking towards German Literature', *Conspirators and Poets*, 1966.

abeyance – possibly because we prefer our authors to confine themselves to provinces or parishes, so that we know what to expect from
them. It is true that Goethe was fond of the sound of his own mind, and
he didn't always distinguish (nor did his Boswells) between the perceptive and the pedantic, for he was interested in everything and had
something to say about most of it. I think that what is often missed,
especially in translations, is the tone of his voice, the humorous or ironic
inflections that modify the utterances of the Sage of Weimar including
Greater Germany (and for some time the Rest of the World). The
reader is aware of his wisdom, but takes insufficient account of the élan,
the intensities and the comedy that go with it. Hence we tend to find
stodgy or platitudinous (granted, Goethe had no objection to an occasional solid platitude) what may be mischievous or ambiguous. Much
the same is true of Thomas Mann: the question is which of them is the
better introduction to the other. Both were public figures, not a good
thing for a writer to be when the romantic idea of him as a slightly higher
species of drop-out still persists: Mann as the representative of the
'good Germany', Goethe as the representative of Germany. And
Goethe was the more diverse of the two, for where Mann researched, he
pioneered – in botany, biology, zoology, optics, mineralogy – besides
taking a lively interest in history, law and the arts, and an active part in
the administration of the grand (though fortunately small) duchy of
Weimar, where he lived from 1775 till his death. (Like Mann, he was
himself in some degree the 'Establishment' which he satirized.) It was
the large view of the world that he took, the largest possible one at the
time, looking for connections or inventing them, rejoicing in the spirit of
life in himself and, in the terms of Wordsworth's definition of the poet,
'delighting to contemplate similar volitions and passions as manifested
in the goings-on of the Universe'. It is impossible to name an English
writer or thinker with whom he can be compared. The nearest thing
would be a cross between Dr Johnson and Shakespeare with traces of
the nineteenth-century Romantics thrown in.

How disconcerting that could (and can) be is not hard to imagine!
Disconcerting even for Goethe himself . . . Having presented *The Sorrows of Young Werther* as a possible state of affairs, he found that it was

being taken as a desirable state of affairs and the young men of Europe were copying not only the hero's dress but also his suicide. As for *Wilhelm Meister's Apprenticeship*: studded with aphorisms and emblems, the book seems to throb with 'meaning', yet the author said of it, 'I should think a rich manifold life, brought close to our eyes, would be enough without any express tendency, which, after all, is only for the intellect.' *Only* for the intellect! Johnson declared 'Great thoughts are always general.' But characters and events in plays and novels need to be particular. And therein lies the weakness of Goethe's other novel, *Elective Affinities*: its events are signs and portents or (as we say with a grimace) symbols, while its characters too obviously stand for general types of humanity or states of mind and heart.

Elective Affinities is bound to strike us as artificial, programmatic and deliberately manipulated. When the married couple, Eduard and Charlotte, have a baby, it resembles the two other people they were thinking of at the time, and the good old parson dies of some symbolic shock to the religious system while baptizing it. Despite which, the novel is a work of considerable power and originality. In the process referred to in its title chemical elements can separate and remarry in different combinations with ease; but not so men and women. The story ends neither in old-fashioned renunciation nor in modern divorce, but in a stalemate resolved only in death, if then. Ottilie, the other woman, accidentally drowns the beloved baby and starves herself to death, re-emerging as a kind of saint with healing powers (not unlike Gretchen in *Faust*), while Eduard dies soon after and is buried by his wife beside Ottilie. The moral is thus 'open-ended', and the conclusion neither happy nor exactly tragic. Goethe said that his nature was too conciliating for tragedy, but here he found no way of reconciling passion and conscience – or, more accurately, love and love.

Even more unsatisfactory to those who don't like theology but prefer it straight will be the ending of *Faust*, whose protagonist evades hell through the combination of a legal technicality and the intercession of a good (and dead) woman's love. But the ambiguity sets in much earlier, and persists through the play's transitions – from an ageing don's discontent with his studies and his bank balance alike, by way of a rather shabby affair with a lower-class innocent, to financial shenanigans at the Imperial Court, a protracted idyll with Helen in Sparta (judging by the resulting offspring, both parties were thinking of Byron at the time), and a final career in German real estate. Such is a possible summary of the story: it mentions neither the passages of sublime poetry nor the shrewd hits and humour that occur *en route*. It also leaves out Mephistopheles, the one totally translatable element here, relatively immune (it would seem) to change in times and manners. Nor of course does it throw light on the fact that, impossible though *Faust* is, it is impossible to imagine European culture without it.

A notable stumbling-block for many readers is the episode towards the end when Faust, busy reclaiming land from the sea and 'opening space for millions', is responsible for the death of the old couple whose cottage is a thorn in his side. In this civic project he has needed the assistance of Mephistopheles – who, as the Lord remarked at the outset, 'excites and works and must, though devil, create' – and the devil will have his due, always striving to turn good into evil. Neither Goethe nor Faust (though he behaves like Henry II in the matter of Becket) condones the fate of the old couple, and it is not their fault that more recent events give the incident a darker dimension. When Goethe is sentimental, we turn away in disgust; when he is realistic (allowing the world what the world will take anyway), we grow indignant. He seeks unity within diversity, an ambition which affronts us somewhat; but then, and with his connivance, the diversity looms larger than the unity, and this in turn confuses us.

A more modest example of the author's versatility, or his shapelessness, is the *Roman Elegies*, a sequence of poems in classical distichs, in which a cultivated and vigorous German tourist, lightly disguised as Propertius, experiences several kinds of awakening. The *Elegies* used to be thought shocking, and two of them were long suppressed. While nowadays they will be found sexually innocuous, if a trifle male-chauvinistic, they still ought to shake the British myth of Goethe as the serene or pompous Olympian. In subject and tone they comprehend tenderness, sensuality, humour, the joys of classical art, ambience and history at the fingertips (followed by further exploration in bed with a mistress, called Faustina by the way), the all-too-human antics of the gods, the ferocity of Amor attached to his prey, the smug domesticity of a settled liaison (how pleasant to have a girl you can trust!). And also a discourse (unanticipated but not incongruous) on the treacherous worm in the grass of venereal disease; in David Luke's translation,

> Secretly there in the bushes he squirms, befouling the waters,
>   Slavering poison and death into Love's life-giving dew.

It is alarming or at the very least discomposing to find oneself plunged into such a rich mixture of matter and modes. And in this respect the *Roman Elegies* are characteristic. It appears that many-sidedness on the Goethean scale is no longer possible, and these days we are required to possess specialist qualifications. What the great German lacked was discretion: he failed to conceal his belief that the world was his oyster. As indeed it practically was.

The Brothers Mann

In this dual biography Nigel Hamilton has undertaken to do something so intimidating as to be virtually impossible; it is not surprising that he has not been entirely successful. When their subject has led a life long in years and rich in achievement, biographers (at any rate biographers of the more reputable kind) often end by losing the life-line under a mass of creases and folds. There is so much to tell, and it gets told whether or not it adds to our sense of the man: but if it doesn't add, it subtracts. Mr Hamilton has taken on two long parallel lives, and he deserves a medal for outstanding bravery in the face of heavy material odds.

Thomas Mann's life is pretty well covered, in English too: there are the monumental *Letters*, the early *Sketch of My Life* and the late *Genesis of a Novel*, the memoirs by Erika Mann and Katia Mann. But Heinrich's life, like his work, is practically unknown here, and Hamilton has done much to rectify this imbalance.

Rivalry between the two brothers evinced itself at an early stage: there is a trivial but bitter tale here about Heinrich's broken toy violin. The elder by four years, Heinrich soon rebelled against the prosperous materialism of mercantile Lübeck, and in the obvious way: he began to write, publishing his first poem at the age of nineteen in a 'radically modern' magazine dedicated to Zola and the new realism. This was in the very year, 1890, when the firm of J. S. Mann celebrated its centenary. Thomas started to write poetry too, and later published his first poem in the same magazine. In 1891 their father the Senator died, plagued by business worries and two unsuitable sons, these latter left to the care of their suitably artistic, partly Portuguese-Creole mother (who paid for the publication of Heinrich's first novel). In 1904 Heinrich remarked, with his brother's first (and acclaimed) novel, *Buddenbrooks*, in mind: 'After having been Hanseatic merchants for two thick volumes, with the help of Latin blood we finally got to Art – according to Nietzsche this always produces nervous disorders and artists.'

Describing the brothers' different reactions to their sister Julia's marriage to a Munich banker, Heinrich opposing and Thomas accepting, Hamilton comments, 'In the isolated, unyielding pride of Heinrich and the ironic, compromising nature of Thomas one can already trace the pattern of their latent conflicts.' Mutual sniping apropos of their literary productions there had already been, as if each brother defined himself – Thomas more obviously – by reaction against the other. In a letter of 1904 Thomas questioned Heinrich's liberalism: 'I understand little about so-called freedom . . . The great works of Russian literature were written under enormous oppression, weren't they? Would they have been produced without this oppression?' (One of those abiding hard questions.) By now Heinrich was resolutely democratic, socialist, European. Thomas was none of these, yet neither was he exactly the opposite. While his fiction often invoked extreme situations – how could *Doctor Faustus* be exceeded in that respect? – the author himself never runs to extremes. A few months later he was writing thus to Katia Pringsheim in courtship: 'I am quite conscious of not being the sort of man to arouse plain and uncomplicated feelings . . . To prompt mixed emotions, perplexity, is after all, if you will forgive me, a sign of personality.'

The rift between the brothers reached its widest with the Great War, which Heinrich abhorred and Thomas supported. Indeed, Heinrich with his essay on Zola, attacking nationalism, and Thomas with his *Reflections of a Non-Political Man*, a defence of irony, demurring pessimism, privacy against *bien-pensant* politics, appeared to be fighting a civil war of their own, progressive idealist versus conservative sceptic. The *Reflections* is a document of large and lasting pertinence, and a much subtler account of it is given by Erich Heller in his study, *The Ironic German*: the feud at the heart of the work is not so much a quarrel between brothers, barely concealed though this is, as 'an interior dialogue between the Germanically traditional two souls in the one breast'. Thomas had said much the same in a letter of 1919 written to someone who praised the *Reflections* at his brother's expense: 'As a critic you have the right to do so, but this is neither the intention nor the meaning of the book, and the antithesis itself strikes me as too important and symbolic for me really to welcome the intrusion of this question of rank and worth.' We can hardly not think of the symbolic antithesis of Naphta and Settembrini in *The Magic Mountain*. That it was the Heinrich-like Settembrini who survived suggests that if extremes were to be run to – as is often the case with antitheses and symbols – then Thomas considered Settembrini's extremes at least preferable to Naphta's.

Postwar developments brought the brothers together. Thomas soon saw where nationalism was leading, while Heinrich was forced to witness the failure of the Republic. Both of them went into exile within three weeks of Hitler's appointment as Chancellor of Germany, Heinrich (who was in more immediate danger) as 'national vermin', Thomas as guilty of 'pacifistic excesses' and 'intellectual high treason' – for instance, by proposing that while Wagner's art was national, its nationalism was soaked in the currents of European art. Thomas had become the *'Zivilisationsliterat'* he had once attacked in the person of his brother.

No one would presume to pity Thomas Mann, but Heinrich's is a saddening story. His greatest worldly success derived from the filming of his satirical novel, *Professor Unrat* (first published in 1905), as 'a dazzlingly perverse celluloid love-story' called *The Blue Angel*. The film was released in April 1930, shortly after Thomas had received the Nobel Prize. There was some irony in that too, for the prize was for *Buddenbrooks* (1901) rather than the more recent and (from the Swedish Academy's point of view) somewhat 'perverse' novel, *The Magic Mountain*. Moreover, while Thomas, the expert in mixed emotions, had married an apparently spoilt rich girl and made one of the most successful matches on record, the straightforward Heinrich's first marriage foundered and friends saw in his second a painful resemblance to the relationship portrayed in *The Blue Angel* by Emil Jannings and Marlene Dietrich. His second wife committed suicide on her fifth attempt. When the English translation of *Professor Unrat* came out in 1931 it was of course called *The Blue Angel*; and when the original was reissued in 1947 Heinrich had to agree to the title, *Der blaue Engel*.

The rest of the story is mainly Thomas's and reasonably well known: although in exile he met with private distresses and public tribulations, he achieved literary and financial success. Heinrich failed in both spheres. He died in 1950, in Los Angeles, while preparing to move to Berlin as President of the East German Academy of Arts – Thomas had recently visited East Germany and felt that the respect Heinrich would be accorded there was preferable to his American obscurity. Himself accused of pro-Communist sympathies and alarmed by the seeming collapse of democracy in the United States, Thomas left California for a second exile in Switzerland, and died there in 1955. His final summing-up of the fraternal situation was not merely pious: 'The stupid Germans are always squabbling over which one of us is really the greater; but the "really" great one would be the one nature would have made had she taken from us both.'

Erich Heller has doubted the possibility of writing Thomas Mann's 'Life' except by writing about his writings, since for him living and writing were virtually identical activities. What little discussion of the brothers' literary work is found in the present book, otherwise minutely documented, is superficial or lame. It is possible that the spirit of fraternity communicated itself to the biographer, inhibiting him from any sharp indication of Thomas's superiority as a writer, in both lucidity and complexity, over Heinrich. The opposite of the self-flaunting practitioner, Nigel Hamilton comes rather too close to complete invisibility.

Thomas Mann: The Making of an Artist, 1875–1911

The difficulty that any biographer of Thomas Mann faces is that the subject has already supplied an autobiography, in the form of the memoirs mentioned earlier and pre-eminently in his fiction – and in language more powerful, complex and telling than anyone else is likely to bring to bear. Little is left for biographers to do except stitch together the pieces, most genuinely self-revealing when seemingly self-concealing.

In an Afterword to her husband's book Clara Winston speaks of the 'startling discovery' he made when working on his introduction to their admirable English translation of the selected *Letters*. A new Thomas Mann emerged. Readers and critics had taken Aschenbach of *Death in Venice* and Leverkühn of *Doctor Faustus* and their coldness, their aloofness from the human condition, as self-portraits. Instead, it was now seen that Mann's personal history 'had all the elements of a great novel'. I am loath to quarrel with the Winstons, but who supposed that Mann was really a cold fish? To begin with, who can believe that Aschenbach and Leverkühn, despite the drain their art has imposed on 'ordinary life', are frigid, unfeeling, contentedly detached? Only somebody constitutionally incapable of reading could miss the pain that suffuses Leverkühn. We do not assume that a writer who is forever throwing himself or his words into orgasmic spasms is truly in touch with cosmic vitality. Conversely, we should not assume that ordered waters cannot run deep. As for the 'great novel' – in the first place that would need to *be* a novel, and Mann, who wrote several great novels, would hardly be gratified to find his life passed off as a rival to them.

But reason not the need for a biography. It may attract new readers to what matters about Mann, and it is a compliment to observe that in reading this partial biography (whose author died in 1979) one cannot always tell where *Buddenbrooks*, say, ends and Richard Winston's commentary begins: he quotes so well, orders the material firmly and writes lucidly. It is not that Mann had no life, as that term is generally understood, but that his was a writer's life, a life not to be separated out from the work, and impoverished to the point of insignificance if it were.

Quite properly, much is said here about the family background (Hanseatic merchant-princes leavened or tainted by a taste for the arts) and, again, Thomas's relationship with Heinrich. Heinrich emerges with credit – a younger brother is more susceptible to envy and the wish to go one better, or one different – and was the greatest single stimulus for Thomas in these early years. At school Thomas did poorly, managing to scrape a school-leaving certificate with 'barely satisfactory' in all subjects excepting Conduct, in which his one grade of 'good' was crossed out in favour of 'on the whole good'.

The family having moved from Lübeck to Munich, Thomas went to work as an unpaid apprentice in the South German Insurance Bank for six months; a year, says Mann in *A Sketch of My Life*, when describing the snuff-taking clerks and the sloping desk at which he secretly wrote his first story. Thereafter he registered as an auditor at the University: he could thus be a student without the nuisance of examinations. At an early stage the ability showed itself to work up a subject for literary purposes (musical techniques, syphilis, in *Doctor Faustus*: 'concrete reality, exactitude, were needed') through research or the soliciting of advice – and the ability, too, to forget it all, once used. Likewise his habit, often to get him into hot water despite his insistence that he 'exposed' himself far more than he exposed others, of introducing bits and pieces of real people and actual happenings into his fiction. Identity lists were drawn up in Lübeck after the appearance of *Buddenbrooks*, and Mann's conception of the artist as swindler (*Tonio Kröger, Felix Krull*) is amusingly linked with his detention as a suspected con man while visiting his native city in 1899.

In connection with his Jewish schoolmates Winston comments at length on Mann's attitudes towards the Jews. Mixed they were: after all, not all Jews are one Jew. Some of his most savage critics were Jewish, so were his publisher and some of his most ardent admirers. The predilection was there early on, for what he later called 'an adventurous and hedonistic note . . . a picturesque fact calculated to increase the colourfulness of the world', and in particular lighten the greyness of bourgeois Lübeck and his own strain of melancholy. Jewishness was 'romance' – to the extent that he married into a Jewish family (there is a charming account of the courtship of Katia Pringsheim here), and promptly fell into embarrassment over his new and 'anti-Semitic' story, 'The Blood of the Walsungs'. In short, 'though not otherwise richly blessed with wholly unequivocal convictions', he rightly considered himself 'a convinced and unequivocal "philo-Semite"', fearing only that a Zionist exodus would enfeeble Europe.

And so the story, though not a 'great novel', moves busily through the hero's connection with the magazine *Simplicissimus*; the composition and reception of *Buddenbrooks* (the publisher wanted it cut by half but finally capitulated, offering a royalty of twenty per cent without an advance); friendships with Jakob Wassermann (later to write *Caspar Hauser*), the novelist Kurt Martens ('he belonged to the few people – I could count them on the fingers of one hand – whom I ever addressed as "*du*"'), and his publisher Samuel Fischer; in 1905 a 'fairy-tale' marriage for love which happened to bring money; research into court protocol for the novel, *Royal Highness* ('the first fruit of my married state,' Mann wrote in *A Sketch of My Life*, and 'an attempt to come to terms, as a writer, with my own happiness': critics found it 'too light'); the births of his children; the 'opera-plot' suicide of his unhappy sister Carla, a three-weeks' stay with Katia in a sanatorium at Davos (later to surface in the shape of *The Magic Mountain*); and finally the writing of *Death in Venice*.

Death in Venice, Clara Winston says, 'was the place to deal with a delicate, perhaps crucial, biographical question' which was 'like so much else in Thomas Mann's life, ambiguous'. It would seem that this delicate question concerned Mann's possible homosexual inclinations. The subject is first raised in connection with his close, even fervid, attachment to Paul Ehrenberg, a young painter and musician, around 1900. At the same time, while visiting his brother in Florence, he enjoyed a tender interlude with an English girl, Mary Smith, and there was some 'talk of marriage'. In 1910, at the age of thirty-five, he made friends with Ernst Bertram, twenty-seven years old and a teacher at Bonn University, engaged on a book on Nietzsche and composing poems in the manner of Stefan George. Mann found Bertram a highly congenial intellectual companion. Beyond that, one guess is as good as another; and none is worth much. *Reflections of a Non-Political Man* owed something to its author's correspondence with 'Dear Herr Doktor' Bertram, who incidentally was to lose his chair at Cologne in the course of denazification in 1946. However, the isolated remark in Mann's diary for 1919 to the effect that the *Reflections* was an expression 'of my sexual inversion' remains merely cryptic.

It is plain that homosexuality, a powerful manifestation of Eros, interested him deeply as a novelist and also (if we are to preserve the distinction) as a man; in a lecture on the homosexual poet Platen he adduced Nietzsche's words: 'The degree and kind of man's sexuality permeate the very loftiest heights of his intellect.' I suppose Thomas Mann could be said to be shifty, even in his very loftiest heights – in the sense that he was given to changing positions, shifting from one mode of experience to another. To talk of 'masks' in this connection is misleading, for the word suggests a procession of deliberate disguises, visors and veils held up across the face, rather than a diversity of natural expressions, expressions of feeling. Behind that stiff exterior – it needed to be stiff – danced a chameleon novelist.

THE STUPENDOUS CANNOT
BE EASY: On Robert Musil

If you were to read *The Man Without Qualities* for the story, your patience would be much fretted: you would probably not hang yourself, you would merely want to hang Robert Musil. The 'story' of the novel ostensibly concerns the preparations being made in 1913 in the Austro-Hungarian Empire to celebrate the seventieth anniversary of the Emperor's accession in December 1918. The preparations are known as the Collateral Campaign because Germany, that uncomfortable neighbour, is also planning a celebration: of Kaiser Wilhelm's jubilee, thirty years on the throne, in July of the same year. Unfortunately July precedes December, hence honour requires the Austrians to turn the whole of the year 1918 into a jubilee. Since, as the author knew (he began to write the work in the early 1920s and the first volume was published in 1930), these celebrations are never going to take place, the story in an obvious sense bears on a non-event.

The view that the work is a study of decadence, revealing the decay at the heart of the Austrian Empire, though it endows the project with a respectable-seeming significance, is a highly doubtful one. It points to what, though marvellously apt, is the least important element in the novel: its setting in time and place. By and large the dramatis personae form an exceptionally bright set – they could as well win the world as lose their little piece of it – and the tone of the work is remote from Orwellian or Brechtian allegory. The inset story of Moosbrugger the sex-murderer hardly supports the view either, despite the opening it offers for the question of whether one is responsible for one's acts, and despite Ulrich's portentous reflection in one of his grimmer moments that 'if mankind could dream collectively, it would dream Moosbrugger'. There being so much civility in evidence, someone has to stand for violence and unadorned insanity.

It says something for a country that, although it customarily regards a genius as a lout, a lout is never ('as sometimes happened elsewhere') regarded as a genius. No doubt the Empire was ramshackle, tottery and given to 'muddling through' – the hero Ulrich, we shall see, is given to thinking through: he however has no other calls of a pressing nature – but Musil was not interested in a retrospective analysis of the processes of decline and downfall. Ulrich even suggests that 'muddling through' may be Austria's world mission. And in fact, despite his virtually continuous irony, Musil is careful to forgo the hindsight wisdom which would have supplied him with irony of the cruder sort in plenty. The analysis that interests him – obsesses is a better word – is that of his characters and their situations as individual and yet (on a somewhat elevated plane) representative beings. He is the most relentlessly analytic of authors, the most sententious (except perhaps for *Wilhelm Meister*'s), and one of the most intelligent.

He did not finish his 'story' because in one sense, a minor one, history had already finished it for him, and in another and major sense it could never end. If his characters died it would be as if humanity died out. Death is as immaterial here (but how useful it is to novelists who have to tell a story and to end it too!) as in a Freudian casebook. Events too are rather crude animals, although they do happen, even to representative figures, and might be thought on occasion to be capable of representativeness themselves. Where events are concerned Musil can make Proust seem as fast-moving as James Bond: why, Mme Verdurin gets to be Princesse de Guermantes and Marcel's grandmother actually dies . . . Yet, like *A la recherche du temps perdu*, Musil's novel is a continuous texture, a vast weave of references back and forth, a seamless expanse of strands of thought which evince themselves at remote intervals and yet have been there, imperceptibly growing, all the while. If you skip, and it is very hard never to do so, you will be made to regret it.

'What this age demonstrates,' the novel tells us, sounding as so often as if it had been written yesterday, in some intellectually richer yesterday, 'when it talks of the genius of a race-horse or a tennis-player is probably less its conception of genius than its mistrust of the whole higher sphere.' The reader should not let himself be alarmed by that fearsome expression 'higher sphere', but merely remind himself that some spheres are higher than others. What is enjoyable in this novel is, happily, what matters most in it, and not just the sugar round the pill. To that extent the heart of the matter is worn on the sleeve and there is, until we make it, no insuperable problem: the novel is highly entertaining. Or the problem is: how sturdy is our appetite for what we are fairly overtly offered? That is to say, intelligence and insight, an 'unmerciful' shrewdness, outright comedy, wit, an all-embracing but by no means merciless irony – in short, a cast of mind, in motion, that we might think of as world-weary were it not for the sheer energy and gusto it bears and is borne by.

If the first characteristic we note of Musil's style is its leisureliness – Volume I begins with a hefty meteorological paragraph which at last summarizes itself in the words 'In short . . . it was a fine August day in the year 1913' – the second is its succinctness. For speed there is little to beat this sentence: 'Two weeks later Bonadea had already been his mistress for a fortnight.' And in two and a half pages we are given a living portrayal of the reluctant nymphomaniac Bonadea, the stuff of a novel in itself. 'She was capable of uttering the words "the true, the good and the beautiful" as often and as naturally as someone else might say "Thursday".' She has only one fault: 'she was liable to be stimulated to a quite uncommon degree by the mere sight of men'; a good wife and mother, 'she was by no means lustful' but 'sensual in the way that other people have other troubles, such as sweating of the hands or blushing easily'. Comic as the tone of this is, we emerge from the three-page chapter knowing that Bonadea is not merely to be laughed at or despised or condemned. Musil's starting-point, the reminder that Bonadea was a goddess of chastity whose temple suffered a transmogrification into 'a centre of all debaucheries', does not initiate the crushing send-up of a trivial, pretentious light-of-love that we might have expected. Bonadea, when she has no one in her arms, is a 'quiet, majestic woman'. Like the goddess's temple, people too are subject to queer inversions and contradictions, and the only infallible way of preserving an empire, of whatever kind, is by petrifying its inhabitants, reducing them to programmed robots *in perpetuum.* The most perspicacious (and perspicuous) passage in Musil's early novel, *Young Törless,* touches on the boy's experience of 'the failure of language' whereby things, people and processes have been fettered to harmless explanatory words from which they may break loose at any moment.

In Chapter 99 of the Second Book the story is told, in passing, of Ulrich's adoptive Aunt Jane, whose dress resembled a soutane and who smoked cigars and wore a man's wig – not in anticipation of 'the mannish type of woman that was later to come into fashion', but because of her early and passionate admiration for the Abbé Liszt. Aunt Jane's heart was 'womanly' indeed. A music mistress, she had married against her family's wishes an improvident photographer and self-styled 'artist', who at least had a 'superb head' and drank and ran up debts like a genius. To him and then to his illegitimate child she sacrificed herself utterly. 'She seldom spoke of that past,' the author interposes: 'If life is stupendous one cannot also demand that it should be easy.' This anecdote – it arises out of a family album Ulrich is leafing through and occupies three pages – is a slice of the very body of life: again, the raw material for a substantial novel of its own, one would say, except that Musil is never 'raw'. That he over-cooks is the objection we are more likely to make. In an interesting essay, 'The Ironic Mystic' (*PN Review*, 22) David Heald varies the metaphor: 'His terrier-like habit of chewing every scrap of flesh and sucking the marrow out of every fleeting insight can irritate . . .'

With one sense of the word 'raw' in mind, we are provoked into perceiving before long that, for all the author's well-bred discretion, or because of it, the work carries a powerful sexual charge – in no way defused by the presence of humour, satire and pathos – and especially in the vicinity of his women characters. 'The tender aspects of masculine self-abandonment,' he remarks, 'somewhat resemble the growling of a jaguar over a hunk of meat.' But then, his women are the most original of his creations, and only brute accident, one wants to say, could bring about the downfall of an empire that had such women in it as Agathe, Diotima, Bonadea and Clarisse. It has to be admitted that Musil turns his sardonic gaze even more lovingly on his women than on his men: this detracts from them less than the reader might suppose in his innocence.

Apropos of Diotima, Ulrich animadverts on 'the mind of this woman, who would have been so beautiful without her mind', and it could hardly solace her to hear that Musil is offering her as an exemplary victim of what he calls 'the indescribable wave of skim-romanticism and yearning for God that the machine-age had for a time squirted out as an expression of spiritual and artistic protest against itself.' Diotima is the spiritual and artistic spearhead of the Collateral Campaign – culture, in the circles to which she belongs, being largely left to ladies – and in quest of a Great and Beautiful Idea, something to do with the Ideal and the eternal verities and, if at all possible, involving 'a positively redeeming exaltation of inner life, arising out of the anonymous depths of the nation'. How gratified the Emperor Franz Joseph will be by a whole year of all that! When Ulrich looks at Diotima he sees a fine woman; in his mind's eye, however, she appears in the shape of a 'colossal hen that was about to peck at a little worm, which was his soul'. Musil's women have a peculiarly potent charm, bypassing or overriding one's intellectual judgement of them; their wrong-headedness is richer than male right-mindedness, which by comparison looks cloddish, pompous or ineffectual.

In fact almost all the characters are endowed with a generous share of their creator's acuteness. Even the patently foolish ones, like those of limited brain-power, are allowed such fluent cogitation that they too strike us as preternaturally observant and self-aware. The 'tubby little general' Stumm, fallen under Diotima's sway, goes to the Imperial Library in the hope of locating a 'great redeeming idea' for the Campaign and finds himself faced with three and a half million volumes. 'You may say,' this simple soldier reflects, 'one doesn't really need to read every single book.' But that won't pass muster. 'My retort to that is – in warfare, too, one doesn't need to kill every single soldier, and yet every single one is necessary.' The Prussian industrialist Arnheim is put in his place by the author as a plausible *vulgarisateur* or at best a talented eclectic: none the less he proceeds to put neatly in their place the 'fat species' of solemn idealistic poets who 'puff out great bales of the eternal emotions'.

In conversation, as when Arnheim and Ulrich dispute together, one character's wits strike sparks off another's sagacity and, at times quite unexpectedly, intellectual honours are more or less equal at the end. What respect for – or what rare generosity towards – one's own creations this shows, among them not a single imbecile or swine! The exceptional subtlety thus implied in the differentiation between characters – levels of intelligence, degrees of good intention – doesn't make the reader's task any easier. Whose side is he meant to be on? He will need to be a reader without qualities, apart from those of insatiable curiosity and immense patience. He will need to be nearly as clever as Musil.

'At times he felt just as though he had been born with a gift for which at present there was no function.' The figure of Ulrich is obviously crucial, and also slippery: he is, one supposes, the author, in large measure at any rate, and the reader's zealous though less than wholly accommodating guide. Over this length, he will require to be more than a guide, a stance or a view-point; he will need to be of very considerable appeal, gruesome or charming, in himself. Is he sufficiently so? He describes himself in a typical paradox as 'a man of faith, though one who believed in nothing'. More strongly he asserts (partly, one may suppose, by way of apology to Bonadea, with whom he is breaking off), 'My nature is designed as a machine for the continuous devaluation of life!'

Ulrich is or was (like Musil) an engineer and mathematician, earlier a cavalry officer, now taking a year's leave from his life in order to find out what to do with it: a youngish man of promise disillusioned with the promises, a dilettante who loves 'intellectual hardship'. He is a detached observer, a juggler with ideas, an intellectual trouble-maker – as his friends discover – and he can run to tedious sophistry and sterile elaboration – as his readers discover. If he appears sexually cold – he certainly isn't abstinent – this is in part, though only in part, because the author skips over the details (we catch a rare period glimpse of ribbons being untied or tied, hooks being unfastened or fastened) and straight into Ulrich's post-coital musings. Against his coldness we set the quickness of his curiosity, as when he pauses outside a shop window to marvel at 'the countless versions of nail-scissors' or the processes whereby a goat's skin is transformed into a lady's glove. In the barely definable relationship between him and his sister Agathe which begins to take over Volume III, he reflects, 'there was implicit not more love for each other than distaste for the rest of the world.' Yet when he is out with Agathe, discussing his dislike of the world, and they stroll through a busy market-place, he exclaims: 'Can one help loving the world if one simply sees and smells it?'

Wherever his mind may be, Ulrich has his feet on the ground, and he is less of a pedant, and in truth probably less of a world-disliker, than the windy idealists and Great Lovers whom he mocks. If he is rather too knowing about women, and – even for a personable thirty-two-year-old bachelor – somewhat over-privileged in that sphere, he likes them naturally, with a liking that can only go with a fair amount of respect, and in their company he never declines into baby-talk or sulks or masculine mysteries. He may fall into silence, however. What is exasperating to the reader, as to his female visitors, is his capacity for thinking, at such length and for the greater part so well. This is indeed quite offensive. 'Let's have more conviction!' we protest, when we really mean, 'Less superior intellection if you please!'

The reader's courage may dim a little when, in Volume III, Ulrich is reunited with Agathe ('sister . . . woman . . . stranger . . . friend'), for alas the siblings have long been separated and have so much to talk about. Moreover Agathe is made of sterner stuff – stuff of a less decipherable pattern too – than his other women friends, and she can give as good as she takes. We are told by Musil's expert translators – they deserve the Nobel Prize for Translation – that this is where he originally intended the story to begin, and so the previous thousand pages are only a form of prologue. What is to be narrated now, Musil declares in connection with the siblings and by way of warning to the slow-witted and hence (he assumes) squeamish, is 'a journey to the furthest limits of the possible, skirting the dangers of the impossible and unnatural, even of the repulsive, and perhaps not always quite avoiding them.' This, though one may not be absolutely sure of what it signifies, is possibly a clue to one reason for the novel's unfinishability. The man who is going to travel that far needs to travel light, and as a symbol, no matter what of, no matter how beautifully managed, incest tends towards top-heaviness.

However, this volume contains splendid material continuative of the foregoing volumes. On the one hand, such ripe comedy as Bonadea's playing truant from Diotima's high-minded academy of love, where general theory alone is taught, to taste the reality of sex in Ulrich's apartment. On the other, an unforgettably powerful scene in which – at the instigation of Clarisse, a highly-strung 'modern' version of Aunt Jane moved by fiercer artistic aspirations but a lesser lovingness – some of the friends visit the lunatic asylum where Moosbrugger is held. As they progress from ward to ward ('this is idiocy, and that over there is cretinism') General Stumm rambles on about the Collateral Campaign and how the War Ministry finds itself co-operating with both the pacifists and the nationalists, the former keen on universal love and human goodness and the latter on seizing the opportunity to bring the army up to scratch. The General himself is in favour of both parties.

There is no facile suggestion that it is the inmates of the asylum who are 'truly' sane while the outside world is 'truly' insane. Musil compares lunatic asylums, 'the ultimate habitation of the lost', with Hell – which 'is not interesting; it is merely terrible'. Those who have attempted to portray Hell, however imaginative they may be, have never got beyond 'oafish torments and puerile distortions of earthly peculiarities'. And Dante, more discreetly, humanized Hell by populating it 'with men of letters and other public figures, thus distracting attention from the penal technicalities'. Asylums are as uninteresting, as lacking in imagination, as Hell itself, and even Clarisse, fired by self-generated excitation and a head full of Nietzschean ideas ('for her this journey was half philosophy and half adultery'), is left disappointed. On the return journey the General remarks, as he lights up a cigar, that he didn't see a single patient smoking: 'People don't realize how well off they are so long as they're in their right minds.'

The advent of Agathe brings about a new seriousness in Ulrich, or a thinning of the flippancy that has invested his seriousness. For a while we wonder whether he is going to develop qualities. He comments on his own scepticism: 'I don't believe God has been among us yet. I believe He is still to come. But only if we shorten the way for Him': that is, we have to meet God half-way. The comment is indicative of Ulrich's 'mysticism', itself a contributory reason for the novel's length. For that mysticism, in so far as it is describable, is of a scrupulously rational species which allows of no short-cuts by way of 'feeling', no leaps into the unknown, but only of hard and rigorous journeys. There follows a sustained passage of considerable solemnity on the theme of morality, which for Ulrich consists in 'order and integrity of feeling'. 'Morality is imagination' and 'there is nothing arbitrary about the imagination'. Men have introduced a degree of order into the workings of the intellect, which is at least able to weigh theories against facts. Cannot something similar be done for the feelings? For 'we all want to discover what we're alive for . . . it's one of the main sources of all the violence in the world.' When Arnheim interrupts: 'But that would mean an expanding relationship to God!' Ulrich asks mockingly, 'And would that be so very terrible?'

It is tempting at this point – but not especially rewarding – to turn back to *Young Törless* (*Die Verwirrungen des Zöglings Törless*, 1906), a book whose curiously high standing may owe something to the guilty sense that its author wrote another novel, much finer no doubt but very much longer and on the face of it less accessible. For it is hard, I would have thought, to distinguish between the *Verwirrungen*, the confusions, of young Törless and those of the not much older author. The unlikeable youth Beineberg – but who in the novel is likeable? – sounds like a seedy pubescent hanger-on of Diotima and her Great and Beautiful Idea when he talks about the soul and how we should restore our contact with it and make better (in his case, probably worse) use of its powers. But it is the author *in propria persona* who tells us that

Any great flash of understanding is only half completed in the illumined circle of the conscious mind; the other half takes place in the dark loam of our innermost being. It is primarily a state of soul, and uppermost, as it were at the extreme tip of it, there the thought is – poised like a flower.

Such Freudian-style talk of light and loam may pass in a boarding school where metaphysics and masochism, soul and sadism, are jumbled up together, but the later Musil is more authentic in his aspiration and more rigorous in his scepticism.

Musil tells us that in his references to the rubble of feelings one age bequeaths to another Ulrich is prophesying the fate of Europe, though without realizing it – 'indeed, he was not concerned with real events at all; he was fighting for his own salvation.' The salvation of a representative being is a theme, a concern, which survives 1914–18 and thereafter: the end is not yet nigh, and it is wholly in character that a fourth volume of translation should be in prospect, containing (we are told) the unfinished conclusion of the work and some unfinished chapters.

Musil's mind is a brilliant, speculative and untiring one, but not precisely the mind of a novelist. Yet if such a mind applies itself to a novel – and it is difficult to think what it could apply itself to more profitably – then the result must be, if not a brilliant novel, then still brilliant. In Chapter 112 of the Second Book Arnheim reflects on Ulrich, his Viennese 'counter-influence' in the triangular relationship with Diotima and a man with whom, paradoxically, he is much taken. His diagnosis of what he persuades himself is Ulrich's weakness may stand as a criticism of Musil himself, so long as we keep in mind that it is highly paradoxical to describe as a writer's 'weakness' what is plainly of his essential strength. Ulrich is witty, 'and wit came from witting, knowing, and here was a piece of wisdom on the part of language, for it revealed the intellectual origins of this quality, and how spectral it was, how poor in feeling.' Arnheim continues: 'The witty man is always inclined to live, as it were, by his wits, overriding the ordained frontiers where the man of true feeling calls a halt.'

Yes, we think, more feeling would surely have served to inhibit, to slow down, even to tire out Musil's wits, and thus to call a halt to his novel this side of the ordained frontiers of magnitude and ambition. But therein, as we have seen, lies the burden of Ulrich's – and Musil's – complaint against 'feeling' and its soulful exponents. When they are moved by emotions they think they are moving towards truth – and never mind frontiers and halts.

The Man Without Qualities is essentially exploratory and experimental rather than programmatic or predetermined. Yet, as we expect novels to have a conclusion, so we expect thinkers to arrive at conclusions. The truth may well be that Musil couldn't end his novel because he hadn't arrived at his conclusions, he was still inching ruthlessly towards them when he died. If he had arrived – ah, then we should have more than merely a great novel, we should possess the great secret of life.

ECHT BRECHT

Bertolt Brecht: Poems 1913–1956

The first thing to say about this scholarly production, which includes notes both by the poet and by the editors, is that it is vastly enjoyable. The second is that it is scholarly – and all that prevents one from regretting the sparsity of explanatory, interpretative glosses (i.e. a little more help with meaning) is that there is patently no room for them in a volume already bumper.

The volume takes in roughly half of the approximately one thousand poems in the 1967 Suhrkamp–Verlag collected edition. The editors tell us that Brecht felt his poetry to be private to him, and they suggest that he also felt it to represent 'a dangerously seductive distraction from the real hard work of writing and staging the plays'. If, as they say, this consideration discouraged him from letting his verse be seen, it certainly failed to inhibit him from writing verse. Indeed, he was so continous, so 'natural' a writer that he could hardly have had the time to arrange for the publication of so immense an output. It could be that what the editors term 'his staggering indifference to much of his own work' was in part sheer forgetfulness.

Even so, I think the editors overstate our ignorance of Brecht as a poet. True, not very much has hitherto been available in English: in fact, as we now see, a mere fraction of the whole. But what there was – notably though not solely H. R. Hays's *Selected Poems* (1947), the poems scattered through John Willett's *The Theatre of Bertolt Brecht*, the selection in *Modern German Poetry 1910–1960* (Michael Hamburger and Christopher Middleton) and in Hamburger's *Tales from the Calendar* – has been much read and (usefully or not) influential. More than a few English readers have at least realized – or come to think, or to suspect – that Brecht is more considerable as a poet than as a dramatist, despite (or in some cases because of) his cult as theorist of the theatre. Obvi-

34

ously not many will have had much idea of the sheer volume and variety of his poetry until now.

Brecht on the run from the Nazis, with his combative and barbed poems, is of course a stirring figure. Brecht *in situ* as a Communist, with his combative and barbed poems, becomes, as the years go by and Nazism recedes while Communism doesn't, if not a sinister at any rate a suspect figure. In her *Unwritten Memories* (published in 1974) Katia Mann remarks, apropos of his defence before the Committee on Un-American Activities in 1947: 'Brecht was very sly indeed'. (Possibly the comment was meant to have a wider application, but either way we might note her next words: 'he pretended to be stupid, and the others *were* stupid'.) Some of Brecht's admirers remoter from the *haute-bourgeoisie* than Katia Mann (there was something lordly even about the Manns' late Leftism) must wonder over the nature of their admiration – and whether perhaps Brecht wasn't a trifle sly and shifty over and above the call of survival.

His poetry is less likely than the plays to arouse such suspicions. Aside from the simple-minded propagandist pieces ('Only in Karl Marx and Lenin could we workers / See a chance of life ahead') and occasional outbreaks of silly bad temper, it has other weaknesses. Notable among these are repetitiousness, the over-insistent and vain effort to make minority art look like *vox populi*, and what we might call an excessive fluency in laconicism. What mostly kept Brecht out of danger as a poet, and what is most potent in him, is that – whether or not you share his attitudes – he talked about his times, he was plugged firmly into a particular reality. This kept him, generally, on the right, decent path. It also preserved him from the mere vapid egotism of poets who pride themselves on their concern with the so-called 'eternal verities' while actually busying themselves narcissistically with themselves. (No offence is intended to the said verities, who, like Brecht's gods, tend to evince themselves in disguise. And not much to Narcissus: the poet does look into his own heart, to find something more than himself there.) But perhaps this is to say no more than Brecht's favourite slogan says: 'The truth is concrete.' His 'Little Epistle' begins, solemnly and mischievously,

> If someone enjoys writing he will be glad
> If he has a subject.

In the early poems Brecht's liking for catastrophe, for 'strong meat', already comes out strongly; and later he was to find plenty of it to hand. Even around 1922 we read this:

> When the tables of the law broke, so did all vices.
> Even sleeping with one's sister is no fun any more.
> Murder is too much trouble for many
> Writing poems is too common . . .

Similarly, his taste for strong cigars, brandy and damnation (all those drowned girls who weigh on his sturdy conscience!): for rotting timbers and 'pestilence and puke and piss'. This goes along with his amusing and surely self-amused 'persona' poems, such as 'Anna speaks ill of Bidi' (*c.* 1919):

> Smokes cigars and reads the papers
> Swigs schnapps, haunts the billiard hall
> Ice-cold, with his airs and capers
> No humanity at all

or, 'You smoke. You shit. You turn out some verse', or of course the famous 'Of Poor B. B.' (in its present form, revised *c.* 1925, when Brecht was twenty-seven):

> Before noon on my empty rocking chairs
> I'll sit a woman or two, and with an untroubled eye
> Look at them steadily and say to them:
> Here you have someone on whom you can't rely.

The comical 'woman or two' is sufficient to modify the horrid 'machismo' of the lines, while the whole poem – despite the newspapers, the tobacco, the brandy – has less to do with any form of virility than with a growing sense of self-chastening unease.

And elsewhere the toughness of the persona is in a fairly undeceptive way 'deceptive', as we give due weight to lines like 'all that lives, lives frailly' and the allusion in a seemingly hard-headed secular version of the Nativity to Mary's

                    bitter shame
                  Common among the poor
                  Of having no privacy.

The two strands, tough subject-matter and tough persona, develop and combine into Brecht's 'news-item' poems. Some of these relate to the past, like the coarsened-Cavafy of 'The Gordian Knot' and 'I'm not saying anything against Alexander' –

                    Only
                  I have seen people
                  Who were remarkable –
                  Highly deserving of your admiration
                  For the fact that they
                  Were alive at all.
                  Great men generate too much sweat.

(Incidentally, 'The carpet-weavers of Kuyan-Bulak honour Lenin' reads like a *bien-pensant* version of Cavafy's *mal-pensant* 'In a Township of Asia Minor', where the citizens adroitly switch their honouring from the defeated Antony to the victorious Octavius.)

Other poems in this genre are drawn from the fairly immediate present: the poem about the eight thousand unemployed miners and their families camped outside Budapest (seemingly written two years after the event), and the one, also written in 1926 and carrying as epigraph 'A dispatch from London says . . .', concerning the three hundred coolies who froze to death in China. I don't know whether the eternal verities feature in these reports; and probably to claim that the truth, besides being concrete, is topical, isn't to make out much of a case for them. 'Letting the facts speak for themselves' is hardly an adequate definition of poetry. Still, at the least such poems are likely, for as long as history survives, to retain some historical interest. And that, if one thinks of the short life-expectancy of the great mass of verse, is something.

                    When the wound
                  Stops hurting
                  What hurts is
                  The scar.

                              37

This book raises a number of questions of radical concern, not only to Brecht's work but to literature in general, its subject-matter and form and tone, the relationship between writer and reader, between the transitory and the permanent and between *Wahrheit* and *Dichtung*. For instance, the temptation common among poets to 'point up', to make a good story even better (which often means making it worse), as when an injured man in history becomes a dead one in the poem, or the Moscow Metro, exemplifying 'the builders in the role of proprietors', is said to have been built in one year instead of the actual three. In some sense the phenomenon is, if not justified, at least acknowledged in 'Bad time for poetry' (1939):

> Why do I only record
> That a village woman aged forty walks with a stoop?
> The girls' breasts
> Are as warm as ever.

'Only an idiot lives without worry': at times Brecht strikes us as worrying mechanically. His didacticism exacted a price, various prices. The Svendborg and other satires are a mixed bunch; the eternal nastinesses certainly haunt some of them. 'Praised be doubt!' he said, and perhaps this tip which he offers us – a defence against his sloganeering – was one of his own defensive measures. If so, it is effectively, and movingly, deployed in 'To those born later':

> And yet we know:
> Hatred, even of meanness
> Contorts the features.
> Anger, even against injustice
> Makes the voice hoarse. Oh, we
> Who wanted to prepare the ground for friendliness
> Could not ourselves be friendly.

Then there are the love poems, highly individual, and the Buckow Elegies of 1953. The latter, with the other late and last poems, suggest that the old Adam in Brecht couldn't for long have toed a line, and wasn't likely ever to locate an Earthly Paradise, however constituted and administered. For one thing, he was too well aware of the old Adam in other people.

Another question raised here has to do with the translation of verse. Technique being more important in Brecht's case than with many modern poets, the editors say, 'we felt it essential to match the original forms as closely as possible': not, that is, to rest content with a flat literal translation hopefully intended to supplement whatever in the way of 'sound and structure' the reader can deduce from the originals. The 'many hands' involved in these translations chose the hard way, and it has paid off in the simplest and purest of currencies: readability.

Bertolt Brecht in America

Chased from my country now I have to see
If there's some shop or bar that I can find
Where I can sell the products of my mind.
Again I tread the roads well known to me

Worn smooth by those accustomed to defeat.
I'm on my way but don't yet know to whom.
Wherever I go they ask me: 'Spell your name!'
And oh, that name was once accounted great . . .*

The poems Brecht wrote in America between 1941 and 1947 tell us much about his mental and emotional life during those years. Now James K. Lyon tells us all, or what seems like all, or even more than all in some departments, drawing on unpublished letters and documents, FBI files, and interviews with the subject's friends, relatives, associates and collaborators.

Brecht's American years were, in his own words, an 'exile in paradise' – he thought of himself throughout as an exile, not an immigrant – and to this we might add, with partial truth, that Brecht was himself the serpent in the garden. The experience of exile is peculiarly hard on one whose life centres on language, and no easier if he finds he has little fame in his new land. (There was a sharp contrast in this respect between Brecht's lot and that of the much-translated Thomas Mann.) The situation is aggravated if the exile is a playwright, and hence in

*'Sonnet in emigration', translated by Edith Roseveare, in the volume discussed above.

need of a theatre; still further aggravated when he has very strong and unshared ideas about 'theatre'. Brecht had lost his natural public, his true students – temporarily at any rate, for much of his writing at this time he saw as lessons laid up in advance for the postwar German people.

As for America, his feelings might have been expected to reflect those conveyed in Goethe's verse: *'Amerika, du hast es besser'*, better than our old continent with its ruined castles, its fruitless memories and vain strife – even allowing that for Brecht hardly any strife was vain. In fact his view approached Rilke's: America was a country of nomads who built homes without intending to stay in them and changed jobs like boots, rootless, lacking a cultural past. Nine days after arriving he wrote in his journal of 'this mortuary of easy going'; a week later, referring to Hollywood, 'Tahiti in metropolitan form'; eight months later: 'I have the feeling of being like Francis of Assisi in an aquarium, Lenin at the Prater (or the Oktoberfest), or a chrysanthemum in a coal mine.' What America could offer him – peace and security – was something he never really wanted, something his nature would soon reject or pervert.

Setting out on his previous visit to America, from Denmark, in 1935, Brecht had compared himself to Columbus, with the implication that it was the New World that was to discover *him*, along with his new kind of 'learning play'. Now, at the age of forty-three, he was stuck in that new world, faced with the prospect of causing himself to be discovered, or (as Lyon puts it) with the necessity of 'producing' himself. That the 'production' failed was largely due to his unyielding didacticism, his emphasis on that un-American activity, class conflict, and his self-will, or what seemed to his indigenous contacts a European 'superiority complex'.

Bertolt Brecht in America details the nature of that failure, in instance after instance, while indicating that in another, longer-term and no doubt more important sense these years *were* productive. Although Brecht described Hollywood as the 'world centre of the narcotic trade', he was alive to the enormous power films could wield in forming or modifying opinion, and he played some part in the writing of more than fifty film stories, the most fruitful of which (though it is impossible to say how much of Brecht's work survived in the end) issued in Fritz Lang's *Hangmen Also Die*. More often such projects foundered: film-making was collective work, but not (as Lyon observes) collective work of Brecht's kind. Early and late he insisted on collaborative effort, but with himself as the Boss, having the whip-hand. Hollywood declined to hand the whip over.

Most engaging was the plan to turn his poem 'Children's Crusade' into a film, with the ballad-story told in a snowbound New England schoolroom. The project failed, seemingly in that it was 'by extension' an anti-war film and would have had to compete with the successful and more wholehearted war pictures then being put out by Hollywood. Another story on which he worked, 'Silent Witness', appears to have had the requisite ingredients to carry it through to the silver screen, notably a strong plot and a happy ending. A French woman, unjustly accused of collaboration with the Germans, is vindicated when recognized as the model for a stained-glass window of Joan of Arc commissioned by a dead but impeccable abbé who worked for the resistance . . . However, Brecht insisted that the leading lady should appear with her head shaven – and no star could be persuaded to do that! Then there was his comedy, *Schweyk in the Second World War*, probably written with an eye and a half on Broadway: but alas, its hero was too unheroic, its humour too European, and the play did not receive its first professional American performance until 1977.

During 1943/44 Brecht wrote *The Caucasian Chalk Circle*, in which the celebrated Austrian-born actress Luise Rainer was to star on Broadway. Their ideas on acting failed to coincide and – even though at this stage only one page of the play actually existed – a violent row blew up. Luise Rainer remembers it thus:

Brecht (roaring): Do you know who I am?
Rainer (calmly): Yes. You are Bertolt Brecht. And do you know who I am?
Brecht: Yes. You are nothing. Nothing, I say!

The customary tangle ensued, with collaborators and translators set one against another and only Brecht's right hand knowing what his left was doing. Having been told by the dramatist that *any* actress would jump at the chance to play the role of Grusha, Luise Rainer withdrew, and two decades passed before the play was seen in New York. Two minor successes – minor in Brecht's table of priorities at the time, one guesses – were the publication by New Directions in 1944 of seventeen scenes from the play *The Private Life of the Master Race*, as translated by Eric Bentley, and of *Selected Poems*, in the fine English versions of H. R. Hays, by Reynal and Hitchcock in 1947.

For Luise Rainer, Brecht was 'cruel, selfish, vain – an awful man'. Apropos of the confusion into which Brecht had thrown the staging of *Master Race* in 1945, Eric Bentley wrote to a mutual acquaintance, with considerable discernment: 'He has neither good manners nor elementary decency. He lives out his own theory that it is impossible to behave well in this society . . . a scoundrel but an artist.' Bentley and Hays both suffered from his blend of the dictatorial and the devious, both retained an unwavering admiration for his writing. And both of them attest to his charm. Not so, however, Auden ('an odious person') or Isherwood ('Brecht simply had very bad manners'). Isherwood also remarked how 'ruthless' Brecht was where his own projects were concerned. Here lies the overriding cause of the many quarrels, complaints and wounded feelings recorded in this book. Brecht was intransigently Brechtian. He knew nothing of the fashionable uncertainty about 'identity': he had it in excess. His attempts to 'depersonalize' professional or political disagreements were not uniformly successful; he got up people's noses, and generally stayed there. His works were to be produced the way he wanted, not how Broadway or Hollywood or the rest of the United States wanted. He was his own worst enemy, at least in the short run. But he was the best friend of his own beliefs and principles.

George Grosz, a friend of Brecht, remarked in his autobiography that 'he would have preferred a good electric calculator where his heart was, and the spokes of a car wheel in the place of his legs.' Professor Lyon is a well-disposed ringside commentator, but still somewhat hard pressed to make out a case for Brecht's warmth of heart. He cites a poem, written in 1947, which begins with a reference to the 'swamp' of Hollywood, or conceivably of drugs:

I saw many friends
And the friend I loved most
Among them helplessly sunk
Into the swamp . . .

and ends thus:

Now I watched him leaning back
Covered with leeches in the shimmering, softly moving
    slime
Upon the sinking face
That ghastly blissful smile.

The poem was apparently about Peter Lorre, addicted to morphine and now suffering a sharp decline in reputation, and since it was found among his papers we may assume the author gave it to him. Lyon claims, not altogether convincingly, that the poem reveals a concern for the actor extending beyond his professional usefulness to the dramatist: 'the poem is for Lorre as a human being whom he wanted to help.' Aside from the one brilliant phrase in it ('that ghastly blissful smile') it savours of the coolly didactic and depersonalized.

Yet it is probable that Brecht was genuinely attached to Lorre, as also to the politically timorous Charles Laughton, whom Lyon considers the single most important person for him during his American exile. If Brecht hid his feelings, he must have had them. He customarily preferred to voice a professional reason for admiring someone rather than a merely personal one; to admit to an objective cause for affection (in Lorre's case, for pity or regret) rather than a subjective one. This was the case at times with his women friends too; they were of interest and significance to him in more ways than one. There is a comical-naughty poem written in America in which he praises an ample peasant-style skirt for its ancient associations and its grace – 'Your lovely movements bring to mind Colchis/ The day Medea strolled towards the sea' – adding that there are other reasons for favouring such a skirt, however: base and lustful ones, which 'will do for me'.

In his chapter on 'Brecht's Women' Lyon is relatively reticent, con-fining himself to (A.) Ruth Berlau and (B.) Brecht's wife, Helene

Weigel, both of them actresses (though then unemployable) and there-fore collaborators, as being the only two women in America who counted in terms of his work. Certainly there would be little point or propriety in leading us through the list of members of the 'harem'. Sufficient on this aspect of Brecht's briskness (and his distaste for the bourgeois/capitalist notion of love-as-ownership) is Joseph Losey's comment that he 'ate very little, drank very little, and fornicated a great deal'. Ruth Berlau ('Brecht's backstreet wife' she called herself) re-turned his devotion but, by this account, gave him dreadful trouble by her exigency, hysteria and utter lack of discretion. A story told here about Helene Weigel is particularly refreshing since it was commonly Brecht who came out on top in arguments with his intimates. She had maintained that women possess greater fortitude than men since they have to put up with menstruation and childbirth. Brecht, who was notorious for his permanent stubble, countered with: 'Men shave.' To which his wife retorted: 'How do you know?'

That Brecht, who could put his hand to practically anything, was obliged to abandon the idea of rendering the *Communist Manifesto* into classical hexameters may suggest that there were limits to his ideological manoeuvrability, and that – for all his foxiness and for all that the old fox had nowhere eminently desirable to run to – he would not have lasted much longer in the bosom of the German Democratic Republic. (At least in East Berlin he had an appreciative audience, even if much of it came from the bourgeoisie of West Berlin.) During his earlier visit to America he reportedly answered Sidney Hook's protest against Stalin's persecution of innocent people with the shocking epigram, 'The more innocent they are, the more they deserve to die.' Alert though Lyon is to Brecht's trickiness, he is content to ascribe the saying to annoyance at Hook's attack on Stalin and the desire to stupefy his opponent – without exploring the possible implication that those who were innocent of plotting against Stalin deserved to die for that very reason.*

Lyon is enlightening on the subject of Brecht's relations with the 'Frankfurt School', also evacuated to America. He might have been

*See Martin Esslin, 'Brecht: Icon and Self-Portrait', *Encounter*, December 1977.

expected to find the group's self-critical, dialectical procedures congenial. However, he regarded them as introverted mandarins, spinning
verbal subversions of the capitalist society in which they (unlike Brecht)
lived in some ease, while they saw him as a 'vulgar' Marxist, a crude and
retarded materialist still committed to the stuffy proletariat. Both camps
had a point to their credit: Brecht in that his politics were at least down
to earth, 'concrete', unlike the school's disembodied theorizing, and
Theodor Adorno in the element of truth behind his gibe that Brecht
spent two hours every day pushing dirt under his fingernails to make
himself look like a worker.

The quarrel between Brecht and Thomas Mann – the greatest
German novelist and the best living German poet, both of them exiles –
is less edifying. According to Katia Mann's *Unwritten Memories* hostility
was born early on, when somebody showed Mann one of Brecht's plays
and the novelist's comment – 'Just imagine, the monster has talent' –
was passed on to the dramatist. The latter came back with a sharper
quip: 'As a matter of fact, I always found his short stories quite good.'
Bad feeling intensified in America. Mann referred to Brecht as a
'party-liner', Brecht described Mann's works as 'clerico-fascist'. Mann
was a pessimist, seeing the Faustian two souls as Siamese twins native to
the German breast; Brecht was an optimist, readying himself to foster a
single-souled Germany just as soon as he could get back there. Mann
was an 'Establishment' figure, or figurehead, in America; Brecht, as
ever, was a rebel, a 'professional "anti" ', in Elsa Lanchester's words.
Yet neither was exactly single-minded or transparent, and it is possible
that what each of these masters of irony most disliked in the other was
his public image. The one dirtied his fingernails every day, the other
cleaned them.

We may still be in doubt as to what Brecht really intended by his
remark about Stalin. He was himself devoted to the play of thesis and
antithesis, but what he generally expected from other people was synth-
esis, or plain simplicity without the frills. When Hans Viertel, a Trotsky-
ist, asked him what would happen to those who declined to accept his
views, he answered: 'They have to be shot.' Given his dialectical nature,
not very many would be left alive in that case. Lyon remarks that it was

Viertel who came as near as anybody to realizing the complexities of the Brecht enigma when he termed him 'a one-man political party'. The description continued: ' . . . in close coalition with the Communists', which now gives it a strong air of paradox. But paradox was in order for Brecht, while orthodoxy was for other people. And what in him was the licence of the 'chameleon poet' would in others be the mark of the turncoat.

Katia Mann's comment on his appearance before the House Un-American Activities Committee is worth repeating: 'He was very sly indeed: he pretended to be stupid, and the others *were* stupid.' Brecht politely stressed his consciousness of being a guest in the United States, freely admitted that he was not nor ever had been a member of any Communist party, and courteously corrected the Committee regarding the date of his birth. Martin Esslin has compared the proceedings to the cross-examining of a zoologist by apes. In which case the apes, too, were courteous. 'They weren't as bad as the Nazis,' Brecht joked. 'The Nazis would never have let me smoke.' Finally the Committee pronounced him an honest and co-operative fellow and a good example to others, one whose links with known Communists were principally on an artistic level – a judgement which normally would have infuriated him but presumably, on this occasion, merely amused. It was undeniably convenient. As it happened, the hearing was held immediately before Brecht's previously arranged departure from the country – a coincidence which, as Lyon notes, gave his going a dramatic appearance. It was as if he were escaping from a witch-hunt. (A hunt from which, in reality, he had just been officially exempted.) He was pursued hotly by an award of a thousand dollars from the Academy of Arts and Letters. And behind him, like a bomb timed to go off later, he left his dramaturgy. 'In one form or another, it was theatre until the very end.'

TOURS DE . . .
On Max Frisch

It was *Stiller*, published in 1954 and translated into English as *I'm Not Stiller* in 1958, that carried Max Frisch into the class of major international writers, eliciting comparisons with Kafka and Thomas Mann which may have been more automatic than reasoned. *I'm Not Stiller* could have been called 'I'm Not Swiss – Or Not Entirely'. 'In Germany they click their heels, in the East they rub their hands together, in Switzerland they light a cigar and strain after a pose of surly equality as though nothing could happen in this country to a man who behaved correctly.' The eponymous (or not) hero, arriving at the Swiss frontier, maintains that he is not a Swiss called Stiller but an American of German extraction called White. The subsequent reaction (held up to scorn) is that anyone who doesn't 'grasp the opportunity of being Swiss as a boon' must be either crazy or criminal, possibly a spy. However irritating this view can be to outsiders, and to some insiders, we ought to acknowledge a core of sense in it. You can scold Switzerland for its complacency and self-righteousness, for its materialism, for what Stiller/White, generalizing from his small, clean prison cell, calls its 'oppressive adequacy', but you cannot reproach it with the class of calamities and evils caused by or occurring in some other countries. There would seem little opportunity for budding Bölls or Grasses among its authors, German-speaking or otherwise.

Even so, it is tempting to think of *I'm Not Stiller* as a study or critique of Swissness, if only because the alternative reading (alas, the correct one) is to see it as an exercise in 'identity' and 'authenticity', the attempt to escape from one identity into another. If Stiller/White were a fascinating individual, one might care more about his identity. His obsessive interest in himself is amazing by reason of its intensity and protraction: the self itself is an enigma doubtfully worth solving. The novel has much in the way of incidental attractions – topographical beauties, insights into other lives, some splendidly mimetic writing – but at its heart is a cloud that grows darker and more diffuse as we proceed. The hero is a menace to others, before long a bore to the reader (the reader at least in whom some sympathetic or needful nerve has not been pounded on); the novel a small spun-out storm in a large tea-urn. Or possibly a late example of Expressionism, humanized – and humorized – perhaps as far as it can be, but not as far as it needs to be.

Montauk (1975) is prefaced by a nicely self-deprecatory passage from Montaigne: 'Thus, reader, I am myself the matter of my book; you would be unreasonable to spend your leisure on so frivolous and vain a subject. So farewell.' And farewell it nearly is, when on the second page one is informed that, to light his pipe, 'he' has to stop briefly and use five matches. Well, it is windy. Is the wind material, then – or merely hot air? But yes, one sees that this may be in line with that 'truthfulness of presentation' on which Frisch insists. (The blowing-out of matches is one affliction in a smoker's life.) What does this truthfulness have to do with fiction – or, since the diary-like *Montauk* is questionably fiction, with truth?

Yet this interrogation of mine verges on pettiness: Frisch is telling us that 'he' is a pipe-smoker and that Montauk Point, Long Island, is or can be a windy place, and all these details contribute to the density of relation characteristic of the author. And one wants an author to have character. One may not warm to the persona that emerges in these pages, where Frisch's remark in the *Sketchbook 1946-1949* that writing is the equivalent of reading oneself applies more directly than elsewhere in his work, but the 'reading' is both unsparing and lucid. 'He' is not Stiller. 'Completely autobiographical – without inventing a single character; without inventing happenings of more significance than his own simple reality; without taking refuge in inventions of any kind; without seeking to justify his writing as a duty towards society. A story without a message . . . He wants simply to tell it (though not without some consideration for the people he mentions by name): his life.'

'He' is amusing on the subject of Max Frisch's fame, an attribute carried lightly. In a sauna bath a man asks him: 'Aren't you Herr Fritsch?' (*sic*), and a German customs official mentions a play of his that he liked – *Der Besuch der alten Dame*, actually the work of Dürrenmatt, the other half of the Swiss twins. At Yale a girl student asks: 'Does Stiller really want Julika to be redeemed, or is he really only interested in being her redeemer?' – a sensible question, one that points to the baffling egotism, the monstrous gratuitousness in Herr Stiller.

The passage on autobiography quoted above is followed swiftly by second thoughts, prompted by the discovery that he has been concealing his life from himself. 'I have been serving up stories to some sort of public, and in these stories I have, I know, laid myself bare – to the point of non-recognition. I live, not with my own story, but just with those parts of it that I have been able to put to literary use. Whole areas are missing . . . It is not even true that I have always described just myself. I have never described myself. I have only betrayed myself.' It's true that what a writer uses becomes the 'reality' for him: to such a degree that he may wonder how non-writers remember anything of their own story. The meaning of the word 'betrayed' in Frisch's passage is uncertain; and that 'whole areas are missing' seems inevitable rather than re-prehensible. Discounting a prurient interest in *Montauk* as 'bare' self-revelation – something Frisch plainly doesn't encourage and the reader would be hard pressed to sustain – the chief interest lies in a strong sense of life or, better, of having lived, backed up by such apothegms, products of having lived, as (concerning the absence in a weekend tryst of serious quarrels as distinct from misunderstandings): 'You need a marriage, a long one, to become a monster.'

There is mention in *Montauk* of a story set in Ticino which 'has gone wrong for the fourth time; the role of the narrator is not yet clear.' If this refers to Frisch's most recent novel, *Man in the Holocene* (1979; in English 1980), set in a village in the canton of Ticino where the author himself lives, it may strike us as strange since there is virtually no narrator in the book – yet not strange, in that the role of the author, remotest of controllers, does remain obscure. Blurb writers earn more kicks than compliments, and it ought to be noted that the jacket copy here is genuinely informative and truly helpful about the author's intentions. If we wonder why there are so many white spaces between the paragraphs – this helps to give the book the look of a primer, but is rather pleasant after the over-populated condition of much contemporary setting – the jacket tells us that 'spaces are made to say as much as words, since they indicate thought leaps and gaps in a flickering memory, reinforcing the hallucinatory character of the story.' Frisch is a writer, one might venture, whose books really need blurbs. Not that, by its author's standards, this one is abnormally difficult to read; much of it consists of sketches of dinosaurs, charts and inset passages in various typefaces taken from encyclopedias, guide-books, local histories, the Bible . . .

Herr Geiser, nearing seventy-four, lives alone in a valley whose history of floods and landslides is reproduced from authoritative sources, alongside an extract from Chapter 7 of the Book of Genesis describing the Flood. There has been heavy and prolonged rain, and the village is cut off, the electricity supply failing intermittently. 'Geiser has time to spare', time to read in his twelve-volume encyclopedia, *Der Grosse Brockhaus*, about the different kinds of lightning (twelve are itemized), geology both global and local, glaciers and mountain ranges, and (a little too much) about the dinosaurs, those tyrants who had nothing to fear on earth and yet whose reign was mysteriously cut short. That the weather prevents the old man from working in his garden may be part of the trouble: the 'he' of *Montauk* noted that 'the older I get, the less I can bear myself when I am not working'. Geiser anticipates disaster, an avalanche that will bury him, his house, the whole village. In the village tavern, however, while they admit that it has been a bad year for wine and for mushrooms too, 'nobody is reckoning on another Flood'.

The progress of Geiser's fears – though fear is not the right word, for he shows little emotion of any sort – is logical enough. What has happened once can happen again. Man lives in the Holocene epoch, which began when the Pleistocene ended, and if the Pleistocene could end, so can the Holocene. Geiser's books are full of warnings, ranging from avalanches in the recent past to the disappearance of dinosaurs in the further past. He clips passages from them which he then pins to the walls, removing his dead wife's portrait to make room.

The reader comes to understand that the approaching doom applies to Geiser himself – not the whole earth, not even Ticino, not even the village in the valley, or the old man's house. He goes to the tavern to buy matches, and forgets: 'Obviously brain cells are ceasing to function.' He drops his reading glasses and breaks them: 'If necessary, one can always use the magnifying glass for reading.' Then he sets off on an arduous expedition to the pass, 1,076 metres above sea level, leaving the house at dawn and returning after a painful trek (cramp in the calves and thighs) past midnight. 'There is always ground, even at night.' This is some feat, a tribute to the old man's indomitability, and perhaps by extension to man's indomitable spirit, but in itself unmotivated, inexplicable. Geiser is not trying to save himself; he doesn't even wish to.

Similarly gratuitous – is the gratuitous a part of truthful presentation? Another hard question – is the lengthy account, late in the proceedings, of Geiser and his brother (now dead) climbing on the Matterhorn fifty years before. Dinosaurs in their prime? Hardly, but in itself a vivid, expert piece of writing.

From the summit there was not much to see. Here and there a break in the clouds: a view of bleak moraines or the dirty tongue of a glacier, elsewhere a green Alpine meadow in sunshine, streams like a network of white veins, and once they caught sight of the little lake, the Schwarzsee, beside which their green tent was pitched, though they could not spot it, a small ink-blue pool glistening in the sunshine, next to some things that looked like white maggots, presumably cows.

Geiser's expedition in old age to the pass might certainly explain, if explanation is required, the collapse he now suffers. Perhaps he has fallen down the stairs, perhaps his chair slipped, he cannot remember, but his left eyelid is numb, he has a feeling of tightness above his left temple. He must have had a slight stroke. The chilly dryness of the writing, its closeness to documentary, is alleviated, as elsewhere in Frisch, by some touches of humour. The crack Geiser sees from his window – 'that is the way landslides begin' – turns out to be a track made by his cat through the grass. Food is running short in the village, but, Geiser observes in his local-historian's manner, 'the cats in this district are seldom eaten'; just as he notes that the last murder in the valley occurred decades ago, and 'ever since the young men have owned motor cycles, incest has been dying out, and so has sodomy.' A little later, and we infer that Geiser has none the less roasted the cat over the fire but found himself unable to eat it. 'Kitty is buried near the roses.' The doorbell rings, the telephone rings, he answers neither. He cannot remember what gave him the idea of cutting out those pictures of dinosaurs and lizards: 'there were never any dinosaurs in Ticino.' The more humane or tender-minded reader will be relieved to hear, towards the end, that Geiser's daughter Corinne has arrived from Basel – 'Why does she talk to him as if he were a child?' – and is making tea.

Concrete, all very concrete. But how much concrete does a reader want in a novel? As conventional fiction – characters, actions, story – *Man in the Holocene* doesn't work, and no doubt doesn't wish to. We cannot feel much sympathy for Geiser – some respect, yes, but less of that after the roasting of the cat, surely an un-Swiss activity – nor shall we take very much interest in the documentation unless we happen to be climbers mad on geology, Ticino, dinosaurs, lightning. The book can be read as a parable about the threat that hangs over us all, the new dinosaurs, and perhaps about the hope of survival too. But this sounds too obvious, old hat, for Frisch, too much 'a duty towards society'. Whatever game is going on here, it is not incontestably worth the candle.

It may be, in Frisch's case, that résumés make the books sound not merely simpler but more engaging than they are. In the reading, his recent play, *Triptych: Three Scenic Panels*, is not notably engaging, although on the stage, with some extra humanity in the shape of human beings actually in front of us, it could well be more so. Once again, the work compels a cool respect, largely through its stealthy ingenuity and its compactness. With its three 'hinged' pictures of death, it is exceptionally tightly knit while conveying an impression of freedom in its personae, a seeming absence of manipulation by the author. Humour, that liberator even of slaves, helps in this respect. In the land of shades there is a flute player who makes the same mistake over and over again; a son, dead at seventy, who is older than his father, stuck fast at forty-one; a convict who assures the clerk whom he shot in a bank raid: 'I'd never do such a thing again, and that's the truth, I'm sure of it'; a clergyman who 'can't understand there's no job for him here'.

This sense of freedom, of autonomous existence, is a rare achievement, and yet it is won at the cost of some gratuitousness – what is freer that that? – and of pointless repetition. Granted, the repetitiousness is a large part of the point: the dead go on repeating themselves, *ad infinitum* one supposes, for 'what has been can't be altered', and they can only consort with those they already knew ('Bakunin and all the rest of them, you'll never meet them'). *Triptych* is a *tour de* something, and I wish I could be sure what the something is. What does it tell us about death, except that there's a lot of it about? What does it tell us about eternity, except 'How ordinary eternity is!'? What does it tell us about life that life itself cannot tell in livelier fashion?

Although he is skilled at skating on the very brink of it, enjoyableness does not rank high in Frisch's order of artistic priorities. This must endear him to those who believe that the profound, the precious and the new are incompatible with ordinary pleasures, and to those who feel comfortable only with discomfort. The rest of us, perhaps by now a minority, can only stare and wonder, or wonder and slink away.

SISYPHUS AND HIS STONE
On Günter Grass and Heinrich Böll

From the Diary of a Snail

Herr Grass explains himself to his children: 'In a devious way I'm uncomplicated.' *From the Diary of a Snail*, though to the undevious reader it may seem somewhat complicated, is in fact uncomplicated, if in a devious way. Grass might be thought to be doing too much in it: but that, it could be, is the impression registered when an eminently intelligent and imaginative writer is actually not doing quite enough.

In part the book is a running account of the author's energetic campaigning for the Social Democratic Party and Willy Brandt in 1969. He covered 31,000 kilometres, which is good going for a snail. Bluntly, the point of the snail – 'Learn from the snail, take your time' – is that it represents the slowness of true progress as opposed to those Dionysiac movements which, exciting as they are at the time, turn into the total stasis of tyranny. 'Signposts with changing inscriptions but identical destination: destroy unmask convert smash eliminate pacify liquidate re-educate isolate exterminate . . .' – this sentence describes the multifold enemy of the snail, of such bruised, sceptical, hopeful, backward-looking progressives as Günter Grass himself. 'Let's look and see whether forward isn't already behind us. Interrogate the rundown heels of our shoes.' Grass's engaging wit must perforce march with his hard good sense, and so he distinguishes between two sorts of snail, 'conservative clinging' and 'progressive mobile': his metaphors have often had to take a dangerous strain.

We may be reminded of the dentist in *Local Anaesthetic*, Grass's previous book, the page proofs of which he passed during the campaign and from which he read (the diary records) at an Evangelical Church Congress in Stuttgart. The dentist was 'conservative' in that he conserved what was worth keeping and 'progressive' in that he removed what had rotted and supplied a bridge: a slow careful process (we remember how protracted the treatment was) and (he believed in anaesthetics) a relatively painless one. A 'radical' would have rooted out the teeth without anaesthetic; or even knocked out all thirty-two of them in the way the SA youths in *Dog Years* knocked out Amsel's. 'I put my money on snail consciousness,' Grass says in the diary, rejecting those various stallions who at various times have galloped under the colours of *Weltgeist* or 'historical necessity'.

Interleaved with this rueful celebration of gradualism and contributory to it are two stories and a meditation. The first and weightiest and very Grassian story concerns the fate of the Danzig Jews and more specifically Hermann Ott (nicknamed 'Doubt') who, a refugee though not a Jew, spends the war hidden in a cellar, where he becomes an expert on snails. Grass has always been given to documentation, to facts, perhaps because they are real things and a corrective to those mystic propensities which understandably he must wish to hold in check, and here much information is dispensed on 'the 112,000 species of mollusc, 85,000 of which are classified as snails or slugs'.

The meditation consists of a commentary, moral, philosophical and political, on Dürer's engraving, *Melencolia*: on Melancholia as the product of sophisticated inactivity or a disillusionment with her sister, Utopia. The argument is rather too complex and fragmented to consort comfortably with the book's other elements. And then there is the other story, of the fifty-six-year-old Augst, inactive member of the SS in his student days, pharmacist, Christian, pacifist and yet missing the soldierly comradeship of the old days, a man of serious concerns, unable to laugh, who kills himself with prussic acid during Grass's meeting in Stuttgart. I must confess to a residual grievance in this connection. It was some time before I realized that, misled by Grass's habitual love of emblems, by Melancholia and Doubt, and indeed by the pharmacist's life-history, I had been misreading 'Augst' as 'Angst'.

The election, as we know, was victorious. In a television film made in 1972 and repeated on the night of Willy Brandt's resignation, the narrator remarked that Grass had 'put his fame at the disposal of democracy'. 'Fame,' said the less simple Grass a little later (and also in the present book), 'is someone it seems fun to piss on.' I hope it will not sound too irresponsible to suggest that Grass would do better to place his literary talents at the disposal of literature. It is not the fate of Willy Brandt that prompts the suggestion: on the contrary, that might be felt to lend a sombre enhancement to Grass's undertaking. No, it is rather that Ott-'Doubt' is pushed into a corner by the busy trivia of the campaign record – 'I wish I could go to the movies,' Grass complains as he talk-talk-talks his way round West Germany, and so do we – and that Grass could have explained himself to his children in private (the book doesn't tell us much more about his attitudes than *Local Anaesthetic* did, and did more powerfully). He is a natural, compulsive writer – 'sentences that lie around, run after me, torment me and demand to be cast in lead' – and, if stuck, he could write exhaustively and with verve about nothing at all. For all the vivacity of its style, its inventiveness and entertaining satire, so much of *From the Diary of a Snail* consists of comments on comments. Politics is the art of the possible, we are told. That doesn't sound a very exciting art. Perhaps the truth is, the snail isn't a very exciting animal, and even Günter Grass can't make it so.

The Flounder

The Flounder is another baggy monster in the line of *The Tin Drum* and *Dog Years*: it may not be what most people consider 'a novel', but it is certainly a meal, packed with spicy ingredients and none too easy to digest. In it Grass blends three histories – of cooking, of the Vistula estuary, and of the roles of the sexes – from the Stone Age up to press date. At the bottom of the cauldron is the Grimm tale of the talking fish who, in exchange for its life, granted the fisherman whatever his discontented and nagging wife desired. The wife's demands grew exorbitant – she even wanted to be Pope, and then God, two occupations reserved to the male – and the couple were returned to their former poverty.

Grass's Flounder begins his pedagogic career as adviser to breast-bound Stone Age men, exhorting and assisting them to wean themselves from a comfortable but humiliating matriarchal rule and to assert the male principle. The author is a mimic of genius, and among other mock-anthropological delights we hear that in those days it was a woman who stole fire from the sky, by concealing it in her pouch – something that no man could have done. Progress is slow: when as part of their emancipation the Flounder teaches men to count ('the hour of algebra has struck'), the three-breasted earth-goddess Awa declares that one hundred and one is the highest possible number, being the number of dimples in her buttocks, and no calculation can proceed beyond it. But with the Flounder's assiduous backing the male cause prevails – as Grass illustrates in a series of parodic portraits of Great Women Sufferers (and cooks) through the ages.

It appears, however, that there exists a second version of the fairy tale, in which the wife is modest and undemanding whereas the fisherman wants to fight wars, subjugate nature, rise above the earth and so forth. The Brothers Grimm couldn't very well legitimize both versions, though both are 'true', and so – not being Sisters Grimm – they chose to record the one we know. Hence in modern times, professing himself shocked by what the male principle and male domination have led to, the Flounder seeks to switch sides: 'Let power change its sex.' He allows himself to be caught by three hardboiled young feminists, who forthwith put him on trial in a disused Berlin cinema for disseminating misogynistic propaganda. The court is entirely female, and the account of the proceedings is the funniest part of the book, a high-speed satire on the splinter groups and the proliferation of jargon that attend any democratically run movement, however undemocratic its aims. The girls are out to get him, but the Flounder, who is both a poor fish and something like God the Father, takes advantage of the situation (and the jargon) to procure security guards for himself and fresh North Sea water for his tank: being obliged to lie in stale Baltic Sea water, polluted with mercury, 'borders on the only-too-notorious methods of torture practised by the modern system of class justice . . .'

Feminists – and indeed others – are likely to consider Grass unfair in picking on the quarrelsomeness of female activists and in making the three leaders not only lesbians but loutish and puerile. Women have of course traditionally done the cooking: cooking is all-important, and demeaning. Thus Sophie Rotzoll, standing for revolutionary woman at the turn of the eighteenth century in Danzig, takes revenge on the oppressors by serving poisonous mushrooms: there is disagreement, we are told, as to whether her last words were 'Long live the Republic!' or 'Venison in aspic!' And even at that, the narrator – eternal man, as his wife is eternal woman – seems to know more about the art of cooking than any of his cook-heroines, and one wonders whether, far from gaining anything, women are going to lose that which they had.

Against this male tendentiousness are set the occasional tenderness and (more often) respect shown towards women, despite the parodic flavour of their 'representativeness' in history, and also a plain if humorously clothed account of what man has done to man as well as to woman. The harshest vignette is the last one, which is not wrapped up in mythic clouds or veils of antiquity. On a Father's Day outing, Sibylle, who cooks for the party and is mocked as 'a femme', 'a butterball' for her pains, is first raped by her three girl friends with the help of a plastic organ, and then raped and killed by seven 'black angels' on motor cycles. Dishonour would seem to be satisfied. Except that the narrator informs us smugly that he has slept with three of the four girls, and the fourth just didn't appeal to him. But then, if he slept with them, they slept with him, and maybe he didn't appeal to the fourth girl – which presumably restores the balance.

Male chauvinist pigs, female chauvinist sows ... Will equality of dishonour and disgrace bring the sexes together, in the way George Herbert saw humanity brought to God, if not through goodness then through sheer weariness? The Flounder is stuck with thesis and antithesis, and *The Flounder* is a progress report, chiefly reporting the weariness, and ending thus: 'What's to become of us? We're worn out, our quarrel has dozed off, it's only talking in its sleep. Little words hang on. Apples of discord roll across the table ...'

Grass can write in lively fashion about anything or nothing; and at times he does just that. The complexity of *The Flounder*, as of *Dog Years* and *The Tin Drum* (whose three-year-old hero appears fleetingly here), is more one of appearance and form than of reality and matter. Grass has said, 'In a devious way I'm uncomplicated.' To which one has to add that the narrator of the present novel, besides being eternal man and omniscient, is also average man, mean and sensual. Though some heavy-handedness persists, the set pieces characteristic of the author are less gratuitous than they have been: the excursus on faeces is at least apropos, as is the eulogy of tripe, and likewise (since not-eating is related to eating) the visit the narrator pays to Calcutta. Food is plainly of the essence, but all the same Grass's obsession with meals and how to prepare them swells into lip-smacking greed – and worse, heartlessness. His collection of poems, *In the Egg*, published here simultaneously, contains an item of 120 lines called 'The Jellied Pig's Head' which one expects to modulate into some kind of Brechtian irony: it doesn't, it remains a recipe.

For me, Grass's most poignant passages come in moments of relative austerity, and austerity is something that, outside *Local Anaesthetic*, he has not often gone in for. Nor is he given to tepidness. And if his private obsessions, flamboyantly indulged, damage his epic intentions, I suspect that they also provide much of the energy and drive required by epic. He is endlessly inventive, monstrously clever, and, whatever you can say against his sophisticated brutishness, he makes his contemporaries look like watercolourists who have added too much water to their colours.

The Meeting at Telgte

'Where princes had disgraced themselves, poets had earned respect. They, not the powerful, were assured of immortality.' It is the year 1647, near the end of the Thirty Years War, and assorted writers, together with a scattering of conventionally ignoble publishers, have risked their lives or their comfort to gather at a town in Westphalia. Their purpose is to give 'new force to the last remaining bond between all Germans, namely the German language' and.(which they see as much the same thing) to read their manuscripts to one another.

While Grass has invented the meeting at Telgte, he assembles real, historical writers, such a galaxy indeed as later literary symposia would be hard pressed to equal. What he sets before us this time is not a tin drum – and hardly an article likely to enjoy the vast success of that rude and raucous instrument – but an embattled lyre. Although a short book,

The Meeting at Telgte has substance. With remarkable economy Grass contrives to evoke and differentiate his assembled men of letters, whose lives and works are characterized in an appendix here by Leonard Forster for the benefit of those unversed in Baroque poetry. By so doing the author imparts conviction to what might otherwise seem a contrived fancy or simply a factitious pre-play of another war-torn scene and another association of German writers, the Group 47 (to whose founder the book is dedicated), exactly three hundred years later in time.

The poets' deliberations and doings belong to that woeful time and place but in essentials are universal and timeless. 'Our stories of today need not have taken place in the present.' With violence and obscenity confronting them daily in life, they debate whether such things should be shown on the stage as well. An expert in prosody lectures on the proper use of dactylic words, inserting gratuitous gibes at a rival theoretician. There is talk of purifying the language and weeding out words of foreign provenance, thus replacing *Kloster* (convent) with the echt-deutsch *Jungfernzwinger* ('virgins' dungeon'). (If this is meant to point us to the denazification of the German language then it is confusingly reminiscent of pre-war Japanese efforts to replace such foreign imports as 'baseball' with good home-grown terminology: the examples given suggest mild raillery on the author's part.) Philipp von Zesen takes refuge in bloated metaphors from the sight of bloated corpses in the river Ems. In a clash roughly comparable to that between edifying realism and aesthetic formalism, the hymn-writer Paul Gerhardt ('O sacred head, sore wounded') champions simple, devout songs for plain people against the high art of the composer Heinrich Schütz, an awe-inspiring figure who has attended in the hope of finding texts to set. (The 'faint *and yet*' still to be wrested, Schütz ventures, from helplessness calls to mind the high G of a cello, the 'last fainting sound', a 'light in the night', detected in Leverkühn's *Lamentation* in Mann's *Doctor Faustus*.) Siegmund Birken reads a poem in which Peace and Justice exchange kisses, and when one listener objects to its overheated rhyming, another asks: since meaning is absent, 'why shouldn't singsong and dingdong exchange compliments?'

While the causes and the course of the Thirty Years War were complicated in the extreme, the division between Catholics and Protestants – Professor Forster remarks – is to some degree analogous to the division after the later war between capitalist West and socialist East. However, the assembled littérateurs do not confine themselves to political prospects, religious reconciliation or literary ends and means. Hopes mingle with despair, 'valeoftearsishness' (Opitz's criticism of Gryphius's sonnets in a cod-consuming scene in *The Flounder*) alternates with gluttony, lamentations over human depravity are succeeded by orgies in the stables with willing wenches – in which the bashful student Scheffler (later known as Angelus Silesius, poet of mystical love) 'poured out his soul with his sperm'.

An unexpected Lucullan feast of roasted geese, pigs and sheep, crystallized ginger and goat cheese looks like the author's old over-insistence on earthiness (all Grass is flesh), but brings out the point that to eat well at that time was something of a miracle, or a crime. It is characteristic – at any rate of the author – that stern Lutherans should be shown unknowingly swigging sacramental wine liberated by the rascally 'regimental secretary' Gelnhausen. The poets assume too readily that acknowledged legislators admire unacknowledged ones, and when they discover that these goodies are not gifts from grateful princes and prelates but the fruits of armed robbery, their sensitive stomachs turn from gorging to vomiting.

It was Gelnhausen who found room at the Bridge Tavern for the symposiasts by representing them as plague victims and thus scaring away its former occupants. Twenty years later he will resurface as Grimmelshausen, author of *Simplicissimus*, the famous plebeian-picaresque chronicle of the Thirty Years War. Present on sufferance in this elevated company, he treats them to a foretaste of his future as a writer: not of 'mincing pastorals', 'sensitive soul-blubber' or 'well-behaved rhymes for church congregations' – no, 'he would let every foul smell out of the bag', 'let loose gruesome laughter', and draw his language uninhibitedly from 'the casks of life'. It sounds very much like a prefigurement of *The Tin Drum* and *Dog Years*.

Libuschka, the landlady of the Bridge Tavern, is an old friend, and more and less than a friend, of Gelnhausen's. Once a camp-follower, seven times married to captains on various sides, now ageing but still operative, she is known as 'Courage', a slang term for the female sex organ, this being the location of much though certainly not all of her bravery as a female warrior. In fact Gelnhausen/Grimmelshausen (or Grass acting for him) has merely taken back from Brecht what was his own creation, the 'Archtrickster and Trollop' Courasche of the novel *Trutz Simplex*, sequel to *Simplicissimus*. We could have done with more of this lively, well-read and disgraceful character. At the end, with the tavern mysteriously on fire, she and her maids mount their mules and join a troop of gypsies, while the poets, 'the other, the true Germany', set out on the journey back to their desks. The manifesto they have drawn up, an appeal for peace, justice and religious tolerance, has perished in the flames. 'What would in any case not have been heard, remained unsaid.'

Once again Grass has surprised and gratified the reader who welcomes or at least doesn't object to something he can get his teeth into. Notwithstanding its low farce, *The Meeting at Telgte* testifies to writing's pertinacious involvement with life, something that in peace-torn times we may come to doubt.

Group Portrait with Lady

How can one describe Heinrich Böll's *Group Portrait with Lady*? To begin with, one might suggest that it looks more like a new novel by Günter Grass. Or even a new novel – and, if corporeality is expected of this literary form, more of a novel than his earlier ones – by Uwe Johnson. Possibly, in a period of consolidation, these novelists are merging together, eventually to form the definitive German Novelist? In which case the German Novelist will be less grotesque than Grass, less disembodied than Johnson, and less staid than Böll. This might seem an excellent recipe. If it is, then it may serve as a tribute, preliminary to some fault-finding, to what is announced as Böll's new novel, here translated by Leila Vennewitz with a splendid air of authenticity.

The book is a portrait, as the title indicates, of a lady, Leni Pfeiffer, at the time of composition forty-eight years old, surrounded by a cloud of witnesses, or 'informants'. The novel takes the form of a closely researched report in depth, in which the author, tongue in cheek, utilizes the most extreme procedures of bureaucracy in full flood. He states early on that '*important* informants will be introduced with exact data as to height and weight'. There are times when the reader is bound to wonder how the author can keep his tongue in his cheek so long without biting it off or choking to death. To some extent the sense of artificiality is alleviated by the fact that the author, or 'the Au.' (as the book has it), comes to take an active if minor part in the action and even falls in love with Sister Klementina, a rather fetching nun who casts off her habit with small reluctance. (There may here be a manifestation of Böll's equivocal feelings about Catholicism, as evinced earlier in *The Clown*.) Even so, some embarrassment remains. In the mode chosen for the relation the Au.'s poker-faced verbatim reproductions of his informants' reports are supplemented by a psychologist's 'psychogram' replete with technical terms and their abbreviations and inverted commas for those lay expressions which still have to be employed, and also by a police officer's deposition. One immediate effect is this: where the author assumes the role of a detective, the reader has forced upon him the role of a voyeur. 'Although obscenities will be avoided wherever possible in this report, for the sake of completeness it may be in order to describe the sexual enlightenment offered to the girls before they left boarding school . . .'

Moreover, these informants and report-writers have something of the loquacity and zeal for detail of Richardson's Pamela. One sees the advantages in this procedure – for one thing it preserves Böll from that faint (though I never thought especially distasteful) sentimentality to which he has inclined in handling a put-upon character whom he admires or pities, and for another, it is itself a comment on our brave new world of insolently brisk computers and identikit psychologizing – but it exacts a stiff price in the way of reader-alienation when pursued through a book of this size.

One difficulty the reader experiences is in establishing whether or not on some particular occasion Böll is being wantonly tongue-in-cheek, superfluously documentary. Do we need specimens of Alois Pfeiffer's patriotic prose ('Such a one was Colonel Günther!'), *c.* 1940? Perhaps we do, if not at such length, since Leni did marry Alois, though in error and very briefly, and she should be cleared of any suspicion of callousness towards him. A lot of what the Au. declares he is or is not 'able to confirm' doesn't matter one way or the other, and his scrupulousness could well be spared – so much is fairly clear. Non-smoking, possibly through association with Hitler, seems to carry some significance as a pointer to character (the Au. himself is a heavy smoker), but do we need to know who among minor characters smokes a pipe, who smokes cigars, who smokes cigarettes? Well . . . at this point the Au. is in the conference room of Hoyser Inc., on the twelfth floor of a high-rise building overlooking the Rhine, discussing the case of 'Aunt Leni' with the two young Hoysers who are about to evict her, despite past obligations to the lady, on the grounds of her 'unrealistic attitude', failure to grasp the profit motive and generally 'sloppy ways'. There follows a highly amusing account of Leni unconsciously undermining the principles of 'our achievement-oriented society, of the free democratic constitutional state':

Side by side with this economic antiprocess – and this is central to the issue – there is a moral antiprocess. It so happens that conditions like those in Aunt Leni's apartment foster communal, not to say communistic, illusions which, not as illusions but as idylls, are disastrous, and they also foster, well, not exactly promiscuity – but promiscuitivism, which slowly but surely destroys modesty and morality and makes a mockery of individualism . . .

The appeal of this impassioned if cliché-starred pronouncement is heightened by the condition of the conference room, its air thick with various brands of tobacco smoke. When the Au. tries to open a window, young Hoyser points out with gentle didacticism that the over-all air-conditioning of the building is an extremely complex affair, permitting 'spontaneous individual airing' only at the lighting up of a magic eye which is not due for another hour and a half. It is all a matter of progress – and '*we* can't do whatever we like, either – we are not permitted to open the windows in our own building whenever we like.' A case of poor little rich industrialist. But we also perceive that, though the phraseology has changed and instead of Blood-and-Soil and degeneracy we now hear about 'achievement-oriented society' and 'moral antiprocess', there is a certain continuity in what is going on underneath. We gather that the sort of disposition which enabled its possessors to thrive under Nazism, not only helped them to ride the defeat of Nazism but also fits them to prosper in the present. Equally, those who never did well out of things, but managed to survive with something like honour, are still not doing well but still surviving with something like honour. Leni is an embarrassment because she has always been her own woman; to those who follow an ideology, whether through conviction or through opportunism, she is bound to seem an 'anarchist'.

'What kind of a world is this?' asks the Au. in the midst of a discourse on life-values and the whys and wherefores of some women receiving two villas, six cars and a million and a half in cash for providing the very same service as has earned other women a cup of coffee and a cigarette costing 22.5 pfennigs in all. 'What has happened to justice?' The saddest instance here of what certainly looks like the absence of justice is the case of Leni's best friend, Margret Schlömer, who lies in hospital suffering from advanced venereal disease, a fearful mess, 'tears might come out of her nipples and urine out of her nose'. Margret was no prostitute, but 'a woman forever entangled in certain masculine desires', and she caught the infection from a foreign statesman whom she was officially instructed to soften (as she did) into a 'treaty mood', thereby benefiting the whole of the 'achievement-oriented society'. Margret dies in a venereal ward, not of the disease which was practically cured, but of blushing. She was, we gather, an extremely modest woman, and her story, though in some ways the reverse of Leni's, underlines the same moral: a love-life cannot be measured in terms of bed-count. Another moral in the air is that you can cure VD, but there is no cure for sensitiveness and a loving nature.

Yet this is by no means a bitter novel: rather the contrary. Grass's *Dog Years* posed the question, 'Who wants to tear open old wounds if the opening of wounds gives pleasure?' It has certainly given rich literary material. While the war is central to *Group Portrait with Lady*, the novel's sweep takes in pre-war and post-war. Most of Böll's 'Group' are survivors, some of them persons of integrity, others not notably so, not one of them a monster. The 'Group' is a varied and meaty one – the reader would welcome an index to supplement the List of Characters – and the way in which each informant becomes in turn the subject of other informants lightens the pressure of scrutiny on Leni and saves the reader's feeling of voyeurism from growing to intolerable proportions.

In fact we do like what we see of Leni, and Böll contrives that the more we see the more we like her. The happy – at least not unhappy – ending is wholly acceptable: 'A garbage collector who rolls, lifts, empties garbage cans, bound in love to a woman who mourns three husbands, has read Kafka, knows Hölderlin by heart, is a singer, pianist, painter, mistress, a past and future mother . . .' To complete this picture it should be mentioned that the happy man in question is an immigrant Turk who already has a wife and four children at home and 'on account of polygamous rights, of which he is aware but of which he has so far never been able to make use, has shown not the remotest trace of a guilty conscience . . .'

The story of the Jewish nun, Sister Rahel (called 'Haruspica' from her ability to read the future in the bowel movements of her charges), and the roses that bloomed out of her ashes every December, might have come from the pages of Günter Grass, as also the fictitious wartime firm which Leni's father created to acquire cement for disposal on the black market and whose payroll featured foreign workers with such names as Raskolnikov, Pushkin, Oblomov, Lermontov and of course Gogol. Also Grassian, one would say, are Boris's sewn-on foreskin (which survived, up to a point), Leni's nightly encounters with the Virgin Mary on the television screen (cf. *Local Anaesthetic*), and (cf. *Dog Years*) the connection mooted between real estate and three or four handfuls of gold teeth. Likewise the exercises in impassive expertise and the mildly self-indulgent 'documentation' devoted to the techniques of wreath-making and the chemical composition of human tears.

Such likenesses are interesting, but scarcely sinister. And it could be argued that if in this novel Böll has moved in Grass's direction, then in *Local Anaesthetic* Grass had already made some move in Böll's direction, tempering his old flamboyance in favour of a new sobriety. What matters about *Group Portrait with Lady* is that it is intelligent, adult, humorous, touching, everywhere humane, and almost everywhere eschewing the easy opportunities. Despite the etiolated bureaucratic/clinical mode, it gives off the mixed smells of humanity undegenerate, unregenerate and, for better or for worse, unremitting.

The Lost Honour of Katharina Blum

Apart from a few obscure references to such technical matters as fluidity, conduction and drainage, this short novel of Heinrich Böll's is a triumph of technique. It is also a triumph of tone over subject-matter, the latter (it must be allowed) being somewhat banal in itself.

The 'story' – Böll's technique necessitates the inverted commas – is of Katharina Blum, 'an unusually nice, smart, virtually blameless person', who falls in love with a young man met at a party, takes him home for the night, discovers that he is wanted by the police, and smuggles him to safety under their noses. Katharina is taken up by the *News*, a popular rag, and her honour is butchered to make a pressman's holiday. She shoots the reporter concerned and, her lover Ludwig having been apprehended, gives herself up.

Possibly, being a well-known champion of the freedom of the writer, Böll felt it incumbent on him to make a clear exception of the yellow side of writing. A number of his old *bêtes noires* suffer glancing blows in the process, including the Church, excessively powerful industrialists, corrupt Army officers, party jargon (whatever the party), and isms, opportunism in particular. What most neatly epitomizes this author's blend of sympathy and irony is his treatment of Hans Schnier in *The Clown*. Schnier is a gifted mimic who could easily make a handsome living by performing his 'Board Meeting' turn in Leipzig and his 'Party Conference Elects its Presidium' turn in Bonn. Unfortunately he prefers to give the latter number in Leipzig and the former in Bonn: 'to poke fun at Boards of Directors where Boards of Directors don't exist seems pretty low.'

In form, *The Lost Honour of Katharina Blum* derives from Böll's previous novel, *Group Portrait with Lady*, which masqueraded almost too successfully as an extended, excruciatingly researched 'psychogram'.

Though younger, Katharina resembles the 'Lady' of the title in possessing an embarrassing honesty and a startlingly simple integrity, and in being one of those characters, rare in contemporary fiction, whom one would truly like to meet. The new novel doesn't have a comparable richness and range, or inventiveness, but it displays a set of virtues the earlier book, taking in some forty years of German history, couldn't accommodate: it is economical, uncluttered, clean-cut and clean-cutting, and runs less risk of losing its readers on the way. And despite its slender proportions, it packs a lot in.

It does run *some* risk. The trick of using an inhuman classificatory-jargonistic mode for the purpose of vindicating or defending the human has something in common with the old witch test: if the subject drowns, she is innocent. The reader has to keep his wits about him, and in particular whichever wit is responsible for interpreting tone. It struck me, in *Group Portrait with Lady*, that the carefully unemotional tone of the exposition might be Böll's way of guarding himself against the faint sentimentality to which he inclines in his handling of a congenial and ill-used character. Again, I think, he has come near, in what is a parody (though not for parody's sake) of 'objective reporting', to leaning over backwards. That he saves himself from tumbling over backwards is proved by Katharina Blum. She may not be a creation of Dickensian density, but she is a living presence, a charming girl whose only fault is her unthinking normality.

'Tone' must seem a somewhat esoteric consideration, and all the more elusive when one is discussing a translation – even one so persuasive as the present, where a cool and ostensibly jocular mordancy, distinctly Böll's, comes through so unmistakably in the English. But 'tone' is bolstered generously – and the reader alerted – by simpler, more straightforward devices, among them the plainly comic. The statements about Katharina made by her friends to the press undergo slight-seeming but substantial modifications on their way to the printed sheet: 'cool and level-headed' turns into 'ice-cold and calculating', 'radically helpful' is politicized into 'very radical'. The headlines modulate gracefully, as if in obedience to some ineluctable law of nature, from Friday's 'OUTLAW'S SWEETHEART' to Saturday's

'MURDERER'S MOLL', while anonymous letter-writers join in with 'Communist bitch', this expression of revulsion followed by sexual propositions of the crudest sort. When an amiable policewoman brings Katharina clippings from the 'quality papers' – restrained, matter-of-fact references to 'a certain Katharina B., a domestic' – she remains unconsoled: 'Who reads those anyway? Everyone *I* know reads the *News!*'

Böll is nicely amusing, just this side of the heavy-handed, on the moral problems posed by wire-tapping – a 'notable and noteworthy process' which before long is extended to all Katharina's friends, well-wishers and contacts (except for the really 'powerful' ones). Young people are encouraged to enter the civil service – and then they are exposed to 'moral outcasts of the telephone' and the risk of damage.

Let us assume that a temporarily suspect person of a vulgar nature, whose telephone is being officially tapped, calls up his equally vulgar sex partner of the moment . . . Is there any provision for psychiatric treatment? What does the Union of Public Services, Transportation and Communications say to *that?* . . . Here at last we have an area where church and trade union might co-operate.

He is similarly entertaining on the media's narcissistic preoccupation with the media. The *News* goes to town with special editions when its reporter is killed, and other papers follow suit: the murder of a reporter is 'something wicked, terrible, wellnigh ceremonial, one might almost say a ritual murder', and not to be compared with the common or garden murder of a bank manager or a grocery clerk.

More humour, and considerably more than humour, derives from Katharina's cool propriety and its unheard-of eccentricity, even impropriety, in the world into which she has been plunged. Since she must be an accomplice of the wanted man, there must be a lot of money hidden away somewhere: the accountant called in by the police to examine her financial transactions is so impressed by her clarity and scrupulousness that he wants to hire her if she gets off. On the other hand, when it is proposed to transfer her to the prison commissary since she has had experience as a caterer, her future co-workers are thrown into dismay: her reputation for integrity has preceded her.

Even Katharina's killing of the reporter is invested with a grim but apposite humour. She has agreed to give him an interview, and when he arrives at her apartment the first question he puts to 'Blumikins' is: 'How about us having a bang for a start?' This decides her. She pulls out a gun (give a girl the name of gangster's moll . . .) and lets him have what he asks for. Such is the death of 'a victim of his profession'.

In the end a lot of damage has been done, some of it irreparable. Friendships and reputations have been laid waste, the seeds of mistrust sown between husband and wife, innocent people have lost their jobs – and one of them declines from geniality and love of life into body odour and bad breath. Katharina's treasured apartment, which she had worked so hard to buy, has been utterly ruined for her, and she flings the contents of her kitchen cupboards against its immaculate walls. Not so – though it might have been ruined – her life. She and her dear Ludwig – whose most serious crime turns out to be desertion from the army in company with the regimental pay – will get from eight to ten years in gaol. They will be in their mid-thirties when released, and Katharina has plans for the future which include the opening of a restaurant with outside catering service. The biggest and saddest joke of all is this: Katharina was dragged into the affair and stripped of her honour and her privacy simply because there could be no two ways about it: she *had* to be a conspirator. She *had* to be a conspirator, in the eyes of the police and the media, simply because in their habituation to 'normality' they failed to credit the possibility of love at first sight, of a mutual *coup de foudre*. Locksmiths may laugh at love. But sometimes hard-pressed love has the last laugh.

Headbirths and *The Safety Net*

Grass and Böll have both amply demonstrated their staying-power and (more strikingly in the case of the former) their versatility. In their new books they have both (Grass more strikingly) turned into what in my childhood were called 'worrits'. Since we can worry well enough for ourselves, and in any case lack no assistance or guidance from newspapers and television, this may strike us as supererogatory. However, these two are at least distinguished worrits.

In *The Safety Net* Böll has the benefit of a degree of 'psychological depth', characters to dip into, and a crowded, anxious story that offers itself to the reader like a dubiously lucky dip. In *Headbirths* Grass has the benefit of himself, or his 'manner', and the Matter of Germany, plus the Third World: his characters here are the shadows of caricatures, extreme instances of the average, the middle-intellectual, the representatively serious-minded man in a typical fairly busy street, while his package-tour of a plot moves too fast for the Grass we know, and nearly always admire and sometimes love, to grow under its hastening feet.

Headbirths bears the alternative title 'The Germans are Dying Out'. Grass has visited China, in 1979, and speculates on how things would be if there were as many Germans as there are Chinese: namely some 950 million. 'Could the world bear it? Wouldn't the world have to defend itself (but how?) against such a multitude?' As it is, there are barely 80 million Germans, counting both Germanies, and so, if you reckon without the resident foreigners ('which was the only natural and obvious thing to do'), you are forced to the conclusion that the Germans are dying out. 'Living space without people. Is such a thought possible? Is such a thought permissible? What would the world be like without Germans?' How Americans – who, I suspect, take more interest in contemporary German fiction than we do – will react to this I don't know. The British reader is likely to give a sour smile: he lives in a country where the essential services are largely operated by 'foreigners' – well, they are 'coloured' – except when white union leaders fall out with white management and a strike ensues. The Germans should worry!

Grass poses the second of his not altogether *outré* questions: 'Isn't there a certain grandeur in stepping out of history, in forgoing progeny, turning into a mere object of study for younger nations?' (The British reader stops smiling sourly and bursts into tears.) Thereupon he creates two characters – headbirths which can hardly have given him much of a headache – two well-intentioned worriers, Harm Peters and his wife Dörte, who cannot make up their minds whether or not to bring a child into 'this world', whose most frequent utterance is 'on the one hand' followed by 'on the other', and whom he sends on a package tour of darkest Asia.

The purpose of their journey is not, of course, to visit temples (though Dörte is temporarily carried away by mysticism arising from self-frustrated maternalism), but to 'confront reality', and – the souvenirs of the serious-minded? – bring bits of it back to show to study groups at home. The travel agency they use bears the name 'Sisyphus', improbable but symbolic (and as such rather more impressive than Grass's earlier Snail): that's what life is, pushing stones uphill again and again, or writing books even though not one of them actually changes the world. Sisyphus specializes in catering for people like Mr and Mrs Peters. It computes for its clients the protein deficiency in each locality, the infant mortality, the per-capita income, and (which the Peterses decide is cynical but honest) for an extra charge lays on such side-trips as a night spent in an authentic harbour-side slum in Bangkok in the company of flies, rats and sewage. Dr Wenthien, the guide (and guru and 'world-crisis specialist'), who would surely have attained to mythic significance had he been given time, congratulates them on the 'courage and love of reality' shown in taking up these optional extras.

To specify but a few, the worries of the Peterses include the Third World, poverty *vis-à-vis* wealth, over-population, the environment, nuclear reactors and NATO. The birth-rate in particular: 'every month a million more Indians' – with a pun, surely their author's, on 'fast breeders'. In this respect the Chinese have done better than the Indians; but then, the Indians have been corrupted by the West, by 'neo-colonialism'; yet the Chinese regulations (no pre-marital or extra-marital sex, the subsidy on the first baby withdrawn if a second comes along . . .) are 'inhuman, cruel, constrictive'. On the one hand . . . on the other . . .

However, a novel, however exiguously a novel, needs a story; the more so when the author contemplates making a film out of it. So Harm Peters is provided with a kilo of German liver sausage to hand over to an old schoolfriend living in Bali: 'I'm sure it will make Uwe happy. You can't get it down there. And I remember like it was yesterday how he loved liver sausage.' Much is made of this 'plot-fostering sausage', or rather much is hinted at: for a brief while it looks as if Harm might get involved in a 'not undangerous sub-plot' connected with his friend's hypothetical smuggling of arms to an independence movement in Timor. But no, 'we won't get mixed up in that,' the author rules: the friend isn't located, the plot-fostering sausage is left to fester. What a pity! We might have had an adventure story as well as a string of elegant ironies.

The author and his headbirths are at one in their antipathy to Franz Josef Strauss and in campaigning for Helmut Schmidt in the 1980 elections. Harm Peters is a 'model democrat', indeed a Social Democrat; yet he declines to espouse one of Grass's proposed reforms – the abolition of compulsory education or miseducation in the hope that unmiseducated children will turn to books of their own eager accord and teach themselves to spell their way through them. On the one hand this is the kind of enlightened measure Harm might be expected to approve of; on the other hand he and Dörte are themselves teachers . . . Grass has another good cause, of his own: the two Germanies should be reunified as one cultural nation – that is, while remaining politically separate, they should come together under the roof of a common culture. (Which would frighten nobody.) 'Only literature (with its inner lining: history, myths, guilt, and other residues) arches over the two states that have so sulkily cut themselves off from each other.'

We have nothing better, Grass continues, than our writers: the dead Heine and the living Biermann, Christa Wolf 'over there' and Heinrich Böll 'over here', Goethe and Schiller, Thomas Mann and Heinrich Mann, Luther and Uwe Johnson – sequences of souls that could surely live in one cultural breast . . . This argument – eminently suitable material for a lecture-tour in China – might seem to have been sparked off by an unfortunate generalization of Franz Josef Strauss's, that 'home-grown apocalyptic', to the effect that writers are 'rats and blowflies'. It is also a hangover from the author's previous novel, in which, as it were a Group 47 brought forward three hundred years, writers assemble towards the end of the Thirty Years War with the intention of giving 'new force to the last remaining bond between all Germans, namely the German language'. *The Meeting at Telgte* is as playful and ambiguous as *Headbirths*, more ambitious it might seem but more modest: the manifesto drawn up by the writers ('the other, the true Germany') is lost in a mysterious fire. And the earlier work has the advantage of 'real' characters (Schütz, Gryphius, Grimmelshausen) who are nimbly differentiated and carry more weight than those paste-board brain-children the Peterses.

Headbirths is a collection of footnotes, endued with Grass's free-spluttering intelligence, satirically pointed but not too sharp-edged. If the author is flagellating himself at all, it is with a feather duster. Conceivably he is mischievously reminding the good that the better can be its enemy and that, in the gradualistic spirit of his Snail, not all things at once does the Highest intend. In a concluding spasm of what looks more like amused resignation than hope and good cheer, 'Murderously we'll survive and be merry,' he says. 'We shall adapt, defend, accommodate ourselves, and take safety measures. We will want to chuck it all and reproduce . . .' And so, it appears, will Dörte and Harm. As for the author himself, he looks forward to his New Year's Eve party, at which (since books alone are certain good, even though they don't obviously do very much) fish will be served: 'Flounder, it goes without saying.' Or, to say it by reference to the title of his last novel but one, *Butt*, or Turbot. Major writers must be permitted a generous helping of solipsism, but at this point Grass appears to be cannibalizing himself.

The worries in Böll's more novelistic novel, *The Safety Net*, are fewer in number, but closer at hand and more pressing and (deliberately or not) verging on the comic in their complications and ramifications. Fritz Tolm, an ageing newspaper owner and newly (and rather incongruously) elected President of 'The Association' – a confederation of tycoons from industry, energy and the media – is, together with his family, the object of terrorist attention. Among the terrorists are several members of his family: an ex-daughter-in-law and her lover for certain, and possibly his two sons, one of whom is a former political activist while the other has joined the 'alternative society'. The police and security men assigned to the case outnumber the potential victims and their potential attackers put together. Despite which, and the consequent inconveniences, Tolm knows 'that all these measures had to be yet would prevent nothing'.

The 'safety net' flung over the Tolms inevitably traps a number of small, irrelevant and apolitical fish. The mildest peccadillo committed by a neighbour comes to light, privacy whether in the present or concerning the past has ceased to exist, and the locals might be held to have stronger reasons for hating the Tolms than do the terrorists. Not that Fritz is what you might call a contented capitalist; he is humane, gentle, he radiates 'capitalist melancholy', he has been driven out of one handsome home because coal was discovered underneath it and is about to be driven out of another to make room for a power station. Another poor little rich man, it might seem. His charming daughter, Sabine, is married to a vulgar, vigorous business man whose 'modes' are made in East Germany and the sweat-shops of the Third World. Like the others, she risks 'psychic damage' caused by fear of terrorists and the eternal presence of policemen. The rich are different from us: they have more worries. Sabine falls in love with Hendler, her security guard – the policemen are a decent lot, and this one is a distinct improvement on her husband, Fischer, the nastiest human specimen in evidence here. So, if there were no terrorists there would be no guards – and hence no great love affair . . .

Böll's creation of his characters, largely through their interior mono-logues, though making for difficult reading (it must be that family 'voices' have much in common), is admirable, even though not so rich and sharp as in *Group Portrait with Lady*. The author's sweetness of nature (there is no other description) is reflected in Sabine and her mother Käthe, and – among the males – in Tolm himself and Hendler. As hitherto, touches of humour and a lemony twist of wryness just save the sweetness from thickening into mawkishness. Sabine is a serious and loyal person, as is Hendler, and Hendler has a good, loyal wife to make him less blissful and more serious. Of Sabine's adultery, her father, thinking of the porn, pop and dope currently in fashion, suggests that 'Perhaps she was longing for the good old sins, the way others long for the good old days'; his wife adds, 'For which we have never longed.'

'Let other pens dwell on guilt and misery,' Jane Austen wrote: 'I quit such odious subjects as soon as I can, impatient to restore everybody, not greatly in fault themselves, to tolerable comfort and to have done with all the rest.' There is something of the same inclination in Böll; at all events he has an endearing preference for a happy, a happy-as-possible, ending for as many of his people as can be so accommodated. Which is not to imply that he cheats. Sabine and Hendler and Hendler's loving and blameless wife cannot all live happily ever after, and Hendler must surely (who is to guard the guards?) lose his job at the least.

As for Böll's terrorists, they turn out to be paper tigers. They burn cars – thus aiding capitalism as much as Communism or the threatened environment. The leader, Tolm's erstwhile activist son's first wife's lover, is a hard man, true enough, but he blows himself to pieces, taking a Turkish policeman with him. (At the very end of *Headbirths* the Peterses nearly run over a symbolic Turkish boy, whose escape is cheered by a symbolic mob of children, all foreign, Indian, Chinese, African.) The first wife herself reaches the Dutch border, mounted on a booby-trapped bicycle (known in the trade as a 'bucket') which she then hands over to the police. And in a final strike Tolm's seven-year-old grandson arrives from Istanbul – a 'time bomb' prepared by 'them' – and promptly burns down the manor house. This is a device which would once have been called 'diabolic', and which smacks of science fiction; it misfires because no one is in the house at the time: as Käthe remarks, 'I could think of worse news.'

True, these revolutionaries don't need to do much, but simply to *be*, in order to tie up half the country. Every telephone call must be monitored in case it comes from one of 'them', every cake that enters the house has to be taken apart lest it should be stuffed with gelignite, the ducks swimming in the pond need to be watched since one of them might turn into a robot-bomb. Is this how the state is to wither away? Stifled under a safety net?

Much as the gentle reader desires the story to end in tolerable comfort, and as little as he wants blood all over the walls or even loud voices prophesying doom, it does seem that Böll is being excessively emollient on the present occasion. It is hypocrisy that chiefly draws his fire – for instance, a local clergyman who inveighs against his parishioners' moral decay while sleeping with his housekeeper – and this is a target he hit more effectively in *The Clown*, his novel of 1963. Fair enough, though – but what happens with such peculiar gratuitousness on the penultimate page needs more accounting for. Tolm confides to his wife that there are two things he has to tell her: first that (as she knows) he has always loved her, and secondly that 'some form of socialism must come, must prevail . . .' The theme is not pursued past the three dots, and the announcement stands out bleakly like those stickers publishers insert on the title verso when they have forgotten to state the ISBN or the name of the printer.

Does Böll feel he has forgotten to tell us something? (And how vague and airy is that 'some form of'!) His admirers may be reminded of the *bien-pensant* element in his make-up, of that conscious 'balance' or too-deliberate, pedantic insistence on being fair all round and being seen to be, manifest in the essays in his collection, *Missing Persons*. On the one hand . . . on the other . . . It could be that in their new books both Grass and (which is less likely) Böll are making fun, directly and obliquely, of the liberal tradition to which they belong. That would really be the way to incur 'psychic damage' – or worse. Sisyphus' stone was given to rolling back, but it is not recorded that it ever rolled back on top of him.

– II –

THE TALE OF GENJI
And Two Women Diarists

The Tale of Genji, the early eleventh-century Japanese classic, is a phenomenon which, in view of its originality and unprecedented scope, can only be likened to a combination of *Antony and Cleopatra*, *As You Like It* and *The Winter's Tale* (with a dash of *Love's Labour's Lost*) suddenly appearing in full flower against a backdrop of *Gammer Gurton's Needle* and *Gorboduc*. To review this new translation by Edward G. Seidensticker, in 1190 closely set but handsome pages, is analogous to comparing the Revised Version with King James's – except that the general drift of the Bible is rather better known.

Since practically every reader is on occasion a common reader, perhaps the reviewer may venture upon a few common and possibly vulgar observations. The hero of Lady Murasaki's *Tale*, or of the larger part of it in that Genji dies two-thirds of the way through, is that not uncommon fictional character, the Great Lover – potent, gifted, irresistible, and nice with it. Genji *is* too good to be true, until sadness sets in. But that *The Tale of Genji* is not a 'romance' in the pejorative sense, that it is not simply a Heian fantasy of an earlier and better Heian world, a more sophisticated opposite number of England's Restoration comedy at its most sophisticated, can be seen by reference to other tenth- and eleventh-century Japanese women writers. In particular, Murasaki's contemporary, Sei Shōnagon, whose *Pillow Book* (a generic term, Ivan Morris suggests, describing an informal notebook kept in a drawer of its owner's wooden pillow) reveals her as an astringent, forthright and unromanticizing witness while also testifying to the general authenticity of Murasaki's more dreamlike impressions.

The impression of reality, as opposed to fantasy, is assisted in *Genji* by the author's periodical cool interventions; for instance, at the end of Chapter 4:

I had hoped, out of deference to him, to conceal these difficult matters; but I have been accused of romancing, of pretending that because he was the son of an emperor he had no faults. Now, perhaps, I shall be accused of having revealed too much.

And more humorously: 'Though no one has asked me to do so, I should like to describe the surprise of the assistant viceroy's wife at this turn of events,' she writes in concluding Chapter 15, 'but it would be a bother and my head is aching.' In Chapter 25 there occurs a passage reminiscent of Jane Austen's spirited defence of novels in *Northanger Abbey* ('performances which have only genius, wit, and taste to recommend them'). After teasing Tamakazura about her fondness for romances – 'Women seem to have been born to be cheerfully deceived' – Genji changes tack:

I have been rude and unfair to your romances, haven't I? They have set down and preserved happenings from the age of the gods to our own. *The Chronicles of Japan* and the rest are a mere fragment of the whole truth. It is your romances that fill in the details . . . to dismiss them as lies is itself to depart from the truth. Even in the writ which the Buddha drew from his noble heart are parables, devices for pointing obliquely at the truth.

No more than Jane Austen did Murasaki approve of running down the very activity she was engaged in.

Heian Japan was 'a man's world' – though apparently less overwhelmingly so than Japan (and the world at large) has been at much later dates – and it was left to the women to write about it. The men were busy with more pressing things, such as governing the country (or in the case of the *Genji* males serving at court), being accomplished and noble, writing 'seriously' or stodgily in Chinese – and seducing women. Women, it has been suggested, were less confined by convention than men, and had more time and licence for scribbling in their native tongue. Murasaki Shikibu was the most remarkable of a group of remarkable females: she has no male counterpart in her own country, indeed no male or female counterpart in any country. Proust is her nearest of literary kin.

None the less, her admiration for her hero is likely to stick in feminist gullets. One would say that she doted on Genji, were it not that such crude, barbarous emotions as that verb implies are never found in her. An attempt on the reader's part to enumerate Genji's love affairs would be incongruously loutish, and in any case frustrated by uncertainty in many cases as to whether the protagonists exchanged only poems or something more besides. Lack of privacy often seems to rule out the latter in these overcrowded compounds: people who live in paper houses should stay in their own rooms, especially when their silk robes rustle so loudly. (Though against this consideration one should perhaps set the Japanese ability to remain blind or deaf to those things it would be incorrect or inconvenient to see or hear.) Murasaki shows not the faintest interest in the physical act of sex. Desire or curiosity on the man's side is indicated, willingness (sometimes but by no means always) on the woman's, a relatively secret meeting has to be contrived, and there we leave them: 'let us not look in too closely upon their dalliance.' We take up the story again with the next morning's exchange of poem-notes or bed-and-butter letters. But Genji's affairs are indisputably many. 'He went on thinking about whatever woman he encountered. A perverse concomitant was that the women he went on thinking about went on thinking about him.'

Genji is not merely good at everything that counts, he is the best at everything that counts: poetry, painting, music, perfumes, dress, bearing, conversation, attentiveness . . . And of course he is the best-looking of all the good-looking nobles who throng the scene. The words of the imperial consort's attendant refer to more than the perfume he happens to be wearing: 'He brings everything all together in himself, like a willow that is all of a sudden blooming like a cherry. It sets a person to shivering.' For Murasaki, Genji is 'the shining one of whom the whole world talks'; and at times it strikes the reader that the whole of this world has precious little else to talk about, and precious little to do except to talk. Admittedly Murasaki does chide the prince now and again, if fondly. 'It continues to be his great defect that his attention wanders.' We note with some amusement that when Genji becomes convinced that a current liaison is illicit, his attention at once wanders to a new liaison in which he anticipates unadulterated joy. Thus, when the fruits of his affair with his stepmother begin to show under her robe, his thoughts turn to a ten-year-old girl, although he knows he is taking risks: 'People would say that his appetites were altogether too varied.'

But, Murasaki insists, one of Genji's great qualities is that he never forgets his women, he does the right thing by them as far as is in his power. 'The result is,' someone remarks, 'that he has a large collection.'

Not that the prince is a carefree Lothario. Oh no, he is Japanese after all, and a sense of the transitoriness of things is never far away, a tear never far from his eye. With a sensibility like his, a little suffering can go a long way: you barely need anything as uncouth as a reason. However, Genji does have his troubles. One unsuitable intrigue leads to his banishment for a period; the effect on his retinue reminds us of the defeated Antony's ability to make his followers weep. Another intrigue scars his soul permanently. Early on, he fell in love with the second wife of his father the Emperor, and the child he had by her is generally believed to be the Emperor's: his supposed brother is actually his son. A form of retribution arrives later, when Kashiwagi, son of Genji's closest friend, gets Genji's wife, the Third Princess (and Kashiwagi's sister-in-law incidentally) pregnant. When this comes to light, there is no duel, no recrimination, no overt recognition of the matter. Kashiwagi has been guilty of a lapse in taste, of bad manners, above all (the cynic might say) the bad manners to be found out. At least he has the good manners to die soon afterwards, just as Enobarbus dies after deserting his master Antony, and the Third Princess becomes a nun. This sequel, it may be felt, is necessary in Murasaki's eyes because it is the shining Genji who is the offended party: he himself didn't die when he got his father's wife with child.

What matters is manners rather than morals, or so it must seem to us, who distinguish more sharply between the two. The aesthetically pleasing way of doing a thing is of more consequence than the thing itself. And shame lies less in being naughty than in being so maladroit as to be discovered. Telling lies or inventing plausible stories in the cause of avoiding trouble and loss of face for either the offender or the offended is quite in order, even *de rigueur*. For worrying over 'what people will say' is almost incessant here: to be laughed at is a fate worse than death. Yet this delicacy of feeling is general, not solely self-directed. Having learnt that his elder brother Genji is really his father, the new emperor is fearful of embarrassing Genji by hinting at his knowledge. And when suffering from malaria, Genji takes care to consult a sage in secret – because, he explains, 'such is his reputation that I hated to risk marring it by failing to recover.'

The exquisiteness and precision of manners, broken on occasion by outbursts of animal spirits and a somewhat brutal disposing of other people's lives, intimates a social precariousness. Yet – and for all the rather mechanical readiness to shed *lacrimae rerum* – what does most to save *Genji* from brittleness and shallowness of soul is the pervasive sense of evanescence, of the fleeting insubstantiality of this world. If a child is intelligent and beautiful, everybody sighs: it cannot be expected to live long. That Genji lasted just into his fifties is a mark of the author's unwillingness to let go of him; even so his ladies muse, 'it is true – the cherry blossoms of spring are loved because they bloom so briefly.' Nor are thoughts of past or future particularly cheering. A 'stupid, senseless affair' is accounted for by 'a bond in some other life', and unsuccessful undertakings or actions injurious to others are put down to 'the disabilities we bring from other lives'. Karma can be thought a useful device for saving face or releasing from responsibility – or, more generously, a tactful and in some cases stoical admission of and allowance for human weakness. There is something of *Rasselas* here: 'Human life is everywhere a state in which much is to be endured, and little to be enjoyed.' Genji's philandering, like the conduct and attitudes of others in the story, can be traced without exercising undue charity to the hunger for human contact in a highly formalized society, for something beyond prescription and propriety, for love and companionship. This hunger is movingly expressed in a poem alluded to in Chapter 47, 'Trefoil Knots', and given by Seidensticker in a footnote:

> A loose thread here to join to a loose thread there.
> If it cannot be so with us, what use is life?*

Truly speaking, it is futile to compare Seidensticker's *Tale of Genji* (1976) with Arthur Waley's translation (1925–33) since the two versions

---

*The next step, the only further step, is withdrawal from the world into prayer and meditation – though hitherto one has considered it (as Donald Keene says) 'not in very good taste to show unusual piety'. Similarly, in Restoration comedy: 'What an odious thing it is to be thought to love a wife in good company.'

differ both in the material worked with and (more important) in their intentions. But it is also irresistible. We shall at times find it hard to believe they are concerned with the same original, even allowing for the work done on the Japanese text since Waley's day. For one thing, Seidensticker's version is complete, whereas Waley abridged, omitted a whole chapter, and frequently elaborated. The effect of his elaboration is generally to help the Western reader by weaving an element of explanation into the narrative. And when we come across a textual crux indicated by Seidensticker, and hence an annotation, the chances are that Waley has quietly skipped the passage – with no apparent loss, it must be said, as far as the general reader is concerned. Seidensticker is scholarly, enormously conscientious and (the lay reader feels confident) accurate. He is much brisker too (which in general is to be welcomed), as may be deduced from the fact that despite Waley's bold abridgements the new translation is actually shorter. This briskness, this economy in words, Seidensticker states, are characteristic of the original. At the same time he pays a handsome tribute to Waley when he tells us that the power of that pioneer version 'has continued to be so great that the process of preparing a new translation has felt like sacrilege.'

Much more than 'nuance' is involved. The difference between their priorities can be indicated, concisely, crudely, but without too much overstatement, by saying that Waley has the reader in mind whereas Seidensticker has Murasaki in mind. Where Seidensticker has the somewhat rebarbative 'Prajñapāramita Sutra', Waley softens with 'Spring Devotions', referring to the Buddhist nature of the ceremony in passing. Waley has 'Lady Murasaki' (the character, not the author) where Seidensticker more allusively and elusively gives 'the lady in the east wing'. The dramatis personae are many indeed, and Waley's habit of identifying them by name makes for smoother reading than Seidensticker's (no doubt literal) 'he' or 'she'. In Chapter 21 Sachūben, a master of poetry reading, is annotated by Seidensticker as 'otherwise unidentified'; Waley refers to him not by name but by office, 'the Under-secretary to the Council', a neat though perhaps unauthorized way of investing him with a little substance. A page later, however, the personage reappears as 'the Chief Secretary of Council'.

When a father is reflecting on his daughter's future, Seidensticker translates thus:

If he is still interested when he is a little older, she would be better off in his hands than at court. I know his Lordship well. Once a woman has attracted his attention he never forgets her.

Waley's version is:

There's this comfort about it, that if Prince Yūgiri is anything like his father he will continue to show an interest in her when he grows up. You know I have always told you that once Prince Genji takes a fancy to people, he never forgets them, come what may.

Waley has spelt out the pronouns and distinguished between the son and the father, thus assisting the reader to keep his bearings. Seidensticker writes elliptically, presumably in accord with the original, and in fewer words. Immediately afterwards he has the advantage in ready comprehensibility with 'I know that people are calling me the unpromoted marvel, and I don't enjoy going to court' over Waley's 'Why should I go to Court if I do not choose to? As a matter of fact, it is very unpleasant to be only in the Sixth Rank. People notice it and make remarks.'

Very occasionally Seidensticker's expressions strike one as obtrusively slangy where Waley's language is bland and timeless, though it may be that some readers will welcome little modern jolts. 'When they are side by side, my husband seems rather short on good looks' comes jarringly from the second daughter of the Eighth Prince: Waley has 'When they are together I sometimes think that Niou comes out of it none too well.' And surely Seidensticker's sentence 'He sought to dismiss it as an ordinary marital spat' offends by mixing two quite contrary modes. When young men are discussing the wiles of women and one remarks that 'The fact is not up to the advance notices', the anachronism shocks more than it enlivens; at the same place Waley gives 'But when we take steps to test their statements we are invariably disappointed', which is long-winded and a shade pompous for the gilded youth who is speaking.

In making these spot-checks, much of the time one is conscious less of inferiority or superiority than of difference, and more to the point would be to suggest that the average reader (who is unlikely to be all that dumb) might still welcome a résumé offering a ready reminder of the story's tangled relationships and its more important events. This is scarcely a book to be knocked off in a couple of winter evenings and the list of 'Principal Characters', though helpful, doesn't go far enough.

Just as Proust is the only Western writer I can think of as bearing any resemblance in manner or preoccupations to Murasaki Shikibu, so the comparison of Waley's *Genji* with Scott Moncrieff's *Remembrance of Things Past* (before Terence Kilmartin's revision) is the only possible one – in respect of inaccuracies and liberties taken, and of triumphs scored – although it would need someone of surpassing scholarship and literary sensibility to assess the implications. At all events, the reader coming fresh to the Japanese novel will meet with very few obstacles in Seidensticker's version that Seidensticker himself can be held responsible for. The reader acquainted with Waley's version will do well to banish it to the back of his mind while engaged on Seidensticker. My guess is that the two translations are going to co-exist peacefully, neither ousting the other.

Two Women Diarists

Sarashina Nikki? Sarashina no Nikki? The Sarashina Notebooks? Lady Sarashina's Diary? Sarashina is a mountainous district in central Japan, the word doesn't appear in the book, and no one seems to know why it was picked on. But 'Takasue's Daughter', as she is usually called, is an unilluminating and lowering designation for the author – as if, says Ivan Morris, George Eliot's sole appellation were 'Evans's Daughter'. The phrase 'bridge of dreams' doesn't appear either, but dreams do (in some abundance) and the whole thing is distinctly (or indistinctly) dreamlike, and so Ivan Morris's title, *As I Crossed a Bridge of Dreams*, is as good as any other, if not better. 'Dreamlike' is exactly what the earlier woman diarist, Sei Shōnagon, was not; and here we must not expect the varied pleasures of *The Pillow Book*, nor the presence of so vivacious, witty and acerbic a female.

Born in 1008 into the Heian administrative middle classes, Lady Sarashina was the daughter of an assistant provincial governor, wife to a provincial governor (she married at the age of thirty-six), and mother of a provisional provincial governor. No wonder that she was addicted to 'Tales' – *The Song of Everlasting Regret* and *The Princess Who Sought a Corpse* are mentioned here besides her favourite *Genji* – and later in life to pilgrimages to celebrated temples. Her husband died or 'faded away like a dream' when she was fifty, and towards the end of her little book, having mentioned his cremation ('he vanished with the smoke'), she writes: 'If only I had not given myself to Tales and poems since my young days but had spent my time in religious devotions, I should have been spared this misery.' That is, or so she seems to mean, she should have gone on some other pilgrimage earlier and then might have become an Imperial nurse in the Imperial Palace. Another dream!

Ivan Morris's substantial introduction and notes occupy virtually the same space as the insubstantial text. The text does often need the explanation it receives, without the explanation rendering it notably more fascinating. He tells us of the Japanese literary women of the tenth and eleventh centuries that 'they reveal themselves to us in all their nakedness': a misleading phrase, particularly so in the case of Lady Sarashina, whose kimono doesn't slip an inch. Her sensibility may be said to be naked, but it is disembodied, and again one has the sense of human wastage, of a quick, feeling and intelligent woman trapped (however 'naturally') in the cocoon of convention, of 'expected behaviour'. Lady Murasaki was immensely talented, of course, an unstoppable scribbler – but even the characterful Sei Shōnagon, for all she gave, doubtfully gave as good as she got. Lady Sarashina is very much the woman of sensibility: apart from what Morris calls her 'remarkably low tolerance for bereavement', she is forever yielding to fits of weeping. Up is the heartening and the strong reply (as Eastern Empson puts it) that we often want to make to her, poor thing.

Poems loom quite as large (or as small) as reality in these pages. 'I enjoyed seeing the Ford of Shikasuga between the provinces of Mikawa and Owari and was truly worried about whether or not to cross.' A necessary note refers us to a poem by Lady Nakatsukasa conveying the depressing message that whether you cross the troublous Ford of Shikasuga or you don't, trouble lies ahead – and informs us that Lady Sarashina was mistaken, it couldn't have been Shikasuga Ford she was looking at. She needn't have worried – but reason not the need. Arthur Waley may have been right when he described her book as 'a much worked-up and highly literary production'. Her own poems, with a few bright exceptions, provoke the response, So what? Ivan Morris takes the blame upon his translations, on those of other people, on the sheer impossibility of translating Japanese poems to any effect. But one wonders ... To know the conventions that govern them is to guess how conventional they are.

He does succeed, however, in transmitting the delicacy of spirit, the muted charm of Lady Sarashina's prose, in her mild self-punishing romanticism and, above all, in her unfussy, strong and exact descriptions of the natural scene. For example, of Mount Fuji: 'Its thick cover of unmelting snow gives the impression that the mountain is wearing a white jacket over a dress of deep violet.' It may be thought that the Japanese have always used their eyes to better effect than their other senses, and these Heian ladies had especially keen eyes.

The Confessions of Lady Nijō is a serious book, and one should start by saying what it is not. It is not an oriental *Fanny Hill* or a medieval *Histoire d'O*. It is not even comparable to Saikaku's writings and the gamy Japanese accounts of life in the floating world and the gay quarters of the turn of the seventeenth century. It belongs to the tradition of women diarists represented by such impeccable dames as Murasaki Shikibu, Sei Shōnagon, Izumi Shikibu and 'Lady Sarashina', and is a worthy later addition to this distinguished if not invariably enthralling line. The original title, it seems, means 'unrequested tale', or something you can't hold in any longer. 'Confessions' is not the aptest of substitutes, given its present associations, and though Lady Nijō served at court and slept with some of the very best people, the jacket reference to her as a 'famous courtesan' (though one sees the point) builds up improper expectations.

For not an improper word is spoken in this narrative, not an improper scene depicted. 'All' is not told; or if it is, then it is told discreetly and obliquely, by way of poems and literary allusions. One advantage of a literary heritage is that the most intimately personal feelings and happenings can be gracefully intimated through a swift, casual-seeming reference to a verse, a legend or a figure in some novel of the past. This may not be seen as an advantage nowadays, when readers have grown used to having the whole thing explicitly in front of them – the blood, the bed, the members of the party in full fig – as if nothing remotely comparable had ever happened before.

The law of diminishing returns having worked its slow but ineluctable effects, the result here is that some of Lady Nijō's 'revelations', couched in a quotation or in her own sparse words, carry quite a charge. The Retired Emperor proposes to her father that the latter's fourteen-year-old daughter should become his concubine simply by mentioning 'the wild goose of the fields', an allusion to the tenth-century *Tales of Ise*. Nijō is confused and distressed (her mother was dead, but why couldn't her father have told her what was in store?), and the first encounter ends with His Majesty (only twenty-nine, by the way) leaving at dawn, disgruntled: 'Now to go back pretending something happened!'; the second ends with Nijō's thin gown getting badly ripped. Not long afterwards, 'I discovered that my condition was not normal': she is pregnant.

Later in the story she is uncouthly grabbed by Ariake, a Buddhist priest (also half-brother to the Retired Emperor), who tells her (or himself) that 'Even when we walk in paths of darkness, we are guided by the Lord Buddha.' She whispers back ('but my words were wasted'), 'Some things are embarrassing even to Buddha.' Before long she records, 'He did have an undeniable way about him, a manner that was both pathetic and appealing': we gather she has ceased to resist. She has remarked, in connection with an earlier suitor, that her heart is 'far from adamantine'. By means of an allusion to *The Tale of Genji* the Emperor indicates that he knows Nijō is pregnant again, this time by Ariake, but accepts the situation.

Lady Nijō's memoirs span the years 1271–1306, more than two and a half centuries after the Heian women diarists. The Heian aristocracy or cultivated middle classes were given to literary allusion, and Nijō has them to allude to as well. Her society was heavily retrospective in its cultural habits and ceremonial activities; she recounts the enactment at a palace party of an episode from *Genji*: the novel had become in effect a combination of Shakespeare, the Book of Common Prayer and Emily Post. The vast number of source-references provided by the stalwart translator, Karen Brazell, inclines one to ask whether Nijō's contemporaries ever said anything in their own words – except, in some small degree, when composing short verses for later generations to invoke.

The complaint may be made that, in journals of this kind, we don't know what the lady *really* felt. Though it is hard to know what *really* really means, I think we do. In outline, the circumstances of these court ladies were determined by uncontested conventions, and they made what they could of life within those conventions. Murasaki and Sei Shōnagon made of themselves very considerable writers, infinitely more memorable as writers and personalities than their male contemporaries – and the thought comes to mind that possibly a 'free life', like free verse, either doesn't exist or is boring, or at any rate does not lend itself to the purposes of literary composition. If when reading these diarists we are conscious of human wastage – and we are – then we have to ask ourselves whether matters are arranged more fruitfully today. If the rather insistent aestheticism of these ladies, their too conscious sensitivity, makes us want to shake them, yet we note the glint behind the tear, and we admire them still. Mrs Brazell comments that 'sleeves damp from weeping soon become soppy'. Certainly melancholy was 'an acceptable tone' in Nijō's day ('Life is more fleeting than a dream within a dream'), and women were expected then (and later) to weep, but Nijō is much less damp than Lady Sarashina.

She is also less sharp and lively and entertaining than Sei Shōnagon, but her life was differently disposed – and she does have a story to tell, however obliquely she tells it. Ingenious and disingenuous she clearly was, and she needed to be, given her independence of mind. When she is pregnant by Akebono, another of her lovers, the Retired Emperor supposes himself the father-to-be on this occasion. Unfortunately there is a discrepancy of two months. The Emperor is told that Nijō is ill and an abortion has proved medically necessary: the baby is carried away by

Akebono and brought up by his wife as her own. It is not that the Emperor would have sought revenge on the lovers, for Nijō's behaviour was not altogether 'unexpected' in view of her circumstances and, as for Akebono, men will be men: the concern was to spare feelings and save faces as far as possible. The Emperor had his own fun, sometimes enlisting Nijō's assistance in it, and he displays a commendable suavity in the matter of her affair with his half-brother the priest. 'After thinking about the subject at great length,' he tells her, 'I have concluded that there is nothing sinful in the relationships between men and women inasmuch as they are usually caused by bonds from former lives and thus defy our resistance.'

The last part of the narrative, beginning in 1289, records Nijō's travels as a Buddhist nun. Her expectations at court have been thwarted and now, she says, she is 'suppressing my emotions by lecturing my heart'. She comes on an island community of nuns who were formerly prosti- tutes, and their ex-madam tells her, 'I was over fifty when some karmic effect suddenly enabled me to shake off the sleep of illusion'; she makes friends with the Shinto priests at the Ise shrine ('We are usually reluctant about allowing people in Buddhist orders to visit the shrine,' one says, 'but you look so tired I am sure the gods would understand'); and she has a touching last meeting with the Emperor. In a dream her father appears to her, reminds her of the many generations of poets in the family, and recites a poem:

> Sow all the words you can
> For in a better age
> Men shall judge the harvest
> By its intrinsic worth.

It was up to her and her journal, undiscovered till 1940 – and with the help of Karen Brazell's excellent translation – to keep the family reputa- tion alive.

FLAUBERT
His Letters and Ladies

Flaubert and an English Governess

The English governess in question in Hermia Oliver's book – very much in question – was Juliet Herbert, governess at the Flaubert home in Croisset to Flaubert's much-loved niece, Caroline, between 1854/5 and 1857. Her acquaintance with the novelist lasted till his death in 1880, which suggests it was far from casual, but the nature of the acquaintanceship is in dispute. The most tender of Flaubert's affairs? Or a non-affair? Miss Oliver believes that Juliet was 'almost certainly' Flaubert's mistress, but her book, a record of indefatigable research and rather meagre revelations, is stuffed with 'probably's', 'may's', 'if's' and 'just possible's', a case of seeking hopefully rather than arriving.

Born in 1829 as the daughter of a London builder, Juliet came from 'the artisan rather than the professional classes,' remarks Miss Oliver, who is faintly surprised that Flaubert should have been devoted (if devoted is what he was) to so humble a being. 'It seemed far more probable that the father of a woman who held Flaubert's interest for so long a period would have been more highly educated, like Mr Brontë.' That is grossly unfair to governesses! – and, I would think, to Flaubert too. However, all is well on that front, for Mr Herbert was a master builder (if a small one) and even, in 1831, enjoyed the professional cachet of bankruptcy. Who could better sympathize with Flaubert, Miss Oliver asks, after his niece's husband's financial collapse? Though that happened in the mid-1870s.

The sad fact, or the fact, is that there are very few references to Juliet in Flaubert's letters and no letters at all between the two putative lovers. Three possible reasons are advanced for this: Caroline resented the closeness of the relationship which she discovered on sorting her uncle's letters after his death, and so destroyed those from Juliet; she suppressed the letters in order to spare the feelings of Juliet and surviving members of the Herbert family; or, an explanation Miss Oliver favours, Flaubert himself burnt the letters in the course of an eight-hour bonfire, at which Maupassant assisted, in the year before his death. (This last being an act which, like any decent biographical writer, Miss Oliver both understands and regrets.) As for the letters written by Flaubert, it is 'almost certain' that Juliet, who died in 1909, destroyed them.

It is known that after Juliet left Croisset in 1857 she paid summer visits there in succeeding years, and also that Flaubert came to England in 1865, 1866 and 1871 and met Juliet then. It is possible, too, that the couple met during short holidays which Juliet took in France at intervals between 1872 and 1878; references in Flaubert's letters to Caroline prove that they met in 1872 and 1874, at any rate. It is the case that during her stint as governess at Croisset Juliet read *Macbeth* with Flaubert and translated *Madame Bovary* into English, though – which was probably just as well for her reputation – the translation was never published. And in 1856 Flaubert wrote to his friend and confidant Louis Bouilhet that 'the governess excites me immeasurably; I hold myself back on the stairs so as not to grab her behind' – by the standards of his correspondence with Bouilhet this is a mild enough confession, or boast – although the first mention of Juliet by name occurred only the following year, in a letter from Flaubert to his niece.

In the accounts of the novelist's visits to England, instead of amorous encounters the reader must rest content with a listing of the pictures he saw at Bridgewater House, Grosvenor House, the National Gallery (South Kensington) and Hampton Court. Flaubert's travel diary is otherwise uncommunicative, but on 6 July 1865 he recorded dining at a restaurant and thereafter a *'retour délicieux'* – to which Miss Oliver appends, 'possibly in a cab'. If Juliet was with him at the time, the reference 'can surely only indicate a relationship that was something other than friendship'. It could merely signify that Flaubert was glad to get back to his lodgings after a hot, stormy day spent touring the Crystal Palace.

Similarly, it may have been Juliet who in 1869 sent the novelist some translated information about the Calves' Head Club which he wanted for *L'Education sentimentale*: whoever it was addressed him in a gloss by the intimate form, '*tu*'. 'If it can indeed be proved that it was Juliet who wrote the covering letter, the use of "*tu*" is itself highly indicative.' There are certainly some similarities between the handwriting of the translation and Juliet's inscription in a copy of Hans Andersen which she gave to Caroline, and 'it may or may not be considered' that the resemblances outweigh the differences. But, as Miss Oliver allows, there can be no proof unless the covering letter can be traced: it 'may be' still in private ownership 'if' it was not lost during World War II.

'It is by now impossible,' Miss Oliver declares, 'to doubt the emotional nature of their relationship.' What does the latter phrase mean? We cannot know what Juliet's feelings for Flaubert were, but 'that she must have suffered anguish, "the torment of love unsatisfied", seems undeniable . . .' Miss Oliver continues: 'We can only hope and suspect that she too received the kind of letter' – then quoted – 'that in 1858 he had written to another woman whose beauty moved him.' Yes, Flaubert was a great letter-writer, and (within limits) a great admirer of women, and the thought is a nice one – but it looks as if research is now aspiring towards the condition of romantic fiction. Miss Oliver's intention is a worthy one: she is, I take it, seeking to do Juliet a posthumous good turn, she would like to prove that this English woman, this mere governess, actually slept with a celebrated foreign novelist . . . in somewhat the same spirit in which not so very long ago she would have been concerned to prove that Juliet had done no such improper thing. Other times, other pieties . . . One must respect the scrupulousness shown in these investigations, for it is not all that common, and the total absence of anything approaching prurience. Even so – and while no one would grudge those involved what happiness they could snatch, from a perhaps constricted life, from a life certainly made over to art – one has to ask: is all this labour in a worthwhile cause? *Flaubert and an English Governess* seems to me an instance of book-making, however superior. But then, ours is an age when books are increasingly made rather than born.

The Letters of Gustave Flaubert 1830-1857

That Flaubert, as a writer and as the kind of writer he was, was born rather than made is plainly indicated by the opening letters in Francis Steegmuller's excellent selection, the first of two volumes. The very first item, addressed to a schoolfriend and written on the eve of 1831, when Flaubert was nine, includes these sentences: 'I'll also send you some of my comedies. If you'd like us to work together at writing, I'll write comedies and you can write your dreams, and since there's a lady who comes to see papa and always says stupid things I'll write them too.' At the age of ten, Flaubert signs off, 'Your dauntless dirty-minded friend till death'. At thirteen he is attacking theatre censorship and restrictions on press freedom: the representatives of the people 'are depriving the man of letters of his conscience, his artist's conscience', and what matters more than people, crowns and kings is 'the god of Art, who is ever-present, wearing his diadem, his divine frenzy merely in abeyance'. Two years later, writing to the same friend, Flaubert displays a peculiarly clear recognition of what was to be more than an adolescent conflict:

... for the most beautiful woman is scarcely beautiful on the table of a dissecting-room, with her bowels draped over her nose, one leg minus its skin, and half a burnt-out cigar on her foot. Oh no, it's a sad thing, criticism, study, plumbing the depths of knowledge to find only vanity, analyzing the human heart to find only egoism, and understanding the world only to find in it nothing but misery. Oh how much more I love pure poetry, cries from the soul, sudden transports and then deep sighs, the voices of the soul, the thoughts of the heart.

Ex ungue leonem . . . All Flaubert is in these first five pages of letters, in embryo. In 1846 he wrote to Louise Colet: 'I am ripe. Early ripe, it's true, because I have lived in a hothouse.' His hothouse – while it embraces the family apartment in the Rouen hospital where his father was director and chief surgeon – was very largely him.

Among these letters, which the editor has knit together with an intelligent and succinct narrative-cum-commentary, the three big constituents are the correspondence with Louise Colet (less love letters than love-and-literature or even love-versus-literature), the travelogue (or brothelogue) addressed to Louis Bouilhet from the Orient, and the letters relating to the trial of *Madame Bovary* for outrages against public morals and religion.

Steegmuller's earlier book, *Flaubert in Egypt*, has treated us to the distinctly alarming blend of the sumptuous and the squalid, the romantic and the clinical, found in Flaubert's account of his travels in Egypt and the Middle East with Maxime Du Camp between 1849 and 1851. He wrote from Constantinople towards the end of 1850 that 'There's nothing like travel for the health': this was after his umpteenth venereal chancre. Incidentally, the apparently total frankness with which he communicated his sexual activities to his male friends makes it seem odd that, if he slept with Juliet Herbert, he should never have mentioned it to them. It could be, I suppose, that he held *les Anglaises* in greater awe than the famous courtesan Kuchuk Hanem and her ilk.

Notwithstanding Flaubert's obvious contempt for the Establishment, the case against *Madame Bovary* in early 1857 was dismissed, though without costs awarded. His counsel made effective play with the distinguished medical careers of the accused's father and also his brother Achille, and Achille saw to it that the Ministry of Justice was fully aware of the importance of the Flaubert family, 'whom it might be dangerous to attack because of the approaching elections'. It sometimes helps to have bourgeois connections. Not that Flaubert was wholly placated: the trial had 'deflected attention from the novel's artistic success,' he complained, quite genuinely, 'and I dislike Art to be associated with things alien to it.'

Most profoundly interesting of all are the letters to Louise Colet. Flaubert met her in 1846 (she was eleven years his senior) and their increasingly troubled liaison ran out in 1855. Passionate, sensual, even violent as these letters are, they are marked by chilling phrases right from the start:

Ever since we said we loved each other, you have wondered why I have never added the words 'for ever'. Why? Because I always sense the future, the antithesis of everything is always before my eyes. I have never seen a child without thinking that it would grow old, nor a cradle without thinking of a grave. The sight of a naked woman makes me imagine her skeleton. As a result, joyful spectacles sadden me and sad ones affect me but little. I do too much inward weeping to shed outward tears – something read in a book moves me more than a real misfortune . . . Forgive me, forgive me in the name of all the rapture you have given me. But I have a presentiment of immense unhappiness for you. I fear lest my letters be discovered, that everything become known. *I am sick and my sickness is you.*

During the first eighteen months of their relationship Flaubert wrote some hundred letters to Louise (a lot of risks run there!), but saw her only six times. As Steegmuller observes, we cannot altogether blame her for her growing bitterness and her expostulations. Art, Flaubert told her, was greater than earthly love, he had never sacrificed anything to passion and never would; and the concentration of thoughts about literature and the artist ('Come now, smile, kiss me. Stop being hurt because I speak to you about Shakespeare rather than myself') will commend these letters more readily to the later reader than they could have commended themselves to the fretful recipient.

In his third letter, Flaubert exhorts her: 'You speak of work. Yes, you must work; love art.' (She was a poet, a journalist, in the way many people are poets, journalists, not in the way that Flaubert was a literary artist.) 'Of all lies, art is the least untrue. Try to love it with a love that is exclusive, ardent, devoted. It will not fail you.' A plain enough intimation of priorities, one would say. And it was to Louise that, in 1852, he delivered this splendid manifesto:

I like clear, sharp sentences, sentences which stand erect, erect while running – almost an impossibility. The ideal of prose has reached an unheard-of degree of difficulty: there must be no more archaisms, clichés; contemporary ideas must be expressed using the appropriate crude terms; everything must be as clear as Voltaire, as abrim with substance as Montaigne, as vigorous as La Bruyère, and always streaming with colour.

'If I weren't so weary, I would develop my ideas at greater length,' he told her in 1853 after a brisk lecture on *Hamlet*. 'It is so easy to chatter about the Beautiful. But it takes more genius to say, in proper style: "close the door", or "he wanted to sleep", than to give all the literature courses in the world.' And, the same year:

The day before yesterday, in the woods near Touques, in a charming spot beside a spring, I found old cigar butts and scraps of pâté. People had been picnicking. I described such a scene in *Novembre*, eleven years ago: there it was entirely imagined, and the other day it was experienced. Everything one invents is true, you may be sure. Poetry is as precise as geometry. Induction is as good as deduction; and besides, after reaching a certain point one no longer errs about matters of the soul. My poor Bovary, without a doubt, is suffering and weeping at this very hour in twenty villages of France.

At the same time his letters do convey passion, tenderness, concern, much gratitude, and indeed riches of other sorts. Including some common earthiness. 'Blessed be the Redcoats' (as the euphemism has it) – from time to time there is anxiety over the failure of *'les Anglais'* to disembark, and Louise thinks of visiting an abortionist (or *'faiseur d'anges'*, as another euphemism goes), while Flaubert is horrified by the idea of bringing someone into the world. Occasionally the personal and the professional come together – 'Then, after ten more pages . . . I'll have finished the first section of my Part Two. My lovers are ready for adultery: soon they will be committing it. (I too, I hope.)' – though not always in a manner wholly gratifying to Louise. 'Yes, for me you are a diversion,' he informs her in 1852, 'but one of the best, the most complete kind.' And late the following year he speaks even more plainly, and serviceably:

. . . in fact everything is bound up together, and what distorts your life is also distorting your style. For you continually alloy your concepts with your passions, and this weakens the first and prevents you from enjoying the second . . . You are a poet shackled to a woman, just as Hugo is a poet shackled to an orator . . . Do not imagine you can exorcize what oppresses you in life by giving vent to it in art. No. The heart's dross does not find its way on to paper: all you pour out there is ink, and no sooner do you voice your sorrows than they return to the soul through the ear, louder, reaching deeper than ever. Nothing has been gained . . . Only in the Absolute are we well off.

The letter ends: 'Do not be upset. The sweet things I might have written you instead of this would have carried less affection.' Louise would no doubt have preferred those sweeter things. No one likes to take second place, not even to Art. No one likes to think that the pleasure he or she can give falls short of the delight the other person knows in writing, in creating – in being both lover and mistress, and the horses on which they ride, and the wind and the sun. Flaubert's mother must have echoed Louise's sentiments (and those of the parents, spouses, friends and well-wishers of many another writer) when she told her son: 'Your mania for sentences has dried up your heart.' (He quoted this remark admiringly to Bouilhet, adding that its sublimity was 'enough to make the Muse hang herself out of jealousy at not having thought of it herself': 'the Muse' was the name they used between themselves for Louise.) But the final remark quoted here should be one of Flaubert's, for it demonstrates both his utter devotion to his art and also a sense of balance, of proportion, something not always allowed him. *Madame Bovary* first appeared in the *Revue de Paris*, edited by Flaubert's friends, Du Camp and Laurent-Pichat, who cut the first instalment for (as they saw it) artistic reasons. Flaubert resented this deeply, and was aghast to discover that in a later instalment the editors had none the less made a further cut, this time (vainly, as it turned out) for reasons of prudence. He sent a firm, dignified protest to Laurent-Pichat, addressing not his 'dear friend' but the *Revue de Paris*, 'an abstract personality, whose interests you represent'. 'You are objecting to details,' he wrote, 'whereas actually you should object to the whole . . . you cannot change the *blood* of a book. All you can do is to weaken it.' And he ended the letter by declaring that while he might break with the *Revue* he would still remain a friend of its editors. 'I know how to distinguish between literature and literary business.'

The Temptation of Saint Antony

When Flaubert read *The Temptation of Saint Antony* in its first (and considerably longer) version to Bouilhet and Du Camp in 1849, as he grew more and more heated, they grew colder and colder. Finally – after thirty-two hours in all, according to Du Camp – he asked them what they thought of it. 'We think you should throw it into the fire and never speak of it again,' said Bouilhet. 'You wanted to make music and you have made only noise.'

It is the much later, third and final version of the work which is translated and admirably presented here by Kitty Mrosovsky. In her introduction, itself a monograph, she not only says what she can for this curious composition but also outlines what others have said in more and less elaborate exegeses. Among them, a Sartrean reading (the creation of nothing but nothingness) by Sartre, a Foucaldian reading ('erudite oneirism') by Foucault, and a Freudian interpretation by a follower of Freud. It would clearly be foolhardy, then, to venture that what the work pre-eminently is, is a mistake, a miscalculation, brave and 'interesting' no doubt in that it sheds light on several of Flaubert's obsessions, albeit a harsh and crude light.

Indignant though he was at his friends' reactions, two years later he was able to write to Louise Colet that in *Saint Antony* he had chosen 'a subject which left me completely free as to lyricism, emotions, excesses of all kinds . . . How passionately I carved the beads of my necklace! I forgot only one thing – the string.' Here he shows himself his own most perceptive critic. There is, in an obvious sense, a string in evidence; and the Faustian beginning, with Antony beset by what appears a diviner discontent, promises well. The saint – an eminently worthy target – is to be tempted to defect by suffering the onslaught of a seemingly endless string of ranting heretics, gods, monsters and bestial, bloodthirsty practices. 'We have martyrs more martyrs than yours,' an assorted crowd of heretics tell him, 'we have harder prayers, higher flights of love, ecstasies quite as long.' But they have no revelations, no proofs, he answers. Whereupon they brandish rolls of papyrus, tablets, strips of cloth. 'What a night!' he sighs.

The temptations are purely negative: the One God is to be driven out by several hundred other gods. Of these 'false gods' Hilarion, the saint's disciple but at the moment standing in for Logic and Science, reflects mildly: 'Don't you feel they have . . . sometimes . . . some likeness to the true one!' And on the sexual front much less temptation is to be seen or felt than revulsion: instances of self-castration abound. The entrance of the Queen of Sheba is one of the many operatic or painter-like set pieces, as it were programme notes for a large, gorgeous canvas, but her attempts at seduction combine overkill with underkill. 'Would you like the shield of Dgian-ben-Dgian, builder of the Pyramids? Here it is! It consists of seven dragons' skins laid on top of each other, joined by diamond screws and tanned in parricide's bile' – that seems an offer fairly easy to resist. And even when she cries, 'I am not a woman, but a world. My clothes need only fall away for you to discover in my person one continuous mystery!', though she sets Antony's teeth chattering, she remains a shadow, remote from the flesh-and-blood Cleopatra of Shakespeare. For Flaubert the flesh was not a temptation but a distraction and something of a nuisance.

He was right about the string. It should have been, could only have been, Antony himself, as a true believer truly tempted. And alas Antony is a bad-tempered mope, or (as Du Camp expressed it) 'a little simple, really quite a blockhead', given to cataleptic fits rather than fits of passion, and to such ejaculations, more appropriate to the reader, as 'How I suffer!', 'What are they driving at?', or – in the course of a lengthy session with Apollonius of Tyana, Jesus's miracle-working rival, 'Something I can't explain appals me.' His finest moment occurs quite early, when he complains that a thirst for martyrdom drew him to Alexandria, but 'the persecution had finished three days earlier'. Valéry wanted to pinch him – but he would only have howled yet again. The outstanding exceptions in this hectic yet frigid phantasmagoria are the Buddha, most respectable, lucid and persuasive of the apparitions, and the Devil who, though he falls short of Goethe's Mephistopheles in mordancy and wit, gets some of the best lines. If God created the universe, 'his providence is superfluous. If Providence exists, creation is defective.'

To these welcome visitors I am tempted to add Crepitus, the god of farting – 'I too was honoured once' – now discredited along with all the classical deities. His appearance raises the question of tone. Has one got it all wrong? Is the work a theological farce – as may be suggested by Isis when she laments that she has found all Osiris's scattered parts except 'the one which made me fertile' – dragged down by its burden of learning? Is it an exposé of the horrors attending on religion? Was Flaubert indulging himself, no expense spared? If the latter, how unlike those splendid letters of his, utterly unindulgent, serving only the cause of art! Similarly baffling is the conclusion to it all, when the face of Christ appears, shining out of the sun, and 'Antony makes the sign of the cross and returns to his prayers'. We are happy for the saint – especially after all the noise and tumult – but what is Jesus doing up there? Is he a metaphor for the sun, or the sun for him?

Kitty Mrosovsky's translation strikes me as being about as good as it can hope to be. Her occasional colloquialisms and anachronisms are welcome: 'nippy as a goat', 'racketeer', 'Shameless woman! clear off! clear off!', where D. F. Hannigan's 'authorized version' of 1895 has 'nimble', 'monopolist' and 'Impure one! begone, begone!' And one is pleasantly taken aback when she brings in the 'haemorrhoidal woman' cured by Christ: Hannigan follows the Gospels, with their 'issue of blood', but in fact Miss Mrosovsky is reproducing Flaubert. The notes she provides, brief and to the point, are helpful, and even essential. This may be more than one can say, hand on heart, for the work itself.

THE HONOUR OF DEFEAT
Villiers de l'Isle-Adam

Born in 1838, Jean-Marie-Mathias-Philippe-Auguste, Comte de Villiers de l'Isle-Adam came of an illustrious Breton line, latterly more distinguished for its poverty and eccentricity. His grandfather, who fought against the Revolution but failed to thrive under the Restoration, wrote to the Minister of Justice in 1815 that, had his name not been so long already, he would have asked the reigning monarch, Louis XVIII, 'to add to it that of "poor devil" . . . a name I really deserve'.

To us Villiers is best known for the grandiloquent pronouncement (his one entry in the *Oxford Dictionary of Quotations*): 'Live? The servants will do that for us.' Admittedly this was spoken by one of his characters. But it was of the author himself that his friend Mallarmé said, after his death: 'His life – I search for anything that corresponds to that expression: truly and in the ordinary sense, did he live?' The strange thing is that, during the first quarter of A. W. Raitt's *Life*, Villiers appears to have written little of any account, his early productions being turgid and derivative, and yet he attained a reputation, among the best people, as *the* great writer of the imminent future. This can only be put down to his personality, his self-conviction, his remarkable charisma. On the other hand he does seem to be *living* – a life of crazy schemes and extremes which earns the adjectives, rarely found in the blurb to a scholarly monograph, 'bewildering, preposterous, hilarious, and moving'. A life, indisputably, that no self-respecting servant would be seen dead living.

Mallarmé also said of Villiers: 'The word "infinite" can only be proffered worthily by a young man looking like Louis XIII, wearing furs and with fair hair.' Villiers, Raitt tells us, 'changed the whole course of Mallarmé's existence', just as a little earlier, 'Baudelaire altered the whole course of Villiers's life' – though his *Life* suggests that no one and nothing could have done the latter. The convoluted weirdness of Villiers's behaviour, and that of many of his friends, is exemplified by the story of Catulle Mendès and his marriage in 1865 to Judith, Théophile Gautier's attractive and intelligent illegitimate daughter, while sustaining his liaison with the beautiful and rich Irish-born musician, Augusta Holmes (or Holmès). Raitt surmises that Villiers may himself have had hopes of Judith, and possibly of Augusta too, in which case he could well have felt that his friend was getting the best of both bargains. None the less, together with Leconte de Lisle (such choice names they had!), he attended the wedding as one of Mendès's witnesses, decorated with a row of enormous medals which his colleague persuaded him to discard on the grounds that he looked like a display case. Once when someone asked him who conferred all those orders on him, he answered: 'I do.'

Villiers then set out to court Judith's younger sister, Estelle, equally attractive, equally illegitimate. Their marriage was blocked by Tante Kerinou, actually the aunt of Villiers's mother, the only member of the family to possess any financial sense and hence – for a while – money. Tante Kerinou was content to subsidize Villiers in his literary career – the whole family encouraged him in that – but not to subsidize his alliance with someone boasting neither pedigree nor cash. 'Right from his childhood he had known with total certainty that there was only one thing to which a Villiers de l'Isle-Adam could worthily devote his life in the shambles of the modern world, and that was literature.' He also knew that he could not support himself by writing, by his kind of writing. So he gave up Estelle, no doubt dropping some natural tears. Six years later Estelle married a journalist, Emile Bergerat, who confessed to Gautier in advance, with trepidation, that he was a natural son. Gautier commented: 'Aren't we all?' Bergerat went on to divulge that his mother was living with a priest. The future father-in-law replied amiably: 'Who better to live with?'

It was shortly after this setback that Villiers found a backer for a periodical called *Revue des Lettres et des Arts* which appeared weekly and lasted for twenty-five numbers. The list of contributors reads like a roll of fame: among others, Mallarmé, Leconte de Lisle, Verlaine, José-Maria de Heredia, François Coppée, the Goncourt brothers, Mendès and his two ladies, besides Villiers himself. (Talking of the work that Villiers was continually 'about' to bring out, Raitt comments that he was 'quite capable of persuading himself that he had completed and even published whole books of which not a line existed on paper'. Possibly this was a disguised manifestation of his idealistic philosophy: unheard melodies are sweeter?) Considering the editor's aims and aspirations, however, we are surprised that the journal survived as long as it did. He told Mallarmé that his object was to 'drive the reader mad' – 'What a triumph, if we could make some subscribers end up in the lunatic asylum at Bicêtre! ... yes, I flatter myself that I have found the way to the bourgeois's heart! I have incarnated him so as to kill him off at leisure and with greater certainty.' The logic of this is quaint, but it bears witness to Villiers's total idealism, his unworldliness, the dimensions of his spiritual ambitiousness. Towards the end of the *Revue*'s life, he and his assistant would wait eagerly in their wintry little office for advance copies with which to make a warming bonfire.

In 1865 Heredia described Villiers as a 'very interesting madman'. A little later Leconte de Lisle found him a madman, though not so very interesting as a writer. And more recently Sartre called him 'admirable but mad'. The adjectives occurring and recurring in the *Life* are idealistic, unstable, turbulent, feverish, ebullient, unpredictable, indomitable, histrionic, capricious, eloquent ('the most astonishing talker of this age', according to Huysmans). No doubt they all apply, but they point to the difficulty the biographer faces in conveying a sense of his subject's personal presence, fascination and power. Many of those who over the years have come to praise Dylan Thomas, for instance, have ended by doing something oddly like the opposite; to such an extent, indeed, that it has become less easy than it was of old to read Yeats's poem, *The Scholars*,

> Lord, what would they say
> Did their Catullus walk that way?

in the righteously scholar-scorning spirit intended.

Villiers was a genuine romantic, as thoroughgoingly the real thing as to look very much like a caricature of it. He was not duplicitous, although the divisions in his nature produced effects that could be taken for duplicity. He contrived first to support the Paris Commune of 1871 and then to oppose it. He was an aristocrat and a royalist – he felt he was born to 'rule', and in 1862, or so he claimed retrospectively, put in a bid for the vacant kingship of Greece – but ready to adopt revolutionary postures *vis-à-vis* the detested bourgeoisie. His ideas on money and on love were high-minded, but he persisted in the hope of marrying a rich heiress – though not a Jewish one, out of care for the purity of his line. This hope, itself high-minded in that it was not wealth he coveted but the freedom to write that money would ensure, led him into peculiarly grotesque antics. In 1873 he signed a promissory note for 200,000 francs payable to a matrimonial agent called Comte de La Houssaye on his marriage (as the agent's receipt has it) 'to the person to whom I am to introduce him', it being understood, in an additional clause, that 'the fortune of the wife of the Comte de Villiers will have to be at least three millions'. In return La Houssaye, rumoured to have engaged earlier in the slave trade, staked Villiers to a repeater-watch, a fur-trimmed overcoat and a set of false teeth, while Mallarmé undertook to teach him basic English: 'since it's a matter of a wedding,' said the ardent wooer, 'I'll only learn the future tense of the verbs.' The language lessons were deemed advisable in that the lucky lady was a Miss Anna Eyre Powell, whose father owned land in both Ireland and England: 'a girl who is a dream from Ossian,' Villiers wrote to Judith Gautier.

After an exchange of letters Villiers took himself off to England, staying at the Grosvenor Hotel in Victoria and at the Eyre Powell country house in Staffordshire, and proposing to visit Dublin as well. Like the great majority of his projects, this one miscarried – for reasons unestablished, but quite probably because, after a briefly idyllic time spent in Hyde Park, the Crystal Palace and Drury Lane Theatre (cf. Flaubert and the English governess), the young woman took fright at the French poet's excitability. La Houssaye reclaimed the watch and the overcoat, but at least Villiers gained a set of false teeth out of it. 'With all his faults of credulity and fantasy, Villiers lived out to the utmost degree of commitment every role in which he cast himself,' Raitt says, 'and this ignominious collapse of his hopes was perhaps the cruellest blow he ever suffered.' Perhaps. There were so many collapses, so many cruel blows, in 'a life studded with disasters'. 'Yet once again,' Raitt continues, 'his indomitable spirit enabled him to overcome his wounds, even if he could never forget them', and a few days later he was striving to persuade a theatre manager to put on his play *Morgane*, 'a spectacular cloak-and-dagger drama'. Without success.

And so his life went on. Or so he went on – terrifying theatre managers, infuriating publishers and editors, or alienating even the best-disposed of them by his continual tinkering with copy. His father had wasted the family resources on such crazy schemes as hunting for treasure putatively hidden by aristocrats during the Revolution and as yet unrecovered. And Tante Kerinou's death in 1871 reduced him to permanent penury. He survived on modest loans and meagre and uncertain earnings – at one stage he worked as a sparring partner in a gymnasium – and through the unobtrusive intervention of friends in the matter of food and clothing. He was not one to notice that a plate of soup had appeared mysteriously on the café table, or that a new shirt had taken the place of a worn-out article. On one occasion, when he attended an elegant soirée with his hands uncovered, a lady guest remarked on what very fine gloves he was wearing. He replied: 'A present from my mother, madam!' Until we come to read his stories, such reported sallies are our only evidence for Raitt's generous estimate of him as 'one of the greatest, most insidious, and most incisive of French ironists'.

Impoverished aristocrats stand in need of wit. And, as sanguine characters have to be, Villiers was marvellously resilient as well. Convinced of what his career was meant to be, *had* to be, he endured the recurrent pattern of encouragement, brink-of-triumph, collapse – at the best, fame without success. In 1881 he stood as a candidate, under royalist colours, for election to the Municipal Council of Paris. From the outset the victory of the sitting councillor, a left-wing republican, was a foregone conclusion, and Villiers later wrote that 'the result of such elections nowadays being well-known in advance, I had accepted only for the honour of defeat.' It was around this time that Marie Dantine, an illiterate widowed charwoman who had been voluntarily looking after him (she it was who switched new clothes for old), gave birth to a son, baptized as Marie-Joseph-Alphonse-Victor-Philippe-Auguste. Villiers was living with a servant! While pride of race led him to invent a story about the child being the result of a liaison with a beautiful unnamed princess, and while only on his deathbed would he marry the mother, he again accepted 'the honour of defeat' and renounced for ever the dream of marrying into riches. And, he may have felt, rather a *domestique* than a dame from the bourgeoisie.

Villiers was intensely fond and proud of his son, an unusually handsome and intelligent boy, and it looked as though Victor, finally legitimatized, would carry on his father's name. He certainly resembled him, founding a little magazine called *L'Idée* and fighting a duel while still at school. Alas, he died of tuberculosis at the age of twenty. Marie lived until 1920 and was buried in a pauper's grave. To conclude this sad story of the demise of a noble line, Villiers himself died of cancer in 1889, not yet fifty-one, but looking as if he were eighty years old. Towards the end Mallarmé, finest of friends, whose understanding of him was preternaturally acute, said: 'Villiers de l'Isle-Adam wrote the last pages of *L'Eve future* flat on his stomach on the floor of a room emptied of its furniture and lit by the stump of a candle . . . Flat on his stomach! But his spirit stood upright. For the spirit, with some people, always forms a right angle with the crushed body.'

Raitt tells of the young Belgians who came to Paris in 1886 to find out what was new in the arts, and found Villiers. Maeterlinck spoke for them all, in recounting later how some were stunned after an evening spent with Villiers in a café, others regenerated by this contact with genius: when he talked, 'it was as if there was in the air the movement of some great invisible thing of which he was the spokesman.' But it was not only talk and personal presence and great invisible things in the air. There was also, now, the work to marvel over.

A model of the Romantic Poet *in extremis, maudit* in any number of ways, Villiers wrote best in prose. *Axël* takes some swallowing: worked on for twenty years, it never reached a form finally acceptable to its author. It must be peculiarly difficult to preserve momentum when one's theme is renunciation, and on such a sweeping scale; and Yeats's description of the work in 1894, though meant as praise, serves as a fair warning: a drama 'written in prose as elevated as poetry, and in which all the characters are symbols, and all the events allegories.' Yet this doesn't indicate the prime weakness – the long-windedness, the relentless pursuit of every implication of every idea, the sense that the author has been carried away not so much by imagination (reckoned to be his chief virtue, and his chief vice) as by words. Having at last dispatched his cousin – his enemy, or tempter – in a duel preceded by so many long speeches that one cannot believe the principals have any breath left for fighting, Axël moralizes thus:

Passer-by, you have passed away. Here you are sinking down into the Unthinkable. During your days of narrow self-sufficiency you were nothing but a dross of animal instincts refractory to all divine selection! Nothing ever *called* you from the Beyond! And you have fulfilled yourself. You fall to the depths of Death like a stone into a void, – without attraction and without goal. The speed of such a plunge, multiplied by the single ideal weight, at this point is ... immeasurable ... so that this stone in reality *is no longer anywhere.* – So disappear! even from between my eyebrows.*

This might be thought an egregious instance of flogging a dead horse when he is down.

Axël and Sara renounce Christianity (at least in its institutional and ascetic aspects), and wealth (the buried treasure that Villiers's father sought in vain), and then love – or love consummated and lived and hence bound to disappoint. This last renunciation or repudiation (you cannot give up what you have not taken) involves them in one more – of life itself. It is characteristic of the author that in the midst of fearful orotundities there emerge fine spare sentences which suddenly focus meaning out of all the blur and glare. Thus, Axël's 'The future? ... Sara, have faith in my words: we have just exhausted it', and 'Man carries into death only what he renounces in life.' The context of the latter declaration, the key passage in the final scene ('The Supreme Option'), is worth quoting for its clarity and force, besides its unblushing arrogance:

Realize this, Sara: in our strange hearts we have destroyed the love of life – and indeed in REALITY we have become our souls! If we accepted life now, we

*Extracts from the drama are taken from Marilyn Gaddis Rose's courageous translation, published by the Dolmen Press in 1970.

should commit a sacrilege against ourselves. As for living? our servants will do that for us. Satiated for all eternity, let us rise from the table, and in all justice let us leave to ordinary mortals whose ill-fated nature can measure the value of realities only by sensation, the task of picking up the banquet crumbs. – I have thought too much to stoop to act!

For all its kinship with *Tristan and Isolde* (Villiers was a fanatical Wagnerian), with Goethe's *Faust* and perhaps with Flaubert's *The Temptation of Saint Antony*, *Axël* is – to say the least – unique. And a representation of the ultimate battle, it must seem, in the ancient war between the ideal and the actual. Raitt reports that, while it still awaits a worthy (an ideal?) production, 'it has met with acclaim on its various appearances on stage, radio, and television.' Despite everything, we would hate it to have died the death.

More acceptable to the modern reader, I would imagine, as to Villiers's contemporaries, are the stories making up the collection, *Contes cruels* (1883). However gorgeous the style, the brevity of the form keeps them from uncoiling into those 'spectacular constructions with metaphysical overtones' so dear to the author's heart. The overtones are indisputably there – less disputably than in ostensibly more ambitious writings – but in these miniatures the lines of construction are uncluttered and sharply incised. There isn't time to explain and justify and embroider every single thought or act.

The *Contes cruels* are surprisingly varied – surprisingly in that such a diversity of attitude and tone is rarely found inside one set of covers – and range from the Poeian horror story, through the occult, the allegorical, the deceptively idyllic (in the shape of a 'bourgeois' *Paul et Virginie*), the sinisterly humorous, to the pungently satirical. To me they seem more clearly and cogently revealing of Villiers's nature, his visions and revulsions, than is anything else. In 'Véra', with its summoning-up of the late loved one, is displayed the power of mind (love, imagination, conviction) over dead matter. 'Two Augurs', as personally felt as everything the author wrote, assaults in ironic fashion the philistinism of the day. 'If you are a writer, you are the born enemy of every newspaper . . . Dammit all, people don't like being humiliated,' the editor instructs the humble aspirant: 'The only motto a serious man of letters can adopt nowadays is this: *Be commonplace*. That's the motto I've chosen for myself. Hence my notoriety.'*

Similar in tenor is 'The Glory Machine', the invention of Baron Bathybius Bottom, which manufactures fame ('myrtles and laurels') for playwrights – 'Let us not forget that the Spirit of the Age belongs to machines' – and, when suitably programmed, even turns out critical notices in advance – 'on the lines of the Prayer-wheel of the Chinese, our precursors in every sphere of progress'. Then 'The Apparatus for the Chemical Analysis of the Last Breath' is another science-fictional device (in this related to *L'Eve future*, a novel in which a human beloved is replaced by an automaton with a soul); the 'Apparatus' is intended to keep people happy or at any rate equable: it familiarizes the young with the sorrows of mourning by collecting and preserving the '*penultimate* breaths' of their elders. For nobody really wants to suffer these days, and 'our motto in all circumstances must be this: Calm! Calm! Calm!' It was of such stories that Huysmans wrote in *A Rebours*: 'All the filth of con- temporary utilitarian ideas, all the mercantile ignominy of the age were glorified in pieces whose poignant irony transported Des Esseintes.'

Several of the tales offer glosses on – more, clarifications of – *Axël*. The couple in 'Virginia and Paul' are Axël and Sara turned upside-down and travestied. Their youthful passion is frankly contained by considerations of prudence and practicality, and in their minds love and the cash that will enable them to love in comfort are virtually indisting-uishable. Even the voice of the famously romantic nightingale is 'sil-very', while the moon is 'a lovely silver colour', good enough to bank. Knowing how all the world loves a pair of young lovers, and lest we should get hold of the wrong end of the stick, 'Hail, divine innocence!' snarls the author. In 'The Unknown Woman' (a tale Raitt considers misogynistic, though if we are to take it in that way it is better termed misanthropic) the heroine, cut off from ordinary life by deafness – and by superiority of sensibility – tells her would-be lover, himself a count, Félicien de la Vierge, and from Brittany: 'Although I am a virgin, I am the widow of a dream, and I want to remain unsatisfied.'

*Quotations are from Robert Baldick's translations, *Cruel Tales*, Oxford, 1963.

If that tale glances at Sara, 'Sentimentality' glances at Axël, and at their creator. In it his mistress, about to transfer her affections to someone else, asks the young poet (another count) whether art hasn't led to an inability in him to *feel* joy or sorrow as a man. 'I should like to discover, before we part, *what gives great artists the right to show such scorn for the ways of other men.*' The poet maintains that artists have identified themselves 'with the very essence of Joy, with the living idea of Pain', and hence are disinclined to throw themselves about in paroxysms of emotion, whether in the arms of their mistresses or on the printed page. Having parted from her, coolly and courteously, he wins the argument by going home, polishing his nails, writing a few lines of verse 'about a Scottish glen', reading a few pages of a new book, and then serenely shooting himself. Incidentally, a later story tells of a man who strangles swans in order to hear their last song: aestheticism reduced to something worse than absurdity. Raitt has remarked on Villiers's use of irony and self-parody as a means of self-defence in his dealings with other people. In the stories such elements rub shoulders with *le grand sérieux* and also with the sheer pleasure in writing that can lead the writer along unanticipated pathways.

The simple truth – simple, we call it – is that Villiers was wholly and fiercely dedicated to literature; and this is a phenomenon which more often than not is accompanied by idiocies and calamities in practically every other department of life. Raitt's expert and exhaustive biography demonstrates the truth with an amplitude that might be thought excessive – but then, excess is part of it. Villiers de l'Isle-Adam was an enormously brave and, in what mattered to him, steadfast man. In closing sentences which could hardly be bettered, Raitt comments on how fully he lived up to the twin mottoes of his family, exhorting to extremity, daring and tenacity: *Va oultre* and *La main à l'oeuvre.*

SANCHO PANZA AND
PETER PAN
On Hašek and Švejk

Cecil Parrott's unabridged translation of *The Good Soldier Švejk* is
roughly half as long again as the previous English version by Paul Selver
of 1930. Hašek's novel, left unfinished when he died in 1923, is no doubt
too long, considering the reading-span of the average human, yet it
would be hard to work up any keen resentment on the point. It is
essentially shapeless, a day-to-day narration of the minutiae of martial
unheroism, and its only imaginable shape would involve the death of its
unhero, which one would not desire, or the end of the war and Švejk's
return to civilian life, which might prove rather tame. Works of art really
ought to have ends, but *The Good Soldier Švejk* is no work of art. Max
Brod grouped it with the writings of Cervantes and Rabelais. The latter
comparison is apt only in respect of the preponderance of belly and
bowels, while the former reminds us that though Švejk is something of a
Sancho Panza there are no Don Quixotes in his world, only insane
generals, imbecile monarchs, pillagers and a few half-way decent lieute-
nants.

How can a novel be so unartistic and still succeed – for *Švejk* has been
here to stay for a good many years now – in leaving a strong and lasting
impression on its readers? A similitude with *Tristram Shandy* proposes
itself, only to be immediately disowned: Sterne is such a very sophisticated fellow, Hašek such a simple direct one; Sterne is an inveterate
stylist, Hašek (or so one would deduce) has never heard of the word
'style' and would hate it if he had. Hašek is being brutish – not nasty,
there is no nastiness here, nothing 'modern' – about brutish people and
brutish events, and as a Czech writing about a common Czech soldier
caught up in Austria-Hungary and the war of 1914 (administrated in the
German language) he was intimate with his subject-matter. There is no

finesse in evidence, no sensitiveness, no anguishing, nothing of Barbusse or Wilfred Owen. Not much of Brecht, either, though this is the most tempting cross-reference so far: it is rather Hašek himself who could be a creation of Brecht's than Švejk; Brecht, for all his camouflage, is more deliberate than Hašek, more of an intellectual, more of an artist. *Švejk* doesn't take a razor to cut down a tree, or an Imperial forest: it is more like a bulldozer charging about in a fashion barely to be described as controlled. Its satire is mostly of the comic-strip variety: WHAM! BOOM!! CRASH!!! It works cumulatively, in the picaresque mode, and since it isn't subtle one tends to trust it more readily. Imprisoned for malingering, Švejk is warned that to try to escape is sheer suicide, 'and by the way suicide's punished too': perhaps *Catch-22* is a child of *Švejk*, a little less innocent or more worldly-wise.

Švejk himself, though not to be called ordinary, is the common man, the common soldier, not some poet intent on exposing the horrors of war in harrowing images and poignant rhythms. There are passing references to the stench of hurriedly buried bodies, but the predominant smell is that of excrement or of drunken vomiting. And there is much more hot air about than hot lead. Švejk spends a lot of time in the cells, he is (unworriedly) in some danger from officials who take him for a deserter or a Russian spy – but he never lays an eye on the nominal enemy. The real enemy is bureaucracy, whether military, civil or religious, the high-ups who dictate policy and the mouthers of official doctrine who require you not merely to listen to but to believe in their big words about the Emperor, the Nation, the Church, Glory, Self-sacrifice and Victory. Quite simply the book, as its vulgar characters would say, shits on all of this. And arrayed against all of this is only the figure of Švejk, together with a few like-minded bad citizens with a taste for unofficial brawls, a full belly, a plump woman in bed – and for survival.

And also, which accounts for Švejk's extra and special dimension, an unflagging fascination for the human scene, a vast acquaintanceship and a reservoir of anecdotes deeper and richer than the latrine pits into which his comrades are always falling. It is only in the act of writing about the novel that one feels obliged to adduce incongruously exalted comparisons, but it may be worth suggesting a kinship with Mynheer Peeperkorn, the incoherent but giant 'representative of Life' in Mann's *The Magic Mountain*, for this indicates one's sense that Švejk is an uncommon creation, that he too is something of a giant – as he needs to be if he is to carry this huge sprawling book on his back. And it must be he who carries it: the rules of art and the devices of good writing certainly do not.

Peeperkorn of course was inarticulate, although he dwarfed the clever chatterers around him. Švejk, within the limits of his discourse, is immensely articulate, and untrammelled by the silken bonds of symbolism. (Remote indeed is that technique, and its tempting offers of what V. S. Pritchett has called 'a quick return of unearned meaning'.) His tongue is not only his pleasure and consolation but his protection as well: he can so bemuse his superiors that they forget to hang him, their minds collapsing under the inexorable flow of red herrings, of considered but often doubtfully relevant anecdote – they just want to run away. He is 'an official idiot', certified as such by a special military commission, his kindly innocent eyes forever glowing with a deceptive gentleness. 'He looked like the Greek god of theft in the sober uniform of an Austrian infantryman.' The stories which pour from him are circumstantial in the extreme, and before long one begins to believe that his habit of conscientiously naming persons and dating events makes the tales more momentous, and one reads on, swallowing the tall stories along with the credible, the dull with the amusing.

One of the tallest stories is the volunteer Marek's, about how he used to be the editor of *Animal World* and, wishing to offer his readers something new, invented such creatures as the Artful Prosperian, 'a mammal of the kangaroo family', and the Septia Infusorian, 'a sort of sewer rat'. Sir Cecil tells us that Hašek himself was briefly editor of a journal called *Animal World*, from which he was fired for writing articles about imaginary animals. Marek, incidentally, gets the job of writing the battalion's history, which he does in advance, reading out to his comrades his stirring accounts of their heroic deaths in action. A more authentic story of patriotism, related by Švejk, concerns a soldier whose field-flask was captured and who entered the enemy camp by night to recover his country's property: 'It was worth it, because during the night the enemy had drawn rations of spirit.'

Whatever the situation, Švejk looks on the bright side. 'Everything was in order and nothing had happened, and if something had happened, it was again quite in order that anything at all was happening.' When Mrs Palivec, in tears, tells him that a week ago her husband was sentenced to ten years for saying that flies had been shitting on his picture of His Imperial Majesty, he replies: 'There you are, then, so he's already served seven days of it.' In Švejk's book, it's a stroke of good luck if you die before someone clobbers you. When his comrades ask him how long he thinks the war will go on, he answers with his customary reasonableness, 'Fifteen years. That's obvious because once there was a thirty years' war and now we're twice as clever as they were before . . .'

Hašek's explicit authorial moralizing on the horror and futility of war, happily sparse, is ineffectual. More in the spirit of the book is a soldier's remark that an ox is better off since they don't drag it to the drill ground and force rifle practice on it before slaughtering it. 'It can't last for ever. Try to pump glory into a pig and it will burst in the end': ox, pig, dog, mule, baboon, half-decapitated cock – the military don't go far for their metaphors. Equally consonant, if somewhat contrived, is the comment that in the Carpathians the excrement of soldiers of all nationalities and all confessions lay side by side without quarrelling. Earlier we have met the general who believes that the road to Austria's glory lies in its latrines and defecation by numbers. An army marches on its bowels and through seas of shit.

Having in mind the author's early anarchism, we might well fasten on this saying of Švejk's as central to the tendency of the novel: 'There are lots of things in the world which are not allowed to be done but can be done. The main thing is that everybody should try to do what he's not allowed to do so that it can be done.' Yes, perhaps, but – apart from it being typical of Švejk's painstaking (and pains-giving) ratiocination – we ought to note that this moral is deduced from the sight of a Red Cross train which has been 'unallowably' blown up.

Sir Cecil's translation, accompanied by Josef Lada's original illustrations and a pleasing scholarly apparatus, restores material previously pruned in English, including such oddments as a bawdy song about the Virgin Mary and the misadventures of a divorce detective. *The Good Soldier Švejk* doesn't need the defence perhaps implied in the translator's surmise that Hašek was sometimes drunk when writing. It is a rich human (though hardly humanistic) stew into which practically everything that came to hand has been thrown, including the kitchen stove, the latrine and a butt or two of brackish rain-water.

As with other real writers, what matters about Jaroslav Hašek is what he wrote. If the reader will put behind him the presumptuous, vain and sometimes lickerish desire to 'understand' the man, then he can enjoy Cecil Parrott's Life as a comic, instructive and thus worthy supplement to that great work of un-art, *The Good Soldier Švejk*.

The Bad Bohemian (not a 'good' Czech, but a true bohemian) starts with one paradox and ends with another, both of them highly respectable manifestations of the ironic spirit. While the combination of irony, entertainment and politics tempts one to a comparison with Brecht, the dissimilarities between the two loom larger than the similarities: Hašek was genuinely a philistine where Brecht only pretended to be, and whereas Brecht had the Theater am Schiffbauerdamm to work in, it would seem that Hašek had an army latrine.

Parrott begins, then, with one of life's little comedies: Hašek is now a 'hero of Communism', and *Švejk* has even been published by *Our Army*, the military imprint. As he suggests, it was very probably Hašek's lack of sustained zeal in politics that has saved him for the Soviet canon. He was a lower-case anarchist, and when he died in Lipnice in 1923, worn out by anarchism and possibly cirrhosis of the liver, the priest would only bury him against the cemetery wall, alongside the suicides and the unbaptized – though he was formally a Catholic. A choir of his enemies from the Czech Legion rendered Beethoven's 'Angel of Love', not the most congruous accompaniment, and later the grave was marked by a stone representing an open book with the inscription: 'Austria, never wert thou so ripe to fall, never wert thou so damned' – not wholly inapposite for an erstwhile Czech patriot, though a more fitting epitaph would have been an adaptation of those words of Švejk: 'There are lots of things in the world which are not allowed to be done: the main thing is that everybody should try to do them.'

There are hundreds of anecdotes about Hašek which, Parrott says, are probably 'more *ben trovato* than true', but the book would have been dull without them – indeed, it would have been remarkably short – and so he has sensibly included a good number of them. He also includes extracts from Hašek's 'autobiography' of 1921, intended to hoist his critics with their own petard, which set the tone admirably:

When I was a year old there was not a single cat in Prague whose eyes I had not gouged out or whose tail I had not docked. When I went for a walk with my governess, all the dogs gave me a wide berth. My governess did not go on taking me out for long, because when I was eighteen months old, I took her to the barracks at Charles Square and bartered her away to the soldiers for two packets of tobacco. She never survived the shame and threw herself under a passenger train . . . As a result the train was derailed with eighteen killed and twelve seriously injured.

To this Parrott adds, summarily and tartly, that the two main occupations of his subject's life were writing and vagrancy. His brother told a story of Jaroslav's vagrancy, tramping penniless about Slovakia in 1903, at the age of twenty. In each village he approached the Catholic priest for hospitality, casually remarking that the Protestant vicar had turned him away. The following day he would apply to the Protestant vicar, mentioning that the Catholic priest had refused help. This simple ruse worked well – but at police headquarters in Prague there was already a growing file on Hašek.

His writing had a vagrant air about it, too. His idea of political journalism was to carry on polemics between the organs of two hostile parties by contributing anonymously to both. When in 1910, exactly like Marek in *Švejk*, he became editor of an informative family magazine, *Animal World*, he soon returned to his third main occupation, hoaxing – even though he needed to keep the job for the sake of his marriage. Instead of writing articles on the disease of roup in poultry, he fabricated a report of herds of wild Scottish collies terrorizing the population of Patagonia, and advertised a pair of 'thoroughbred werewolves' for sale – the office was swamped with would-be customers.

Shortly afterwards Hašek launched one of his best hoaxes. He founded a new political party called 'the Party of Moderate Progress within the Bounds of the Law' and offered himself as its candidate in the Imperial parliamentary elections. The initial objective was to boost the business of a café-bar situated at a Prague crossroads where the three other café-bars served the three traditional parties. For Hašek its real purpose was to cast ridicule on all the existing parties. In his electioneering speeches he demanded that animals should be rehabilitated, in particular they should no longer be maligned by having their names applied to human beings. (In *Švejk*, apropos of the terms applied to recruits – 'Engadine goat', 'ox-headed toad', 'Yorkshire porker' – Marek remarks on how 'the zoological knowledge of the NCOs and officers increases every day'.) 'When a heckler shouted at the candidate of another party, "Shut up, you ox", it was important to realize that an ox weighing seven hundred kilos was much more valuable than a candidate weighing about eighty. For the one you got four hundred guilders, whereas for the other you'd be lucky to get even a guilder.' Another item in the platform of his 'party' was abolition of the entrance fee for public lavatories, on the grounds that it forced needy citizens to use 'more public places' and be fined by the police for doing so – very Švejkian in spirit.

After lengthy opposition on her family's part Hašek married Jarmila Mayerová in 1910. The marriage broke up two years later when, during a visit from his in-laws, Hašek offered to go out to buy some beer and never returned. Instead he set up as a cabaret artist. Then in early 1915 he was called up for the Austrian army. His subsequent experiences bear a distinct resemblance to those recounted in *Švejk*: Hašek's army file carried the entry, 'A swindler and deceiver'. In September he was captured by the Russians on the Galician front. Having bid goodbye to the Austrians, he now joined the (Russian-sponsored) Czech Legion, a preferable alternative to the prison camps. He became a recruiting commissioner in Kiev and, apparently, a sincere exponent of Czech nationalism, anti-Austro-Hungarian and pro-Tsarist.

After the October Revolution of 1917 Hašek threw in his lot with the Bolsheviks and was proclaimed a traitor by the Czech Legion. He was sent to the little town of Bugulma, to the east of the Volga, where he rose to the rank of Deputy Commandant. He laboured conscientiously, gave up drink, behaved like a responsible revolutionary, and took a Russian wife, Shura – though without telling her he was already married. He also wrote the 'Bugulma stories', rough and ready sketches making game of the Soviet authorities, which were published after he had left the country.* Towards the end of 1920 he returned with Shura to Czecho-slovakia, where the revolution had failed to happen, and where he was considered a deserter, a 'Red Commissar' and a bigamist. He also returned to drink and his bohemian ways, and to work on the final (though unfinished) version of *Švejk*. In the little time left to him he did his best to live down his sober and Soviet past.

Perhaps understandably, in view of the time he must have spent in the company of Hašek and Švejk, Sir Cecil is more than faintly disapproving of his subject. 'Among all the talents and even the few virtues with which he was endowed, one essential quality was conspicuously lacking – a sense of responsibility.' Hašek sponged on friends shamelessly; there was a 'perverse and tasteless strain' in him; he was indifferent to culture, art or scholarship; his taste for lavatory humour and practical jokes suggests that he 'stayed fixed in the pre-pubertal stage'; he was ('a psychiatrist would say') a classic example of 'a creative psychopath', and (a better, at least more intelligible label) 'a kind of black Peter Pan'.

If Parrott's explanation of Hašek's behaviour is rather lame, it is to be preferred to impertinent and extravagant speculation, whether *à la* creative novelist or in the style of what 'a psychiatrist would say'. Hašek was left fatherless at the age of thirteen, and this, so we are told, 'more than anything else, was to leave its fatal mark on his development'; and the 'unyielding stance' of Jarmila's father, an honest self-made bourgeois, in the matter of his desire to become his son-in-law 'certainly helped to drive Hašek deeper and deeper into his bohemian way of life'. While there may be something in this theory, it is hardly more persua-sive than the story of How the Leopard got his Spots. Jarmila, who

---

*Some of these have been translated by Cecil Parrott under the title *The Red Commissar*.

certainly suffered from Hašek's irresponsibility, regarded it more simply as the inevitable price to be paid for his kind of originality.

None the less the able and forgiving biographer concludes with the decent wish that the man whose writing has given such pleasure to millions could have had his share of happiness too. It is good to be happy, but even better to have written *The Good Soldier Švejk*.

CHINESE FICTIONS –
AT HOME AND ABROAD

The Golden Lotus

Legend has it that the anonymous author of the sixteenth-century novel, *Chin P'ing Mei*, impregnated the corners of the manuscript with poison and sent it to the Prime Minister, an enemy of his, in the expectation that the recipient, licking his fingers avidly to turn the pages, would meet an interesting death. Colonel Clement Egerton's translation, *The Golden Lotus*, appeared in four volumes in 1939, with the naughty bits rendered into Latin: he apologized for any exasperation thus caused, 'but there was nothing else to do'. These passages have now been turned into (somewhat ornate) English – except for two lines on p. 213 of Volume 2 which escaped the notice of the counter-censor – and can easily be located since the inking tends to be fainter. They look as if they have been well licked.

Having admitted that such passages seemed more exciting in Latin, when the linguistic skills acquired at school from the study of Caesar's *De Bello Civili* were applied to them, I shall not need to dwell long on the novel's famous eroticism. The descriptions are – or sound – rather more sophisticated or arcane than those found in modern permissive writing, covering most of the exercises known to readers of fiction today and contributing at least two extra gimmicks. Since these are unlikely to find favour in a society where women incline to be low on docility, I shall not report them. (Not that the women swarming here are shrinking violets: 'Soon she whispered, "My darling, my dearest, would you like to enjoy the flower of my bottom?"') The sexual encounters are generally grotesque in that oriental manner to be observed in male-glorifying Japanese erotic prints. Yet such grotesqueness is equally Western, for no pornographer can afford a sense of humour.

Indeed, oriental fantasists are in a sense more modest than occidentals: their sexual champions have open and unashamed recourse not merely to 'interesting pictures' but to unlisted drugs, magic powders, bamboo splints, gold and silver bells, improbable surgical transplants (see the decidedly brisker seventeenth-century novel, *The Before Midnight Scholar*, or 'Prayer Mat of Flesh', which introduces canine reinforcement, hot from the dog) and other aids not yet on sale in our sex-supermarkets. Our native champions generally reckon to stand on their own feet, going naked into the bedchamber, and thus laying themselves open to a degree of scepticism.

Some Western scholars – Chinese scholars have shown less concern for this side of their literary heritage, novels being thought a vulgar pursuit – have managed to identify a working moral in *The Golden Lotus*. It relates the history of the prosperous family of Hsi-men Ch'ing and its ruination through strenuous concupiscence, worldly ambition, vanity, greed, corruption and diverse malpractice and mayhem. 'There is no escape from the fatal circle of Wine and Women, Wealth and Ambition' – or, as the concluding verses have it:

> The record of this house must make us sad.
> Who can deny that Heaven's principle
> Goes on unceasingly?

This admonition, lurking underneath 1,500 action-filled pages, is about as forceful as that delivered in *Fanny Hill*: 'Truth! stark, naked truth, is the word . . .' Other and more prudent scholars have prized the novel ('the translation of such a book would render superfluous any other book upon the manners of the Chinese': Henri Cordier) for its elaborate accounts of domestic life, ceremonial junketings and business deals, and its meticulous descriptions of buildings, furnishings and clothing. True, it is interesting to hear that ginger-broth was given to women who had tried to hang themselves, and to gather that in these polygamous households (Hsi-men had the run of six wives, their maids, and singing girls *ad lib.*) much more fuss was made over a missing shoe or wine-jar than over murder, torture or sexual practices so extreme as to cause the less-than-fragile Plum Blossom to complain, 'You mustn't do this again. It is not simply fun. My head and eyes swim so that I hardly know where I am.'

For the literary-minded the most engaging aspect of the book may well be the idiomatic. Aside from sexual euphemisms – 'Striking the Silver Swan with a Golden Ball' sounds to be in a different class from Tossing Cream Puffs – there are some fine (if occasionally cryptic) expressions. 'He is one of those men who can see a bee piddling forty miles away, but not an elephant outside their very own doors'; 'Strike the gong for a day, and be a priest for a day'; 'If a bitch will not have it, the dog cannot get his way'; 'She is talking out of her queynt'; 'When the butcher is dead, you must eat your pork with the bristles on it'; 'If the only poker you have is a wooden spoon, and a short one at that, it is still better than using the fingers'; and 'The stream of matter from his nostrils looked like chopsticks of jade.' That last euphuism, it should be explained, refers to a holy man, the Indian Monk who supplies Hsi-men with the medicines which 'give ease to men' – before finishing them off.

Some readers may doubt the trustworthiness of social and cultural history which is so thickly interspersed with gobbets of unrealistic sex. Yet we should not disallow the possible coexistence of highly dissimilar genres, and it may be a sign of the book's exhaustiveness as history that at the end of it the reader feels quite old and tired. As the author remarks in the course of Volume 4: 'Heaven abhors extremes.'

The Yellow Peril

William F. Wu's all too well attested thesis is that the Yellow Peril (to wit, the real or supposed threat to the United States posed by Asians and more particularly Chinese) is 'the overwhelmingly dominant theme in American fiction about Chinese Americans' between 1850 and 1940. It was in the late 1870s, on the West Coast, that the fictional stereotypes hardened – in such novels as *Almond-Eyed: The Great Agitator* ('A Story of the Day') by Atwell Whitney and Robert Woltor's *A Short and Truthful History of the Taking of Oregon and California by the Chinese in the Year A.D. 1899*. Prince Tsa Fungyan, the leader of the invasion in the latter pseudo-history, is said to bear less resemblance to a human being than to Milton's Satan (perhaps the first appearance of that piece of stereotyping); while a story called 'The Battle of Wabash' (1880) by one Lorelle depicts an America with three Chinese to every white, the decapitation of a chicken replacing a hand on the Bible in oath-taking, and a Chinese billionaire running for President in 2080, followed by the eponymous battle ending with five million Chinese casualties and virtually no whites left at all.

The social factors behind what was to be a long succession of less than truthful fictions are believed to be the fear, particularly pronounced among Irish immigrants, of a flood of cheap labour from war-torn China, and the radical differences between the Chinese and other immigrant groups such as the Poles, or the Irish. The Chinese were unChristian, unmonogamous, given to strange foods and (if the need arose) infanticide, and hideboundly unassimilable – especially when given precious little chance to assimilate. Much of this instant characterization derived from disappointed missionaries and frustrated diplomats. Chinese immigrants were for long disqualified from testifying in courts of law and therefore unable to defend themselves: fairly naturally, this accounts for the growth of traditional-style benevolent associations and the rise of the less traditional and less benevolent tongs or 'secret societies'.

For writers, the Chinese became the new and local exotic, throwing Shylock's ménage into the shade, even surpassing in its attractions the Italian dukedoms (poison, adultery, incest, corruption notwithstanding) so dear to our Jacobean horror-dramatists, and reducing the indigenous Red Indians and blacks to fodder for the kiddies. In what seems no time a notably industrious and long-suffering people (miners, railroad labourers, servants, launderers), civil, respectable and if not exactly God- then ancestor-fearing – the people who in a recent British sociological study were termed 'the invisible Chinese' – were transported into Chinatowns reeking with slave-prostitutes, murder, treachery, opium-smoking, and pervasive degeneracy, including gambling and inscrutability. It was *The Golden Lotus* all over again, less the more recherché frills.

In the early years of this century Jack London wrote about unsavoury Chinese shrimp catchers around San Francisco Bay and also about

China, in the shape of 'a flood of yellow life', invading the rest of the world in 1976: 'his socialism is not evident here,' comments Dr Wu. The world is saved only when an American scientist comes up with a device for dropping the germs of every known form of plague on the Chinese, who are then completely eliminated. London can scarcely be said to have rectified the balance in two stories involving Chinese immigrants in Hawaii – not quite the US of A? – amiable though these are. One of his heroes, Chun Ah Chun, works hard, amasses a fortune, is barred from a fancy hotel in Macao on the grounds of race, buys the hotel and sacks the management, produces (quite monogamously) fifteen children who are half-Chinese, one-sixteenth Italian, one-sixteenth Portuguese, one-thirtysecond Polynesian and eleven-thirtyseconds Anglo-Saxon, and finally retires to live in solitary peace and quiet in his native Amoy.

An exceptionally mean sub-category of stories would seem to be directed against the theory that, say whatever else you might, the Chinese make good domestic servants. An author called C.E.B. (1884) has a launderer who spits water on the clothes when ironing them and Mary T. Mott (1882) features servants who variously wash their feet in the dishpan, spoil flannels by boiling them, and use the oven to cremate polecats whose ashes then go into native medicines. Even worse, sometimes they get fresh with white women by kissing their hands – this is pardonable, one tale implies, if the woman is Italian – though such misconduct may occasionally be offset by saving white females from earthquakes, fires and other domestic calamities. Loyalty is a well-known Chinese characteristic; as is also treachery.

No doubt, where there's smoke, there's fire (or, give a dog a bad name and soon he will be eating puppies as well as rats), but popular fiction has rarely succeeded in producing so much smoke out of one minor industry. Sometimes, however, it was a different story. Thus, in his tales of western frontier life, Bret Harte showed himself sympathetic towards the Chinese: at the worst, as in 'See Yup' (1898), his orientals are smarter at cheating than the whites who set out to cheat them; while Ambrose Bierce, though he never presented the Chinese positively, made what Dr Wu calls 'negative efforts' on their behalf: that is, he was less for the Chinese than against their persecutors. Then there were the missionary authors, much agitated over the buying and selling of young women and the use of opium, that notorious religion of the poor, but eager to show the salvatory effects of conversion on their erstwhile heathen characters. In this mode, Nellie Blessing Eyster's *A Chinese Quaker: An Unfictitious Novel* (1902) describes both the evil aspects of San Francisco's Chinatown and the good that, with the help of Christianity, can come out of it. For once we hear of a complexion blending the rose with the olive, a skin not pock-marked but as smooth as ivory, and large, soft and dark eyes: '"A Chinese Adonis!" she mentally exclaimed.' Even so, Dr Wu is obliged to reproach the author for asserting that the Chinese eat rats and are deficient in family affection.

More accurate in their details were the occasional stories written by American Chinese or half-Chinese, like Edith Eaton ('Sui Sin Far'), who was born in England in 1867 to a Chinese mother and an English father but moved to the United States as a child, thus acquiring 'a clear understanding of bicultural pressures'; and likewise H. T. Tsiang, the titles of whose novels of the 1930s indicate his sympathies with the Communist Revolution in his native land: *China Red* and *And China Has Hands*. The realism stemming from actual knowledge of the situations portrayed ('a rare and valuable contribution to the fiction on this subject,' Dr Wu remarks coolly) is also seen in *Lim Yik Choy* (1932), the fictional biography of an orphaned immigrant who turns Christian, tangles with Irish Americans (the natural enemy, it appears), proves a fine football-player despite racist opposition, befriends a black shoeshine, and goes to Canton to run an orphanage. The worthy author, Charles R. Shepherd, was himself superintendent of a home for orphaned Chinese American boys in California.

Some incidental entertainment is provided by Dr Wu's complaints about minor inaccuracies in his chosen field, or swamp. In 'Behind the Devil Screen', an 'action-packed melodrama' of 1921, James Hanson commits the solecism of giving a Manchu a Cantonese name and dresses tong killers in tweeds, silk shirts, striped socks and fedoras *à la* Mafia. In C. W. Doyle's series of stories, *The Shadow of Quong Lung* (1900) – by way of introduction the author proposes that San Francisco's Chinatown ought really to be burnt down, 'but the scheme is too

Utopian to be discussed in a mere preface' – one of the plots hinges on a scribe who writes people's letters for them because they use a different dialect from the recipients. Alas, dialects exist only in speech and do not affect the written language. Incidentally, the villain of the title, who is a graduate of Yale and a barrister of the Inner Temple (London), and also a tong leader, could well be an ancestor of the great Fu Manchu. He comes to grief when accidentally falling against an electric chair intended for somebody else. Dr Wu does show qualified admiration for Mary E. Bamford's well-researched novel, *Ti: A Story of San Francisco's Chinatown* (1899), in which the evangelizing author explains knowingly that Chinese gamblers, being superstitious, will never read any book, including the Bible, because 'shü' ('book') is a homonym for the word meaning 'to lose'. Unhappily she 'fails to relate gambling and opium-smoking to social and environmental pressures'.

Dr Wu's book bears traces of its origin as a doctoral dissertation, albeit one of uncommon enterprise and liveliness. Despite the admirable dispatch and even lucidity with which the plots are potted, the reader begins to feel he is suffocating under a yellow flood of homogeneous pulp. Luckily, just in the nick of time, along come the two great figures of this curious genre, the fine flowers of popular orientalism. Between them they sum up the whole proceedings, one standing at each pole: the evil Dr Fu Manchu (the name alone makes you shudder), created by our very own cheese-and-beer-loving Sax Rohmer (for further details of his colourless life, see *Master of Villainy* by Cay Van Ash and Elizabeth Sax Rohmer, 1972); and the good, equally well-named Charlie Chan, brain-child of Earl Derr Biggers.

Fu Manchu (*fl.* 1913–59), that grander ancestor of the neurotic Dr No, was of British provenance, neighbourhood of Gerrard Street; he emigrated to the United States and rose to be the hero/villain of books sold in millions, films, radio and TV adaptations and comic strips. Described by his creator as possessing 'a brow like Shakespeare and a face like Satan', 'the yellow peril incarnate in one man', he was a large-scale international adventurer and mischief-maker (busy in one novel engineering the election of one of his white servant-stooges to the Presidency), specializing in ingenious (and, one might think, chancy) assassination by means of animals (scorpions, adders, baboons, mice), and giving offence – in reality, this – to the humourless government of China ... Moreover, he fathered Fah Lo Suee, prettier but morally no superior, owner of 'an unforgettable hand, delicious yet repellent, with pointed, varnished nails', 'a long oval contour' and 'slight, curving hips' etc., sexually available (in this doing the image of Asian womanhood no good at all) and treacherous in the extreme.

While he too appeared in serial and feature films, Charlie Chan (*fl.* 1925–32) was Fu Manchu's opposite in practically every respect: to begin with, a Chinese Hawaiian (sharing the relative innocuousness of, say, a Channel-Islands Frenchman) and, as a police detective in Honolulu and San Francisco, supporting white law and order and white supremacy. A white man's Chink, in short. If Fu Manchu, tall and lean, resembles Satan, Charlie Chan is closer to Mr Pickwick: short, fat and pink (not yellow), with cheeks 'chubby as a baby's', affable, mild, calm, very much a family man. He has a disarming propensity to aphoristic utterance in the style of 'Confucius say' and to flowery language: 'Relinquish the firearms, Mr Jennison, or I am forced to make fatal insertion in vital organ belonging to you.' Fu Manchu of course speaks impeccable English, altogether superior to that of the wretched whites who litter his path. What the two great Chinamen have in common is an egregious share of cleverness.

To quote that no doubt oriental proverb, Where there is opium smoke there is conflagration. And the sinister stereotype of the Chinese was confirmed by the treacherous attack on Pearl Harbour in 1941 (Japanese, Chinese, what's the difference?) and again by the Korean and Vietnam wars. What is now needed, Dr Wu says in winding up, is that serious attention should be paid to fiction written by the Chinese Americans themselves, 'the source material that can best counter the racist presentations of characters such as Fu Manchu and Charlie Chan.' By all means – but he doesn't actually mention any names. One springs to mind: the semi-fictitious Maxine Hong Kingston.

History has a habit of transferring the boot to the other foot – though usually after the original kicker and the originally kicked have departed the scene. I remember how, some twenty years ago on the Chinese island of Singapore, Han Suyin (half-Belgian, please note) was in disgrace with the authorities for promulgating 'yellow culture', as it was officially known, through such sexful fiction and non-fiction as *A Many Splendoured Thing*. Concurrently I was myself in trouble for semi-facetiously protesting against the ban on juke-boxes (well, there was more to it than that) and teaching Wordsworth and Milton. The term 'yellow culture' embraced any form or channel of foreign influence or foreign values deemed likely to imperil the correct development of a brand-new and pure-minded (also single-minded) nation. Han Suyin was teaching at the Chinese-medium Nanyang University, and I at the older, colonially established University of Singapore. Between us, you would have thought, we had contrived to turn two respectable educational institutions into veritable Chinatowns, with all that that dread name implies. Like Fu Manchu, we were yellow perils incarnate! As Confucius says, More different, more same.

The Woman Warrior and *China Men*

The subtitle of Maxine Hong Kingston's first book, *The Woman Warrior*, embodies a pun: 'Memoirs of a Girlhood among Ghosts', that is to say, among Chinese story-ghosts and also among non-Chinese, who by definition are ghosts if not demons. 'Those of us in the first American generations have had to figure out how the invisible world the emigrants built around our childhoods fits in solid America.' In her books Mrs Kingston comes near to suggesting that it is America which is invisible – populated by the Mail Ghost, the Newsboy Ghost, the Garbage Ghost – while China, the China of her parents, or the China her parents told her about, is the solid world.

This raises a question which, though it sounds prissy, is legitimate: how much of this 'China' is true, how much is tale-telling or, as Mrs Kingston puts it, talking-story. For the insider, whatever country he is inside, there is no settled boundary between actuality and myth: all is part and parcel of life as it is lived. While realizing this – for we all have our legends – the outsider still likes to know, of a country he is outside, which is which. We are sufficiently able to distinguish (say) between

Hans Andersen and the real, geographical country of Denmark: we have heard tell of both of them more or less concurrently since we were children. But China is a different kettle of mysteries.

Just as the last English gentleman is reckoned to be, if not an Indian, then an Englishman living in India, so Mrs Kingston, born in Stockton, California, in 1940, is possibly more Chinese than the Chinese in China. There is nothing like emigration and expatriation, especially when it shows in the face, for bringing out one's nativeness; 'characteristics' are accentuated in a way they never were at home. 'What is Chinese tradition and what is the movies?' One is moved to reply that one Chinese tradition is never to explain Chinese traditions to benighted foreign barbarians. Such refusal or reluctance can evince itself as arrogance. Or, in a politer person, as modesty. Outsiders won't be able to understand: or, outsiders surely won't want to be bothered with understanding. Being a true writer, Maxine Hong Kingston has no truck with either of these considerations.

One way for Chinese girls to escape being merely wives or slaves was for them to be swordswomen. Mrs Kingston weaves a story about herself as heroine, based on the tales her mother told of Fa Mu Lan. In a small epic along the lines of *The Water Margin*, she is a version of Maid Marian as Robin Hood ('My army did not rape, only taking food where there was an abundance. We brought order wherever we went'), or a female avenger, at times a Bruce Lee in drag. She defeats a giant who then changes into his true shape, a snake, whereupon his disgusted soldiers pledge their loyalty to her. Her followers, she remarks in a nice aside, never knew she was a woman: 'Chinese executed women who disguised themselves as soldiers or students, no matter how bravely they fought or how high they scored on the examinations.' Finally she overthrows the emperor and beheads him, then inaugurates the peasant 'who would begin the new order'.

The 'new order' sounds rather like Communism. Under it a male chauvinist baron loses his head too, exploiters of the people are tried, and ancestral tablets are torn down. 'We'll use this great hall for village meetings . . . Here we'll put on operas; we'll sing together and talk-story . . . This is a new year, the year one.' No wonder, as she says when the tale ends, that 'my American life has been such a disappointment'; if she tells her mother she has got straight A's at school, her mother replies, 'Let me tell you a true story about the girl who saved her village.' To make matters worse, news comes from the old country that the revolutionaries have taken an uncle's store away from him and killed him, along with other members of the family, for the crime of selfishness. 'It is confusing that my family was not the poor to be championed. They were executed like the barons in the stories, when they were not barons.' In her role as female warrior, 'we would always win,' she had declared: 'Kuan Kung, the god of war and literature, riding before me.' Now, it appears, war and literature have gone their separate ways.

From time to time there comes a thin mosquito-like sound of feminist grievance. No husband of hers – the author announces – will say that he gave up his cherished career for the sake of the wife and kids. No one will have to support *her* 'at the expense of his own adventure'. But 'then I get bitter: no one supports me; I am not loved enough to be supported.' Even now her feet are bound, figuratively speaking. Just to get dates she has to 'turn myself American-feminine'. So she refuses to cook, or if she has to wash the dishes, she contrives to break them. Chinese women have more cause than most to complain of their status and treatment. It took a whole revolution to nurture a Chiang Ching. (It must have taken all hellishness to breed a Chinese revolution.) Mrs Kingston dwells on those hurtful old expressions like 'Better to raise geese than girls', 'When fishing for treasure in the flood, be careful not to pull in girls' and 'Girls are maggots in the rice'. In *The Gate of Heavenly Peace* Jonathan D. Spence mentions the young revolutionary poetess, Qiu Jin (Ch'iu Chin), who wrote in 1904:

We, the two hundred million women of China, are the most unfairly treated objects on this earth. If we have a decent father, then we will be all right at the time of our birth; but if he is crude by nature, or an unreasonable man, he will immediately start spewing out phrases like 'Oh what an ill-omened day, here's another useless one.' If only he could, he would dash us to the ground.

Three years later she was captured by government troops, tortured and beheaded. In the case of the young Maxine, one feels sorry for her mother; and not merely because she was closer to such events. Mothers tend to experience the dirty end of both sticks, masculism and feminism alike.

Brave Orchid, the mother, is a great character, a teller of myths but herself no myth. She had been a doctor before coming to America, the Gold Mountain, in the winter of 1939/40 to join her husband in running a laundry. On receiving her diploma from the To Keung School of Midwifery, she went to market to buy herself a slave. The parents who were selling their children liked to talk with buyers. 'If they could just hear from the buyer's own mouth about a chair in the kitchen, they could tell each other in the years to come that their daughter was even now resting in the kitchen chair. It was merciful to give these parents a few details about the garden, a sweet feeble grandmother, food.' The little girls who were being sold by a professional dealer might stand in a line, bowing together, while the older ones chorused, 'Let a little slave do your shopping for you', or singing 'a happy song about flowers'. Brave Orchid picked a healthy girl with a strong heart-beat, who pretended to be less than wholly competent in order to bring the dealer's price down. The slave cost her the equivalent of $50, and she found her a husband before leaving for America. The author cost her mother $200 in hospital bills at birth.

Here is a subject for someone to study: the ways whereby Eastern people have managed to clothe their fearful hardships and humiliations in something approaching dignity, in ritual, in the necessary and some-times almost elegant *euphemism*, when nothing else remained to them. No doubt what discourages any such study (cf. the stridency of affluent reformers and educated revolutionaries) is the fear of seeming to con-done the conditions which bred this precarious civility. But there is quite enough unpalliated horror in the chapter about the Lady Doctor: we hear of a baby without an anus, left in an outhouse (euphemism for latrine) to die, and the box of clean ashes placed beside the birth bed in case the baby was a girl – suffocation by the midwife or a relative was 'very easy'.

The account of Brave Orchid's sister promises to be rather more jolly, chiefly because it shows first-generation Chinese Americans as viewed through Chinese eyes. In her late sixties, Moon Orchid arrives from Hong Kong in search of her errant husband whom she hasn't seen for thirty years. He is suitably terrified, having married again and being a citizen of a country where bigamy is frowned on. Moon Orchid is useless in the laundry, and upsets the children by trying to smooth their hair or leaning over them when they are studying. 'They're so clever,' she exclaims: 'They're so smart. Isn't it wonderful they know things that can't be said in Chinese?' But then the story turns sad. Moon Orchid imagines that Mexican 'ghosts' are plotting against her life, and has to be put away. She was too old to move; her spirit, her 'attention', was scattered all over the world, her sister explains. 'Brave Orchid's daughters decided fiercely that they would never let men be unfaithful to them.'

Mrs Kingston's second book, *China Men*, in which (the blurb announces) she 'turns her attention to her patriarchal forebears', starts off menacingly with a fable about a man who is looking for the Gold Mountain but finds himself in the Land of Women, where he is forcibly rendered female: holes bored in his ear lobes, his feet broken and bound, his womb improved by vinegar soup. There follows a short anecdote telling how the narrator and her brothers and sisters mistake a stranger for their father, whereas (we take the implication to be) they would never confuse their mother with another woman.

The suspicion or expectation that men are about to get it in the neck is strengthened by the beginning of the next chapter. The narrator's father swears a lot, in the (not exclusively) Chinese manner: 'bag cunt', 'your mother's smelly cunt' . . . The narrator wants him to tell her 'that those curses are only common Chinese sayings, that you did not mean to make me sicken at being female', that he was not referring to her or her mother or her sisters or grandmothers or women in general. The narrator herself is no sensitive plant, and this doesn't ring altogether true. If it isn't ritual sensibility or a sign of acquired American delicacy, it may be an excuse for what follows. Since BaBa is given to silence or to few words (and those, apparently, obscene), she will have to tell his story for him. 'You'll just have to speak up with the real stories if I've got them wrong.' In the event she does men no wrong at all.

BaBa – the story goes – passed the last Imperial Examination to be held, turned to village teaching, married, got fed up with his pupils, listened to yarns about the streets that were paved with gold, emigrated (legally or otherwise: the narrator gives alternative versions), was detained at the Immigration Station outside San Francisco, started a laundry in New York, was joined by his wife fifteen years later, then was cheated out of the laundry by his partners and left for California, 'which some say is the real Gold Mountain anyway'. If women have a right to complain, it looks as if men have a right to curse. Except that later, mind you, the author says her father was born in San Francisco in 1903. Then what was all that about the Imperial Examination? Just a good story? And what about the two children, brother and sister of the author, who (we were told) died back in China? Dream children are one thing; dream children killed off as testimony to historical hard times are another.

I do not think it was solely because I read it immediately after *The Woman Warrior* that *China Men* struck me as the less fresh and persuasive of the two. One item here is a Crusoe-like story which adds little to Defoe and looks rather like padding. Another, 'The Ghostmate', takes a theme common in old Chinese stories, a love-affair between a young man and a beautiful woman who turns out to have been dead for centuries, and treats it conventionally, except perhaps for mention of a song we would like to have in full – 'What Does the Scholar Do with His Bagful of Books After Failing?' – and a concluding comment which blends Chinese realism with the author's modernity: 'Fancy lovers never last.'

But Mrs Kingston gets into her stride when she moves to her great-grandfather's adventures while clearing forests in Hawaii, the Sandal-wood Mountains. The chapter contains an authentic description of the state of mind induced by opium-smoking, the only dubious touch being that Great-Grandfather experienced these effects after his very first (and last) session. Even stronger is the story of the grandfather Ah Goong, who worked on the construction of the Central Pacific Railroad in the Sierras during the 1860s. It was the time when dynamite had been invented, and was being tested by or on the railroad workers: 'chinamen had a natural talent for explosions.'

'Stupid man to hurt yourself,' they bawled out the sick and wounded. How their wives would scold if they brought back deadmen's bones. 'Aiya. To be buried here, nowhere.' 'But this is somewhere,' Ah Goong promised. 'This is Gold Mountain. We're marking the land now. The track sections are numbered, and your family will know where we leave you.'

Ah Goong lost his citizenship papers in the San Francisco fire of 1906, returned to China and lived to be bayoneted in the head by a Japanese soldier. This left him a bit queer – not surprisingly, since he must have been a hundred years old by then.

The author was a small child during World War Two but remembers how her father was exempted from service – the draft, she says, was one reason for leaving China in the first place, the other was having to pay taxes with grain – because he was too skinny. She also remembers when the AJAs, Americans of Japanese Ancestry, were released from the relocation camps at the end of the war. One such family lived on her block:

We had not broken into their house; it had stood shut for years . . . They gave us their used comic books, and were the only adults who gave us toys instead of clothes for Christmas. We kids, who had peasant minds, suspected their generosity; they were bribing us not to lynch them. The friendlier they were, the more hideous the crimes and desires they must have been covering up. My parents gave them vegetables; we would want them to be nice to us when the time came for us Chinese to be the ones in camp.

Yet the finest chapter, a noble conclusion to the book, concerns her brother, a high-school teacher who was drafted into the Vietnam War and resolved to 'follow orders up to a point short of a direct kill', on the grounds that it was better to be a pacifist in the Navy than a pacifist in gaol. As his ship nears Asia he has dreadful dreams in which he is unable to distinguish between villains and victims: they all have 'Chinese faces, Chinese eyes, noses, and cheekbones'. He visits the Philippines and Korea, and also Taiwan, 'a decoy China, a facsimile', where nevertheless he meets apparently real Chinese who tell him how lucky he is to be an American. Planes from his aircraft-carrier bomb Hanoi, but he can't see the bombs falling. Then he is promoted and transferred to Taipei: he has been cleared by Security, which in turn implies that the whole family is truly, securely, American, despite all the black marks (real or imagined) in its history. Mustered out, he returns to Stockton. 'He had survived the Vietnam war. He had not gotten killed, and he had not killed anyone.'

Here, in Keats's words, there is no 'irritable reaching after fact and reason', for fact and reason are safely within the reader's reach. Elsewhere, it is because Mrs Kingston's subject is real men and women, a real and long immigration, and a real nation or indeed two nations, that one feels some uncertainty and hence some irritation. Her mother once told her: 'You can't even tell real from false' – and if she cannot, then how can we? At other times, and much of the time, poetry doesn't smudge truth, and we rest content in the spirit of another of Keats's sayings: 'What the imagination seizes as Beauty must be truth – whether it existed before or not.'

– III –

SCHOLARSHIP, SEXSHIP, SHITSHIP
Misadventures among Words
Sexism in Children's Books

Since I still believe that Mother is a woman, with breasts, and Father is a man, without, I am not the ideal customer for this collection of documents edited by the Children's Rights Workshop. Any attempt to wean – oh dear, a sexist metaphor – to lead children away from this primal sexist stereotype seems to me doomed to failure. I hope.

As defined in the McGraw-Hill Guidelines which conclude the book, sexism originally referred to prejudice against the female sex but now covers 'any arbitrary stereotyping of males and females on the basis of their gender'. Fair enough, and there is much in this compilation to which one is compelled to assent. If it is true that most picture books for pre-school children 'are about boys, men, and male animals, and most deal exclusively with male adventures', then the whole industry needs shaking up: such uncreativeness and slavish dependence on the past must be unparalleled in any other field of human endeavour. But in fairness to Maurice Sendak (*inter alios*), who is ticked off for making his 'adventuresome' hero a boy instead of a girl, it has to be said that, if writers – some of them – stand at the growing-point of the race's consciousness, they still have to connect with things as they are. Even if they are writers of science fiction, in which incidentally feminist themes have proved felicitously apt. By and large boys *are* more adventurous, more active, I suppose, for better or for worse. The report on 'Sex-Role Socialization' remarks that girls in picture books are often restricted by their clothing, 'skirts and dresses are soiled easily and prohibit more adventuresome activities'. (There are repeated references in this connection to one 'Ronsome', 1968, who incurs reproach for dressing his Princess in a long gown whereas his hero, the Fool, is dressed 'in a sensible manner'. Investigation reveals that the guilty author is Arthur

Ransome.) Girls may be restricted by other things too: they have babies – if that is a restriction.

The 'narrow role definitions' which the Children's Rights Workshop complain about are the mark of an unimaginative writer; and someone should ask this question: Where does the animus against imagination and enterprise in children's books come from, and who is responsible for serving up flavourless pap? When it is suggested that books 'might show little boys crying, playing with stuffed toys and dolls, and helping in the house', one can only agree that at times books should do just that – there are even dolls that can cry – although (and I doubt this should be kept from the kiddies) there are biological reasons why girls play with dolls and doll's prams more commonly than boys do. The material gathered here is largely of American provenance – we British 'have a long way to go yet before a local education authority can be prosecuted for the use of sexist materials, such as is now happening in the USA' – but a paper of local authorship points out that the female world of children's books is almost entirely confined to domestic activity, cooking and child care, despite the fact (is it?) that 'the majority of women in Britain are in paid employment outside the home'. Still, I would think that unless *someone* is shown cooking the food and running the house, the child-reader is going to feel very uneasy. Why is that little boy crying, mummy? Because he is hungry, dear.

A little more hard thinking would have removed what is ridiculous, petty or slack in this book. The 'Sex-Role Socialization' paper numbers among its grievances a children's book from which 'Mrs Noah, who had an important role in the biblical story of the flood, is completely omitted'. In the Bible, unless it has been rewritten to conform with Anti-Sexist Guidelines ('Our Parent which art in heaven'), Mrs Noah features merely as an entry in the Ark's manifest. The complaint could have been brought that the writer was stuffy and failed to avail himself/herself of later legends. Yet if the writer had represented the lady as the shrew and gossip of the Mystery plays, wouldn't that have been considered a most offensive piece of stereotyping? Oddly enough, nowhere is there any mention of the most famous book of all, and the most famous character – a girl called Alice.

McGraw-Hill's Guidelines, issued in 1974 'for the benefit of their editorial staff and authors', is the most interesting section here and, notwithstanding its allowance that 'the language of literature cannot be prescribed' and the recommendations are intended primarily for teaching materials and non-fiction works in general, perhaps the most alarming. Reasonable generalities which can be left to work on a writer's reason decline into ludicrous or pernicious or boredom-promising particularities and also, one notes, a disinclination to differentiate between stereotypes and types. Thus the sentence 'Henry Harris is a shrewd lawyer and his wife Ann is a striking brunette' is stamped NO, while the following is stamped YES: 'The Harrises are an interesting couple. Henry is a shrewd lawyer and Ann is very active in community (*or* church *or* civic) affairs.' The man is allowed to retain his shrewdness (lawyers are typically shrewd), but the woman forfeits her crowning glory in exchange for a social conscience that will send childish readers to sleep. The fine old expression 'distaff side' is NO, while the tepid 'female side or line' is YES. 'Cleaning woman/lady' must give way to 'house *or* office cleaner', 'housewife' to 'homemaker' – 'or rephrase with a more precise or more inclusive term': yes, precision is likely to be a casualty in these operations!

'Man' is in deep disgrace, and hence also 'mankind', which should be replaced by 'humanity' or 'people'. 'Manmade' must yield to 'artificial' or 'of human origin' (is this lampshade of human origin?), and 'manpower' to 'human power' or 'workforce'. Since 'man' is unacceptable as a suffix, the rich word 'statesman' must be replaced by the impoverished 'leader' or 'public servant' – the preferred terms so often belong to the jargon of bureaucracy – and 'chairman' by the clumsy circumlocution 'the person presiding at (or chairing) a meeting'. Wouldn't it be simpler for us all to agree that 'man' can equal 'human' when the context so indicates? Then of course there is the sad fact that English, horrid manmade language, 'lacks a generic singular pronoun signifying *he* or *she*', and therefore the sentence 'The average American drinks his coffee black' has to be rephrased as 'The average American drinks black coffee' – which seems to me to carry a distinctly different meaning. It would have been nice to hear English commended for its freedom from embarrassing gender in nouns: *une erreur, ein Egoist* . . .

The element of plain justice in this crusade makes it hard to resist. But resist one must whatever smacks of Agitprop and Index, in the nursery as elsewhere. Gradualism is the only process that works, not mechanical prescription and proscription; and facts are not changed by changing words. One fact is that a good writer, ignoring guidelines, will produce something good and humane and valuable, while a poor writer, following guidelines, will produce rubbish or worse. And, one is forced to ask, what about the insistent lowering sexuality of entertainment and advertising, in which women (and men too) feature as *objects* to a degree never known before in history – 'Every night they take off their XYZ tights for us' – and to which children are exposed continuously? Yet porn or near-porn appears to have been accepted, while the Children's Rights Workshop agitate over words like 'policeman' and 'poetess'. There *is* much to be done, there are many wrongs to be righted – or, humanity being what it is, not much better than mankind, to alleviate at least – but I fear the Workshop are starting at the wrong end. The wrong end is often the less arduous: intellectuals are easier to impress and intimidate than traders.

Maledicta and *Bad Mouth*

Maledicta calls itself 'The International Journal of Verbal Aggression', but the worst thing about it is its editorial huffing and puffing. It sees itself as a band of frank, gallant and daring intellects battling vigorously against the 'envious, mindless, cacademoid prissy pricks' of some putative stuffed-shirt Establishment. In truth *Maledicta* (the best thing about it is its name) is the old Teutonic philologizing shakily transferred to the dark side of the tongue: the sort of volte-face so popular when once safe. It is typically academic in keeping up the old game in which scholars stockpile future reasons for their existence. Thus, 'It is time to consider why psycholinguists have not examined dirty words and what researchers can do to learn more about this frequent phenomenon' (Timothy B. Jay, North Adams State College); 'Although there is an extensive body of literature dealing with the diverse aspects of the engineering profession, none of it deals with what is one of its well recognized but neglected aspects, namely the use of sexual terms to describe actions, motions or parts of machinery or equipment' (Norman B. Friedman, Richard J. Daley College); 'Looking at current bibliographies, one will soon be convinced of how shamefully "erotology" is neglected in the field of lexicology' (Edgar Radtke, presently completing his doctoral dissertation at Mainz University); '*Shit* has not had its share of serious scholarly attention' (Margaret Fleming, University of Arizona); 'As is true of every other aspect of the new transdisciplinary science *Maledictology*, we also lack a system of classifying terms of abuse on the basis of their *provenance* or *literal meaning*' (Reinhold Aman, who 'has mortgaged everything except his wife and daughter' to keep *Maledicta* going). The thought that *Maledicta* was a sustained anti-academic hoax did cross my mind, but the genuine fury with which the editor turns on its critics removes the suspicion.

Academic is the word, in one sense, for Professor Fleming's 'Analysis of a Four-Letter Word'. When she showed a first draft of the article to a class of teachers or prospective teachers of English, one of them, 'a retired military man', thrust it away in disgust, observing that his old Sunday School teacher used to tell him, 'Cecil, there is filth in the world, but you don't have to wallow in it.' Professor Fleming comments, 'Could there be a clearer example of mistaking the word for the thing?' Well, one would rather have the word thrown at one than the thing – but the word does signify the thing, it puts us in mind of it. Professor Fleming concludes with the pious hope that her article has served to direct attention away from the 'dirtiness' of *shit* and towards 'its usefulness as an index of social and linguistic behaviour': she has done her tidy best to clean the word of its prime quality – its meaning.

The operation of the dread law of diminishing returns in the sphere of obscenity is starkly revealed in 'Dialogue between a Pederast and a Libertine', presented in French original and English translation by 'Robert Saint-Vincent Philippe'. This is indecisively attributed to Voltaire and inaccurately described by 'R.S.V.P.' (it all begins to sound like those euphemistic ads in newsagents' windows) as 'a compilation of dirty words, true, but written with considerable charm and ingenuity', moving along with 'sprightly and mounting interest', and delineating with skill 'the basic character of two vastly different social types, neither of which is too well known to the academic world'. A Professor from the Sorbonne seems nearer the mark in surmising that the Dialogue was 'a *tour de force* to use all the words for male and female parts, for bordels and whores, for toilets, venereal disease': it reads like a flaccid dramatization of the 'Répertoire' to Harrap's *English-French Dictionary of Slang and Colloquialisms*. The Pederast and the Libertine consume a vast amount of sexual argot, say little, and mean less. An index of social behaviour? It is high time that somebody researched into the reasons for the grinding inanity of porno- and scatolinguistics.

However, *Maledicta* contains passages of genuine interest – and also some entertainment, as when Professor Jay explains that rudeness (like many other things) is relative, and *jesus-fucking-christ* 'may be very offensive in a nunnery' whereas *cock* 'would be inoffensive on a chicken farm' – yes, *rope* can be mentioned freely in a circus but is best avoided in the house of a hanged man – and Peter Tamony points out, in a lively piece on the semantics of the rag trade, that while fashion spies in the early twentieth century were called 'keeks' (Scots-English-Irish dialect), Stevenson was not employing the locution exactly in this sense when he wrote in *Kidnapped*: 'Let's take another keek at the red-coats.'

In a serious-minded paper on 'Xenophobic Ethnica', John Algeo speculates on such terms as 'gringo': apparently a variant of *griego* ('Greek'), hence 'stranger'; 'honky': origin uncertain, possibly a variant of 'hunky' (from 'Hungarian'), probably *not* from the white employer's habit of honking the car horn when picking up the black maid at her house (I had vaguely supposed an allusion to the white man's nose or way of speaking through it); and the mystery word 'bigot': which the *Dictionnaire Robert* explains as a Norman surname from 1155, presumably brought back from England ('by God!') and acquiring its present sense in the fifteenth century. Quoting Byron on the high incidence of adultery in places where the climate's sultry, Professor Algeo claims a hot-country etymology for 'cyprian', meaning 'prostitute': the derivation is more precise, from *the* Cyprian, Aphrodite, whose principal seat of worship and first home on *terra firma* was at Paphos, whence 'Paphian', 'of (esp. illicit) sexual love', as the *Concise Oxford Dictionary* has it. On 'Lesbian', from Sappho's warm island, and the love that dare not speak its name, Algeo comments acidly: 'Nowadays it not only speaks, but jabbers incessantly, and with episcopal benediction.'

'Paths of Pathos: The Urethral in Speech' is altogether wilder in its exploration of venereal whys and wherefroms. Its author opines that 'we have no difficulty in tracing to the urinal syllable' – viz. 'piss' – 'the popular slang expression for its female organ' – i.e. 'pussy'. While acknowledging that some believe the nickname to derive from 'a favourite synonym for cat', he contends that, on the contrary, the cat is called 'pussy' 'on account of its feminine fur reminding of the human female's centre'. That scarcely seems plain speaking. Even less plainly, and more circuitously, he submits that the common origin of the verb and the noun 'pass' is confirmed by the way the noun, as in 'mountain pass', can still evoke from our unconscious 'the likeness of the *Mons Veneris*'. 'Beau' is allowed to come from the Latin 'bella', but 'bella' impresses him as 'another abstraction from a lost Latin variant of *belly*, basically standing for the womb'. (The fuddy-duddy derivation is from 'benus'/'bonus', as summed up by the French etymologist L. Clédat in the pious aphorism, *'Une bonne peinture est une belle peinture'.*) We are heading for a total identification of *lingua* with *lingam*.

The author continues: 'Why hesitate to transpose *l* for *r* as countless children, not only the Chinese and Japanese, do and recognize in *fear* a close relative of *feel*, thus visioning in the *flame* of both our *flow*?' It would be the act of a spoil-sport to point out that why Chinese and Japanese sometimes 'transpose' when speaking English is because their own nearest sound falls somewhere in between our *l* and *r*, and the Chinese tend (only *tend*) to pronounce *r* as *l* while the Japanese tend (or more than tend) to pronounce *l* as *r*.* Incidentally, the author is A. Bronson Feldman, a man of many parts, of many articles on e.g. Stalin, Freud, *Secrets of Shakespeare* and *Hamlet Himself*, and he calls his footnotes

---

*Travellers in the East will have heard about, or even heard, the Japanese stewardess informing passengers that 'frying time will be three hours', or even 'three howls'. Over-compensation can take place: occasionally in Japan I was myself transposed into 'Enlight'.

'hindnotes'. Again, one begins to suspect the sincerity of these scholars. Roy T. Matthews's complaint that obscenity has become so much a part of everyday speech that a man doesn't know which way to turn when he wants to explode isn't the only piece here that makes one wonder whether Dr Aman's collaborators are invariably loyal to him. 'My modest plea, then, is for us to coin a new set of obscenities and vulgarisms so that we can get back to the basics that have made our country so strong, so powerful, so much a land to be honoured and imitated.'

That one can write cleanly about dirt – wisely, wittily, though disturbingly too – is shown by *Bad Mouth*, 'Fugitive Papers on the Dark Side', which touches on points raised more breezily and dropped more promptly in *Maledicta*. The edifying scientific intentions of the obscenologist, Robert M. Adams observes, 'corrupt and simultaneously sanitize' the specimens he is studying. 'Even when he picks up words like "shit" and "fuck" for inspection, he touches them only with gleaming, stainless-steel forceps (represented on the still-sanitary page by quotation marks), in a solemn clinical atmosphere, the very reverse of the exceptional rage and disgust which usually authenticate such words.' The desire to break the laboratory hush may account for the factitious *saeva indignatio* emitted by the editor of *Maledicta*. Mr Adams echoes, more feelingly, the plaint of Roy T. Matthews: for writers, for all of us, 'it's hard to stay out of the obscenity-sweepstakes, but each new success renders it harder to win.' His epigraph from Stendhal on ice-cream is nicely nostalgic: 'But it's perfectly delicious! What a pity it isn't forbidden!' How can you express yourself these days when you hit your thumb with a hammer?

Other essays here are concerned with the related oversupply of the ugly in the arts, the inflation and devaluation of 'shock'; with the arts of political lying ('frankness of manner' combined with 'total vagueness about specifics'); and with the strategies of insult and invective. Adams cites as 'proper' insults J. P. Mahaffy's reply to a rudely interrupting, incontinent student at Trinity College, Dublin: 'At the end of this corridor you will find a door marked GENTLEMEN – but don't let that stop you', and Dorothy Parker's retort to a young actress's muttered

'Age before beauty' as the latter stood aside for her: 'And pearls before swine'. These are insults for the recipient to take home and think about.

Mr Adams is no mere *laudator temporis acti*, and when he remarks that in some circles today it is considered 'élitist' to be anything short of stupid, he also observes that some words, such as 'cretin' and 'idiot', have taken on new colourings as a result of new humane attitudes to mental sickness. He knows how very tricky the subject is, and that it calls for more than simple-minded word-lists. 'Anyone who talks about the way we talk can't help becoming part of his own subject. Sometimes this puts one in the position of trying to open the refrigerator door fast enough to see if the light really goes off when it's shut.' He is scrupulous in weighing the evidence and tentative in coming to conclusions, but his elegant and sinuous prose is sinewy as well, and makes itself heard plainly. On the question of the famous 'indivisibility' of 'free speech' he says: 'The pimping pornographer who claims to be fighting the battles of some future Proust or Joyce doesn't deserve much of our sympathy. If there wasn't good cash to be turned from his pious pose, one would soon see how much he cared about Proust or Joyce, supposing he had heard of either.'

Mrs Byrne's Dictionary of Unusual, Obscure, and Preposterous Words

Words alone are certain good, said the poet (who had not seen *Maledicta*). Almost any book about words will have something to offer, especially at a time of shrinking vocabularies. It has to be said, though, that by no means are all the words in Josefa Heifetz Byrne's dictionary either unusual or obscure or preposterous, except perhaps to an absolute *abecedarian* ('a person learning the alphabet; a beginner'). *Abattoir, almoner, aperient, autodidact, benison, blancmange, burble, cairn, chockablock* – such inclusions make one wonder whether vocabularies haven't declined further than one had feared.

But plenty of instructive or entertaining items are to be found here. *Jeff* ('printers' dice game using pieces of type metal') throws light on a dark mystery, while it is fascinating to be told that *pozzy-wallah* is British slang for 'a jam lover' – Eric Partridge glosses *pozzy* as 'jam: military; perhaps ex a South African language', so *pozzy-wallah* may originally have referred to the quartermaster of a South African regiment serving in India – and that *ingle* can bear the meaning 'a homosexual boy-in-residence'. Not Angles, nor angels, but ingles.

The blurb claims that the *Dictionary* is 'a most helpful reference for students, writers, or anyone unable to locate just the right expressive word in a standard dictionary.' This – as long as one knows the word in the first place – cannot be gainsaid. For the writer of school yarns there is *tolly* ('to light candles after hours: British school slang') and *epistemophilia* ('abnormal preoccupation with knowledge') – 'Take that, you epistemophiliac!' – not to mention *randle* ('a nonsensical poem recited by Irish schoolboys as an apology for farting at a friend'). For the teller of tales involving Red Indians and fishing rights there is *Chargoggagoggmanchauggagoggchaubunagungamaugg* ('Indian name for a Massachusetts lake: "You fish on your side, I fish on my side, nobody fish in the middle" '). The romantic novelist will be grateful for *acronical* ('happening at sunset or twilight'), despite its restriction by other dictionaries to the rising or setting of stars, and for *kalokagathia* ('a combination of the good and the beautiful in a person'), *suppalpation* ('gaining affection by caressing') and *humicubation* ('lying on the ground in penitence'), to be followed by *thalassotherapy* ('an ocean cruise as therapy'). Essential for the historical novelist are *acutiator* ('in medieval times, a sharpener of weapons') and *awm* ('forty gallons of wine in old England'), or – if specializing in the grandeur that was Rome, the glory that was Greece – *centesimation*, although it carries only one-tenth the sensation value of 'decimation', and *petalism* ('the custom in ancient Syracuse of banishing a citizen for five years').* Waiting for the problem-novelist are such treasures as *philematophobe* ('a woman who dislikes kissing'), *cagamosis* ('unhappy marriage'), *agunah* ('a woman whose husband has deserted her and who may not marry without divorce or proof of his death'), *basophobia* ('inability to stand because of a

---

*It is left to more orthodox dictionaries to explain that *ostracism* in Athens was effected by writing the name of the proposed exile on potsherds, whereas in Syracusan *petalism* the name was written on olive leaves. Blackballing is our equivalent, outside the Home Office.

fear of falling'), and *xylophobia* ('fear of wooden objects; fear of forests'); while authors of a more extreme tendency will seize on *ipsism* (much more gripping than 'masturbation'), *anililagnia* ('sexual desire for older women'), *arpagee* ('a raped woman'), *blissom* ('to copulate with a ewe'), and of course *anhedonia* ('the inability to be happy').

We shall all of us be happy with *seeksorrow* as an alternative to the ugly-sounding 'masochism', *quakebuttock*, for 'coward', *bovrilize* as a more flavoursome substitute for 'epitomize', *agomphious beldam* instead of the well-worn 'toothless old hag'. Also with *clinomania* ('excessive desire to stay in bed'), which surely ought to be worth a doctor's certificate, while *matutolypea* ('getting up on the wrong side of the bed') is another ailment to bear in mind. One never knows when *didine* ('dodolike') might come in useful, or *doseh* ('a Mohammedan custom of riding over the prostrate bodies of dervishes'), or *yepsen* ('cupping the hands; the amount cupped hands can hold'). *Spousebreach* makes a change from 'adultery' (and if you need a rare word for its opposite there is *hereism*), though *adulterine* is doubtfully an improvement on the uncouth 'bastard'. This unhappy condition is often due to *gamophobia* ('fear of marriage') or *agenocratia* ('opposition to birth control'). Incidentally, when reproved for bad language, you can now say: 'But *fukfuk* merely denotes an animal's innards. Mrs B says so.'

I do not wish to be a *smellfungus* ('a grumbler or a fault-finder': Sterne's name for Smollett), but is a *balaclava* really 'a full beard: British slang' and not a woollen hood?* Mrs B defines *decameron* as 'a collection of a hundred stories written by Boccaccio', whereas the point is that they were told in ten days. And *forel* one would deem an old term signifying the case or binding of a book or manuscript rather than that modern accessory, 'a book jacket'. Mrs B's treatment of *undinism* seems a trifle squeamish: is 'the association of water with erotic thoughts' (cf. the waves that used to crash against the rocks in the pre-permissive cinema) really all it means? On the other hand, her definition of *wyvern* is unexpectedly vulgar: 'a two-legged dragon with a snake on its ass' –

---

*It has both meanings. Mrs B is right: in his *Dictionary of Slang and Unconventional English* Eric Partridge has: 'A full beard: *c.* 1856–70; ex the beards worn by those soldiers who were lucky enough to return from the Crimea.'

when we come to *onolatry*, 'ass-worship', we could well make donkeys of ourselves. (The word is basically different from *pygophilous*, 'buttock-loving'.) Like many otherwise decent and respectable people, Mrs B may be touched by *grammatology* ('worship of letters or words'), she might be thought a bit of a *logolept* ('a word maniac'), but there is not much *aischrology* ('"dirty" language') in her *Dictionary* – she herself, by the way, is defined as the daughter of the violinist Jascha Heifetz – nor does she pander to *grapholagnia* or 'a more than passing interest in obscene pictures'.

There is a certain oddity in the phrasing of some of her definitions. Is the description of *lycanthropy* as 'insanity in which the patient thinks she's a wolf' a feminist tit-for-tat or she-for-he – or is Mrs B satirizing the female sex (woman is a wolf to woman)? It is not her doing that *pinchpin* indicates both 'a married woman who insists on her rights' and 'a prostitute', for Partridge assigns a similar (but more explicit) definition to *pinch-prick*, low colloquialism, obsolescent. *Sermocination*, 'a speaker quickly answering her own question', leaves Mrs B's intentions in doubt, but the faint scorn in *antinomian*, 'a Christian who believes that faith alone will see her through', suggests a low opinion of women, and so do *philodox*, 'one who loves her own opinions; a dogmatist', and *autologophagist*, 'one who eats her words'. Can these unhappy conditions be specifically *thelyphthoric* ('that which corrupts women')? On the other hand, *rep*, 'formerly, a dirty old woman, now, a dirty old man', may point to an awakening of pro-female feeling,* and *bovarism*, 'man's romantic conception of himself', looks like a total turning of the tables. But then *frotteur*, in spite of its masculine ending, is defined as 'someone who gets her kicks by rubbing against people in crowds' ... The truth is, I fancy, that Mrs B – caught on the horns of that sexistolinguistic dilemma facing all mankind (no, all humanity) – is only trying hard to be fair in her apportioning of awful examples.

The poet also remarked that words without thoughts never to heaven go. They help us to think right, they connive at our wrong thinking: we

---

*No, Mrs B is merely being correct: *rep* appears to have shifted sex. Partridge describes it as obsolescent in its male application, while by 1850 it was already obsolete in its female application.

cannot leave the thinking to them. Out of context and on the loose, they are trickier than ever, and if *catachresis* ('incorrect use of a word or phrase, especially from any etymological misunderstanding') is to be avoided, those setting out to write about or to collect words must be perpetually on their guard. Mrs B is sometimes off hers. To define *Realpolitik* as 'militarism' *tout court* is so wounding as to be near *verbicide*. And to give 'a reformed prostitute' as the sole meaning of *convertite* is simply wrong: when Jaques remarked, 'Out of these convertites/There is much matter to be heard and learn'd', he wasn't proposing to join a band of Magdalenes. (One wonders whether Mrs B can be a *shaconian*, a term she explains as describing 'someone convinced that Bacon ghosted Shakespeare's plays'. Can this be? Or does the term refer to those who believe that Shakespeare ghosted Bacon's essays? Is it another instance of handwriting misread? Can Mrs B's *Dictionary* itself be in part *allonymous* or 'ghostwritten'?) One's faith in Mrs B's reliability is shaken when one meets the entry for *mont-de-piété*: 'a public pawnshop; French = mountain of pity'. Oh no – one cries, with the dreadful, imprudent exultation or exaltation caused by the sight of a *grammatolater/tress* going off the rails – 'mountain of piety', less humane but much funnier! This is the more disturbing in being one of the very few cases where Mrs B gives the etymology, for in her preface she tells us sternly that hers 'is not a book in which one may find romantic stories about word origins' since 'etymological books abound and proliferate like drosophilae'. The unusual word *Drosophila* is absent from her *Dictionary*, but refers to a genus of fly, one moreover much favoured in laboratory studies of heredity.

But a dictionary without etymologies is a poor thing. One misses them the more in Mrs B's, not only because one would dearly like to know the romantic story behind the use of *zondek* as a slang term for 'pregnancy test', but because of an uneasy suspicion that Mrs B is a shade *ultrafidian*, or gullible, and at times her unusual words are simply foreign ones, her obscure words archaisms, and her preposterous words technical terminology or (like the long-winded enzyme requiring 1,913 letters which, to avert an outbreak of *jeff*, I refrain from quoting) scientific formulae.

Enough of this *logomachy* ('1. war with, or about, words. 2. a word game'), for I fear I too am growing long-winded – or, as Mrs B more pleasingly has it, *aeolistic*.

A Dictionary of Catch Phrases

While confessing that he doesn't really know what a catch phrase is, Eric Partridge defines it as 'a saying that has caught on, and pleases the public'. Catch phrases may be sentences or even single words. They are to be distinguished (if not very certainly) from clichés and proverbial sayings: 'All depends on the context, the nuance, the tone.'

Since the world is full of catch phrases and a lexicographer is only human (a c.p. missing from Partridge, though 'he's one of us' is listed as a homosexual c.p.), it will be petty to complain of c.pp. missing from Partridge. And if one does complain, one may well be told that they are clichés or proverbial sayings. 'A standing prick has no conscience' began as 'a low c.p.' but by 1920 had achieved the status of (unofficial) proverb, while 'you'll have your work cut out' is a c.p. only when addressed to a (commonly Australian) mother about to have her third or fourth baby – otherwise it is merely a cliché. An instance of (not itself found in this dictionary) Catch-22? But we shouldn't take the mick(e)y (another absentee) out of Mr Partridge. Oedipus schmoedipus (also missing), what's it matter so long as he loves his mother tongue?

Better to enjoy what is present, and in particular the catch phrases one hadn't come across before – thus proving one is not a mere member of the public. But first, a juster matter for complaint, let us remark on a few oddnesses in this compilation. 'Alone I did it' is described as latish C19/early C20, and Partridge states that his only early record of it occurs in a play by Alfred Sutro of 1906. If Sutro, why not Shakespeare (1607-8)? –

> like an eagle in a dovecote, I
> Flutter'd your Volscians in Corioli.
> Alone I did it.

Of 'are you keeping it for the worms?' ('a Canadian c.p., dating from *c.* 1940') Partridge remarks that it is 'accidentally reminiscent of Shakespeare's famous attack on the value of virginity as such'. Shakespeare? Much more reminiscent of Marvell's playful ploy, 'Worms shall try / That long preserv'd Virginity'. On 'look you!', a Cymricism 'well known since C16 at latest', he comments: 'so much so that it occurs frequently in the plays by James Shirley (1596-1666).' More to the point, it occurs very frequently indeed in Shakespeare's *Henry V* (1599): eleven times in the scene in which Fluellen makes his first appearance.

That in his historical notes Partridge tends to adduce popular instances and sources – Noël Coward, Wodehouse, Terence Rattigan, Edward Albee, I T M A – is perfectly apt. But I think he underestimates the influence on the popular tongue of writers more elevated. *Hamlet*, as we know, is made up of catch phrases, among them (as Partridge notes) 'for this relief – much thanks!'. It is pleasing to come across Stevie Smith's 'not waving but drowning' admitted as a highbrow c.p. 'of *c.* 1958-70'. Shortly before her death Partridge wrote to her to ask whether she had coined or adopted the phrase 'a good time was had by all'. Miss Smith replied that she had taken it from parish-magazine reports of church outings, and asked in turn, 'Are you the Eric Partridge of the Slang dictionary. But no! he must by now be dead.' Better read than dead.

Partridge suspects that 'better Red than dead' was suggested by Hilaire Belloc's epigram,

> When I am dead, I hope it may be said:
> 'His sins were scarlet, but his books were read.'

Not a self-evident derivation, I would say. Solzhenitsyn credits or discredits Bertrand Russell with this updated version of 'A living dog is better than a dead lion.' Basil Brush ought to have got a mention in the entry on 'don't get your knickers in a twist', if only as the popularizer of the c.p. for a younger generation. (There is no connection between this and the probably older c.p., 'you come home with your knickers torn and say you found the money!': 'indicative of extreme scepticism'.) And the entry on 'some like it hot', *c.* 1965 – originally applied to the kind of jazz now often described as 'cool' – should surely have mentioned the immensely successful film of the name, with Monroe, Lemmon and Curtis, made in 1959.

But, no flowers – by request! (Well, Partridge tells us that this jocular c.p. means 'no complaints, *please*!') For 'to -er is human' (a pun involving 'the slurred sound of dubiety'). So let us look at some entertaining and unusual commonplaces, such as the very first item in the book: '*à d'autres!*', an early and brisk version of 'tell it to the Marines!' fashionable among English coxcombs and coquettes *c.* 1660–80. Or, in the twentieth century, 'hell hath no fury like a woman's corns'. 'Les be friends' (lesbian) was new to me, but so was 'as easy as shaking the drops off your John' ('essentially masculine'). So were the (mostly Australian) phrases, 'the more firma, the less terra' (used by those nervous of air travel since *c.* 1950) and 'give her twopence!' By the latter hangs quite a tale: it is used 'on sighting a beautiful female child' and suggests that the (male) addressee should provide her with the necessary coins to ring him when she reaches the age of consent. Though often indelicate in import, catch phrases are at least mercifully brief.

I cannot say that I have often caught the not-so-brief phrase 'she is so innocent that she thinks Fucking is a town in China', reported to be 'a mostly Londoners' c.p. dating since *c.* 1940'. Or 'that'll put your back up', meaning (via cats fighting) 'that'll make you amorous'. Or even the tongue-twisting 'twinges round hinges through binges': since *c.* 1950 and referring to rheumatism and one of its causes. Since 'trot the udyju Pope o' Rome' went out in the year I was born, I can be forgiven for not knowing that, by way of back- and rhyming-slang, it indicated 'send the wife/female home'. A notably grim, resonant c.p. is 'the hills are closing in on him', *c.* 1953–5 (or earlier?) among UN troops in Korea, referring to the forbidding landscape and signifying the onset of madness. But it is amusing to find that the stale gibe against marriage, 'why buy a cow just because you like milk?', has a highbrow companion: 'why buy a book when you can join a library?' (Cf. the genteel 'the day the omelette hit the fan'.) One does rather wonder whether Partridge's occasional esotericisms truly qualify according to his definition of a catch phrase. How big is 'the public' they please? But after all the reader will want to learn, and a dictionary confining itself to what he already knew wouldn't be much fun.

Though he occasionally makes heavy weather of historical backgrounds, as in the entry on 'have at thee (*or* ye *or* you)', Partridge's commentary often takes an agreeably personal turn. He tells us *en passant* that Colley Cibber's play *Love's Last Shift* was translated into French as *La dernière chemise de l'amour*. (I recall seeing a poster in France, *Le Reveil de la Sorcière Rouge*, advertising a sea-film, *The Wake of the Red Witch*.) The c.p. 'my wife (*less commonly* my husband) doesn't understand me' provokes him to expostulate: 'What are *they* complaining about? It would be damned awkward for the speakers if they *were* understood!' On 'a fart's the cry of an imprisoned turd' he comments that the c.p. is 'as essentially poetical as it is superficially coarse . . . clearly an allusion to the cry of a bird imprisoned in a cage'. Hence one is a little surprised when he jibs at 'it's a poor arse that never rejoices' – equally poetic I would have thought, but, according to Partridge, the property of 'those "gangs" or cliques or fraternities of would-be wits in which public houses abound'. He is disapproving of casbahs too ('come with me to the Casbah!', possibly originating in a Hollywood film, to be spoken leeringly): 'supposed to be a scene of romance, but usually disappointing and dangerous'.

The use of 'at this moment in time' he rightly considers nauseating, and one of his correspondents damns 'the name of the game' (to be distinguished from the game of the name) as smug and knowing – epithets I could wish he had also applied to 'didn't they do well!', 'nice one, So-and-so!', and that sports commentator's cant, 'what a turn-up for the book!' The expression 'his nose is always brown' is glossed as 'he's a sycophant of the lowest order', with the comment 'and so is the c.p.'. (Cf. 'I didn't think that was sun-tan on your nose': 'a C20 – and esp. Suffolk – c.p.'.) Of 'looking for maidenheads' (i.e. for something exceedingly scarce) Partridge remarks, 'since World War II becoming increasingly difficult to find, hence now somewhat nostalgic and obsolescent'. He pursues the theme of *autres temps* in the entry on 'think of England': advice to a young bride ignorant about the facts of life, 'very little needed since 1945'. And apropos of 'as the actress said to the bishop' (and vice versa) he ventures the opinion that 'only very slightly obsolescent by 1975, it is likely to outlive most of us'. Quite true. Like 'famous last words' – 'one of the most memorable and trenchant of all c.pp.', ascribed to the RAF, 1939 onwards, as a rejoinder to such 'fatuous statements' as 'flak's not really dangerous' – it fits practically anything. As the bishop said to the actress.

Another Dirty Word

Change and decay in all around we see. But not all change is decay, and some decay turns into new life . . . The trouble with amiably tolerant attitudes – towards language as towards other things – is that, like Dr Johnson's theatrical delusion, they have no certain limitation. Geniuses may misspell, but is misspelling a sign of genius? As a publisher's editor, I noted the lordly assumption of certain writers that somebody else, some dull hireling, could put their tiny oversights right – and their indignation if nobody did. Granted, tolerance is nicer than objection, and safer, for complaints and corrections can easily degenerate into what Jan Morris has called an 'odious mixture of the hectoring, the condescending, the patronizing, the sarcastic and the self-satisfied'. After giving a radio talk some years ago on common misspellings, I received an irate and disgusted letter from a listener: 'I thought you were a poet . . . how can you concern yourself with such petty matters?' My ingratiating admission that among the words I had to look up in the dictionary every single time I used them was 'misspelling' had failed to work.

It might, by the way, be worth collecting common notions of 'the poet'. For example, 'What! You're a poet and you watch *television*?' (for much of the time the only sort of vision available to one), or 'You actually travel on the *Underground*?' (a rich compost for poems and, if you can get a seat, a chance to write), or 'You mean you work in an *office*?' (a place made to work in). A contrasting set of notions of 'the poet' is held by the rather more sophisticated, who quietly remove breakables, lock up the liquor and send their daughters out to the cinema.

In the course of that radio talk I recited a short list of common misspellings, drawn from a long and varied experience as both a marker of essays and a marker-up of typescripts. My seven blunders of the world were: 'liason', 'irresistable', 'comparitive', 'cemetary', 'accomodation', 'seperate', 'exhilerate'. (I hope I have got them wrong.) Room should have been found for 'dessicate' – and for 'miniscule', a word which suddenly became fashionable and simultaneously wrongly dressed, perhaps betraying the influence of the once popular (now possibly recrudescent) miniskirt. Since this form of the word can be seen in the highest circles – I don't refer merely to *The Times*, which once upon a time could be used with confidence in lieu of a dictionary – it may be that behind one's back it has been decided that 'miniscule' stands for 'very small indeed', while 'minuscule' is now reserved for a kind of cursive script developed in the seventh century.

Speakers on television and radio may be held to bear a special responsibility towards language, and by and large they display commendable care. In any case it would be futile to quarrel with them. Usage, they might say, always carries the day – and lo and behold investigation shows that their mispronunciation or misuse has carried the day and is indeed usage. Such is the potency of those commentators who (for instance) tell us about 'the de*cade*', virtually wiping out the old '*dec*ade'. One perceives the rationale here, though, since more often than not the speaker is dwelling on some deplorable aspect of a 'low dishonest decayed'. The stress shows the strain.

The following are a few mispronunciations or pronunciations heard recently on television, not the fruits of long perquisition, and coming not from the laity (who, faced with a camera or microphone, can be forgiven anything) but from professional broadcasters. 'Forte' ('strong point', from French) as two syllables, probably by confusion with Italian 'for*te*'; 'com*mun*al' (to do with people communing, presumably, and to be distinguished from Communism); 'la*men*table'; 'ha*rass*'; 'in*teg*ral'; '*es*timate' as verb, instead of '*esti*mate*'; 'Grorn Prix' (which began in motor-racing but has since spread to show-jumping). I would have included 'lichen' pronounced as 'litchen' except that the latter is now permitted: my *Shorter Oxford English Dictionary* describes it as 'now rare in educated use', but that was in 1947.

In a different category are such eccentric accentings as 'St *John's*

Wood', although no other wood or saint is involved in what is being communicated. Similarly, 'between you and I' (but after all, the speaker has got the polite bit right and didn't say 'between me and you'); 'reserved for Whites only'; 'which today is scorned upon by many' (a telescoping of 'look down upon' and 'pour scorn upon'?); and 'the crowd have gone literally mad' (which could mean what it says: you need to be half-way round the bend to go to a football match in the first place) . . . Not a large haul, but still a contrast to the care broadcasters take with complicated foreign names.

I was about to opine that the rate of yielding to changes or decays of English appeared to have increased of late, and that these days one gives in to practically everything. But then I remembered a small victory over the powers of darkness, a victory albeit inexplicable and perhaps accidental. Some while ago I had a hand in publishing a powerfully imaginative work of fiction, set in Dickensian London, and called *The Albatross Muff*. The muff in question was made from the plumage of an albatross, the sinister symbolism of which will not elude the reader. Trouble set in long before the book saw the light of day. The title, such was the message, would not do: the word 'muff' had obscene or (worse?) extremely vulgar associations. It then occurred to me that they were not in fact entirely unknown to me, but it had never crossed my mind that anyone could suppose the novel to be a variation on the theme of Leda and the Swan.

To start with, I had to break the news to the author; which was embarrassing, since she had no idea of what I was talking about. Then I tried the title on passers-by. The innocent among them could see I was talking smut and grew annoyed because they couldn't grasp it. The serious-minded urged me to stand firm, to fight for the rights of a perfectly decent and even indispensable word. But others, more worldly-wise, advised me: 'Why kick against the pricks? You can easily find something else.' The author and I stood firm. And though the title may conceivably have alienated publishers in the USA where this particular obscenity has wider currency, in this country not a single snigger or snort or cry of outrage greeted the book's appearance. We are of course a nation of bird-lovers.

But that was not the end of it. In due course an offer was made for the paperback rights – on condition that the title was changed. For a new dimension of reproach had revealed itself: the title was 'offensive to certain women readers' in that it incorporated an example of male filth-aggression against the female body. This *démarche* struck me as less an advance in enlightenment than a miserable capitulation. But the matter was out of my hands: who dare stand in the way of paperbacking?

Subsequently I composed an indignant and self-soothing piece to the effect that:

in this 'liberal' age, word after word is acquiring obscene connotations, and soon the Oxford Dictionary will be the dirtiest book ever published. A new sort of censorship is threatening to set in: we shall be free to speak our dirty minds – but not to speak our mind. We must watch over our words, we must fight. To begin with, let us have some help from the intellectual public

and so forth. Happily this was not published, for when the paperback edition appeared it bore the title, *The Albatross Muff*. When one wins a point, or a point is won for one, one hardly likes to inquire how it came about. Perhaps nobody could think of an alternative? Perhaps it had been realized that, for all those 'associations', the title was exactly right for the book?

Just as *Wuthering Heights* was the right title, although someone must surely have remonstrated: 'It won't do, Miss Brontë. It's all very well your telling us it's a *significant provincial adjective* – people will think it's a misprint for Withering . . .'

USAGE
Good, Common, and Most Uncommon

On Language

A seasoned word-warrior, William Safire fires his opening salvo on the half-title verso. The page in question is headed 'Also by William Safire', and William Safire footnotes for our benefit that this does not refer to a book called *Also*, by William Safire. 'The line, which appears unchallenged in thousands of books, should read "Other books written by the same author".' But there could be an element of misrepresentation there, in that some authors go on writing much the same book under different titles. Better perhaps is 'By the same author', even though authors can change in the course of their lifetime, and though the phrase may suggest that the person preparing the prelim copy had forgotten the author's name. Never mind. Worse things happen in books. The jacket of a book recounting a British officer's adventures on the run in wartime Holland carried a picture of a badge inscribed 'S.H.'. The blurb stated that these letters stood for 'slecht hoerend', translated as 'hard of hearing', the point being that the fugitive wore the badge to cover up his ignorance of Dutch. Shortly after publication a distressed Dutch reader wrote to the publisher, explaining that what 'S.H.' really stood for was 'slecht horend', and that 'slecht hoerend' alas meant 'bad whoring'.

In any case, can the present book properly be said to be written by William Safire, seeing that a good third of it consists of excerpts from readers' letters to him? Not that anyone is going to complain, for *On Language* would be the poorer without the sense of community and 'on-going' linguistic life gained through this collaboration. As Safire himself is the first to admit in the last line of the book. Talking about words owes its fascination to the fact that, in a uniquely immediate way, it is talk about life. (I should have watched words, and said 'talking

164

sensibly . . .') And we do not live alone, we do not talk to ourselves. (Well, not all of the time.) As for the exasperations accompanying the fascination – as one correspondent says here, 'C'est la langue.'

'Because I both write to live and live to write,' Safire declares in his preface, 'I have taken an interest in the implements of my craft.' He stops short, thinking perhaps of all those readers poised to pounce, and asks himself why he didn't use the shorter word, 'tools'. Because it would have drawn him into the cliché, 'tools of my trade'. But it is better to use a handy cliché than to be seen straining to avoid it. So he amends (emends?) to 'tools of my trade', more honouring himself in the observance than in the breach.

This nervousness is a malady most incident to the language 'purist'. 'We Never Make Misteaks.' As he well knows, people are all agog to hoist him with his own petard. As a *memento mori*, Safire keeps by him . . . Start again. Safire keeps by him, as a *memento mori*, a list of 'fumblerules' said to have been culled from teachers of English (not, or not all, I hope, from 'English teachers', Mr Safire!) – among them, 'Remember to never split an infinitive', 'Reserve the apostrophe for it's proper use and omit it when its not needed', 'Never, ever use repetitive redundancies', and 'Last but not least, avoid clichés like the plague; seek viable alternatives'.

Elsewhere Safire confesses, or is made by his assiduous public to confess, to errors of his own: 'a firm hand on the rudder of the Ship of State' (a mixed-metaphorical cliché), the repetitive redundancy of 'a hollow tunnel' and of 'the cynosure of all eyes'. I am not convinced that this last is mortally tautologous. A musician could be the cynosure of all ears; and the word = 'dog's tail', something one might suppose to be of compelling interest only to other dogs' noses. At all events, do unto others . . . and Safire ought not to have objected to the saying 'the smile on your face' in that it couldn't be anywhere else. A lady reminds him of the smile in Irish eyes; and I remind him of Browning's 'good gigantic smile o' the brown old earth' and Shelley's 'Heaven's blue smile'. Not that he is customarily illiberal in such matters. (He not only allows, he espouses 'hopefully', on the grounds that 'hopably' – cf. 'regrettably' – doesn't exist. And gets trounced for his misplaced pains.) 'An idiom,' he says, 'is language's way of telling logic: "Sorry, Charley, that's the way life is in the 8os".'

The trouble is, one man's idiom is another's illiteracy. Like Jacques Barzun and like John Simon (Safire's harder-hitting counterpart on *Esquire* and author of the recently published book, *Paradigms Lost*), Safire is unrelentingly opposed to the locution, 'I cannot help but'. A slovenly confusion of two different idioms, 'I cannot but' and 'I cannot help', it is itself, he maintains, 'confusing, redundant and sloppy'. And yet and yet . . . the first of these 'authentic' idioms is impossibly archaic or poetical, while the second sounds slightly petulant or else frivolous, unfit for the more anguished circumstances in which we may have need of some such expression. 'I cannot help but' bears a hint of pathos, a sense of resisting unsuccessfully, of being *compelled*. Compare the three: 'I can't but love you', 'I can't help loving you', and 'I can't help but love you'. Which, if you had to, would you use? I cannot help but think that Safire and his mighty cohorts are barking up the wrong tree.

Most of the time Safire's eye is sharp, and so is his ear. Observing that the *New York Times* has dropped the would-be grand term 'investigative reporter' on the grounds that all reporters are supposed to investigate something or other, he cites a piece of nomenclature which has mystified many of us: 'Distinguished Professor'. You don't mean there are undistinguished ones? Then there's that common absurdity, 'literally' used to mean its opposite, 'metaphorically', as with the sports commentator quoted earlier: 'the crowd have gone literally mad!' One of Safire's 'Lexicographic Irregulars' proposes, with doubtfully appropriate sublety, that the confusion arises out of the association of 'literally' with 'literary', a word which in turn suggests metaphors, hyperboles and other poetically licentious language. When asked whether sloppiness in speech was caused by ignorance or by apathy, an English teacher (teacher of English?) replied: 'I don't know and I don't care.'

Safire's relations with his 'Irregulars' are spirited and help to generate much of the comedy in this almost continuously entertaining book. They can be very sharp with him; he is generally tolerant towards them, even allowing one of them to misspell his name unchecked. Discussing the common confounding of 'flaunt' with 'flout', he quotes President Carter's statement, as reported by the *New York Times*, that the Government of Iran ought to realize that it 'cannot flaunt, with impugnity, the expressed will and law of the world community'. (Never mind 'impugnity': it was a mistranscription.) An Irregular thereupon informs Safire that according to the *Third Merriam-Webster Unabridged Dictionary* and also the *Unabridged Random House Dictionary* 'to treat contemptuously: to flout' is actually one of the meanings of 'flaunt', and so he can only conclude that, in rejecting 'accepted American usage', Safire had 'let political partisanship colour his amateur linguistics'. (Definition of 'political': epithet to clobber opponent with when all else fails.) Safire makes no reply: he loves his children even when they answer back rudely. But if the use of 'flaunt' to mean 'flout' is 'accepted usage', then it didn't ought to be. And the same goes for *Webster's Third New International Dictionary*'s definition of 'Hobson's choice': 'the necessity of accepting one of two or more equally objectionable things'. If dictionaries are going to flaunt misusages as accepted usages then we shall have to flout them. Or at the very least – is that what *Unabridged* means? – abridge them. 'So much for the use of native informants' – as another Irregular remarks here. He had asked his teenage son, 'What's a metaphor?' and was told, 'To graze cows in.'

The Lexicographic Irregulars are a colourful band of men and women. When the Commandant devotes a column to the art of euphemism – 'pre-owned Cadillacs' and 'experienced cars', 'sophisti-cated' instead of 'sweetened' apple juice, 'household technicians' for domestic servants, 'impact attenuators' for bumpers – one of them chimes in with 'evading the issue' for birth control, and with that most ingenious and ancient evasion of the issue, 'life insurance'. Still on this subject, another reports, apropos of 'airline-ese', that since 'fire extinguisher' implies fire, early planes were fitted with green (not red) cylinders bearing the inscription 'Smoke Eliminator'. Even so, those passengers versed in that accumulated wisdom which we call 'clichés' might have whimpered to themselves, 'No smoke without fire.' As soon as identified as such, euphemisms can be distinctly alarming: 'terminate with extreme prejudice' seems nastier than 'liquidate', 'liquidate' seems more disagreeable than 'assassinate', though 'assassinate' does sound grander than 'kill'. I am not sure that the Swedish delegate to the United Nations Disarmament Committee was altogether right in objecting to the euphemistic language adopted by military strategists. 'This has the effect of throwing dust into people's eyes. Everybody knows what a cannon or gun is, but what is conveyed by terms such as Mini-nuke or Mirv, or Honest John or Fat Boy?' (*The Times*, February 4, 1981). Personally I wouldn't trust anyone with names like those; technical acronyms, or 'alphabet soup', are more truly insidious.

Not that euphemisms are all bad. The example cited in *Collins English Dictionary* of 1979, 'relieve oneself' instead of 'urinate', is surely legitimate, and a rabbinical Irregular observes that the Talmud refers to a blind person as possessed of 'extra light'. Yet it may be that good euphemisms are not euphemisms at all, but something quite different, like nuances. A somewhat recherché anti-euphemism is passed on by a Californian Irregular: 'love in a canoe', signifying weak coffee, i.e. 'fuckin' near water'.

Though not exactly in that way, Safire's own style is occasionally a little too rich for comfort. 'Oldsters may find it hard to discuss the old spine of self-reliance' – it must be hard to discuss a spine unless you are an orthopaedist – 'or to adapt to the tieless-in-Gaza dress codes . . .' It is axiomatic that slaves wear only loincloths; no one at the mill would wear a tie, except conceivably the overseer. Perhaps Safire has been led astray by that more recent phenomenon, the Gaza Strip. Or is he merely teasing? That he should remain 'in two minds' about the word 'ambivalent' is permissible. (Cf. Bergen Evans: 'Confronted with a choice between *choose* and *opt*, my impulse is to *opt* for *choose*.') What is not permissible is 'permissable', a lapse drawing a reproach from a poetic reader:

> In language Safire's a dick
> In tracing abuses that stick:
>   Like colons and dashes –
>   and hyphen mish-mashes;
> He writes permissable (*sic*)!!!

And while technical jargon – the tools of others' trades – is always of interest, at least to the outsider who isn't constantly subjected to it, and we are amused to hear that in the world of show biz 'gorilla' = smash hit, i.e. a monster success, I remain in more than two minds about Safire's account of 'gorilla' as originally 'a Greek word for a race of hairy women'. Less sexist on this point but more racist, my dictionaries derive it from a Greek word, 5th/6th century B.C., for a hirsute African tribe. 'Let Greeks be Greeks, and Women what they are', as quoth Anne Bradstreet.

Etymologically speaking, Safire doesn't always push far and hard enough: roots tend to go down deep. Of that hot word 'feisty', applied leech-like or doggedly to Menachem Begin in particular,* he notes the two dictionary definitions: (1) touchy, excitable, quarrelsome, and (2) spirited, frisky. He then repairs to the word's root for clarification: 'a "feist" is a small dog of mixed ancestry, a flatulent mongrel.' Since mongrels can be either frisky or quarrelsome, this leaves us where we were, with 'a Humpty-Dumpty word, a voguish befuddler, meaning what the speaker chooses it to mean'. That is well said. All the same, 'flatulent' is something of a euphemism here: *Collins English Dictionary* reveals that the dialect word 'feist'/'fist', small dog, is related to Old English 'fisting', breaking wind. These days 'feisty' may owe its uncertain force, by a process of *fausse amitié*, to other words it brings to mind – 'fist', 'fizzy', 'yeasty', 'fighter', 'fiery', as well as 'frisky'. In view of its roots, or the roots of its roots, we should do well not to employ it at all, except in such ambiences as 'that feisty tyke is stinking the place out'.

Safire assures us at intervals that mistakes in his pieces are not deliberately planted to catch readers out or stir them up. I am not convinced by these assurances. Such errors as 'redundency' and 'diety' (not even, he comments later, a word for a very thin god) are unlikely in a man of his concern and skill, while the appearance of those recurrent tricksters 'transcience' and 'gutteral' has too much educational value to be inadvertent. 'Transcience' may owe itself to transient memories of 'science' and 'transcendant', and 'gutteral' to the assumption that people who talk like that were born in one, or (more charitably) to the sound of water running down a drain. In similar spirit, his statement that

---

*Jeffrey L. Sammons describes the 'public self' portrayed in one of Heine's prose works as 'wry and bruised, but . . . ultimately in balance, gay, feisty, even confident'.

'media' is the only possible plural of 'medium' must have been intended to draw the Irregulars' fire – what would you use when referring to two or more intermediaries between the dead and the living? (*Collins* lists 'mediums': 'medium-dated gilt-edged securities'.) But one cannot suppose him less than totally sincere when he asserts, in one of his rare pedantic moments and mistakenly, that 'the lion's share' means 'the whole thing' and *not* the greater part of the spoils. True, in Aesop's fable the lion, claiming under various heads, gets the lot. But we are concerned with an idiom, not with literary exegesis or the facts of a fable. Sorry, Bill, that's the way life is.

I remarked earlier that it was damaging for a language purist ever to make a mistake. Not necessarily so. Safire admits to his slips so frankly, and apologizes so charmingly, as to build up a store of moral capital. When he confesses that several weeks earlier he wrote 'hearkening back' instead of 'harkening back', some of the hearkening backs he had put up must have relaxed. (I don't wish to seem holier than he, but I suspect it ought really to be 'harking back'.) He is then all the freer to make merry over the lapse in linguistic rectitude suffered by the chairman of the Carter-Mondale Presidential Committee when, in the course of a vote-winning speech, he referred to Jimmy Carter's 'moral turpitude'.

John Simon, who is ever ready to take a bull by the lapel, believes that whenever you overhear somebody, albeit a total stranger, saying 'Between you and I', you should step in and put him right. This is the way to make linguistic martyrs – and no doubt every cause needs martyrs. William Safire is a gentler, more cajoling soul. In this matter he has sought advice from the editor of the latest edition of *The Amy Vanderbilt Complete Book of Etiquette*. 'If the Mary Joneses correct the John Smiths of this world, I think it hurts,' she instructed him, attaching a sort of kinship table of propriety: 'Parents correcting children; teachers correcting children [not older pupils?]; employers correcting employees; married people and lovers correcting each other to help the other person out.' Between you and I, you had better strike up a fairly intimate relationship with that stranger at the very outset – or else confine yourself to tiny tots.

Be all that as it all may, I cannot agree with Melvin J. Lasky's defeatist view (*Encounter*, February-March 1981) that, while 'word purism' is undeniably a pleasant pastime, 'on a serious level it is a lost cause'. On some levels, yes, but not on *serious* ones. So keep it up, Mr Safire – you're a regular guy, and so are your Irregulars.

On Clichés

Readers are warned that *On Clichés* (subtitled 'The Supersedure of Meaning by Function in Modernity') is not one of those books about English As She Is Spoke that alarm, amuse, instruct or make you feel holier than ye. It may even be that readers find they are unable to read it. It is sociology, written in a mixture of sociologese and unstylish lay lingo. On the first page we are told that clichés and their social and political use have always 'triggered' the author's curiosity. And again and again – hammered in as if only what is told thirty times and thus rendered a cliché is true – that 'the most remarkable feature of clichés lies in their capacity to by-pass reflection and to thus unconsciously work on the mind, while excluding potential relativizations.' You can say that again! – preferably without splitting the infinitive. Anton C. Zijderveld seems to believe, not merely that infinitives may occasionally be split to secure a particular stress, but that by inexorable law they must be split on sight and without exception – reminding us of the character in Peter de Vries who 'splits infinitives like they were kindling wood'. He also believes in spelling the word 'exhilirating' (a change from 'exhilerating'), and spells it frequently since it is introduced at regular intervals to brighten the proceedings up – though alas at some remove, since exhilaration goes on in biochemistry and astrophysics and even the sociology of yesteryear, but never in the arts, the humanities, the politics or the sociology of today.

Yet there is a lively mind somewhere under all this verbiage, with something to say under all that is said and said again. The thesis is fairly simple: clichés do not *mean*, but they have a function. The nature of modernity fosters the functionality of clichés, and in turn clichés mould consciousness and behaviour in ways 'very appropriate and functional to the speech, feeling, thought and action of truly modern human beings'. This sounds like what, if one dared, one might call a vicious circle. (Why the emphasis on modernity? Perhaps because clichés are always here and now and, if not here and now, are not clichés.) Against this drab- or even sinister-sounding functionalism Professor Zijderveld sets what he calls 'aura'. For instance, TV dinners have no aura, and frozen food is 'very functional but totally lacking in aura'. The word might seem merely to mean 'flavour', but the same applies to 'blue jeans': originally they had a meaning, since – unisex, uniclass, unigeneration – they symbolized the 'counter-culture', but now they are no more than a functional article of clothing, 'indeed the cliché of modern fashion'. (Well, so long as your clichés keep you warm and decent . . . a point that Zijderveld is working up to.) More seriously, since they are no longer safeguarded by traditional values, modern man is able to dispose with ease of relationships such as friendship and marriage, which are now based only on 'the desire to consume emotions instantaneously and continuously', and thus bear very little aura and are 'doomed sooner or later to reach a point of saturation'. In an endearingly moralizing murmur Zijderveld adds: 'Loyalty is almost as old-fashioned a virtue nowadays as honour!'

It was religion that kept function tied to meaning while meaning 'remained tied to tradition through the institutions'. In those times clichés had a greater art of permanent meaningfulness (indeed, as in the case of treason that prospers, no one would dare to call them that) – but then, what didn't? One wonders whether Zijderveld needed to drag clichés into the old sad story, especially since he is a trifle uncertain as to what *is* a cliché. 'Jesus, our Lord' and 'Jesus, our Saviour' are not 'semantically empty words': they are words you may or may not believe. It is not their fault if they are tossed around automatically by jaded or half-hearted preachers. Come to that, what other expressions are there for 'Jesus', 'Lord', 'Saviour'? (And one has one's mean reservations about Zijderveld's dealings with the 'cliché', 'the home is where the heart is', which he considers so corny that it could only be found genuinely touching by a foreigner not well versed in the English tongue. Is nothing sacred to him?)

On occasion, and rather pleasingly, Zijderveld lapses into personal confidences, albeit apologetically. Supermarkets may lack aura (to use them you don't need speech at all, there may be no 'social interaction' whatsoever), but we should beware of sentimentalizing that little village grocery where the shopkeeper chats about the weather and local politics and personalities and knows his customers inside-out. Although the reader shouldn't be interested in such trivialities, says Zijderveld, he must admit if pressed to disliking the 'alleged cosiness' of those little shops; their inefficiency, charming if you are on vacation, soon palls, and the gossip that goes on in them 'can be extremely vicious, its effects of social control very tyrannical and stifling'. He concludes, 'However, this normative belief of mine is irrelevant to the discussion'. Would he were more often irrelevant! And would he had given more time to discussing Mahler's use of kitsch to transcend kitsch, his subduing of musical clichés by using instead of being used by them.

Professor Zijderveld is not out to abolish or banish clichés. Far from it. Clichés are indispensable to social life and human communication, and the man who renounces them is as tiresome as the man who tries to be funny all the time: he ought to 'retreat from social life radically, like the anchorites of old'. In our world norms and values, meanings and motives, have slipped their moorings. Modern man is 'up in the air', cast away on 'a vast sea of cognitive vagueness, emotional instability, and moral uncertainty'. And clichés at least serve as beacons, providing the individual – in lieu of 'traditional institutions' – with a degree of clarity, stability and certainty. They tend to function as '*substitutes for institutions*' ... Then why not just say that they incorporate little bits of permanent and important truths? Admittedly, they do not tie the individual to long-term commitments – 'I love you more than life itself' rarely means what it says – they do not insist on loyalty and responsibility. (What does, outside the most dire of penalties?) But they soothe, they offer a painless (and cheap) illusion of meaningfulness. And Zijderveld goes further, claiming that clichés are useful to all concerned, to the government, the Establishment, the bureaucracy, *and* (what can't be cured must be endured?) to the poor devil caught up in them. So, although they may not *mean* much, they do work; and in the absence of a truly functioning meaningfulness we ought to be grateful to them. 'Feign then what's by a decent tact believed . . .' Meaning is dead, long live the cliché! Or – which may serve as a summary of this book – God is dead, and we have to make do with the half-life of clichés. So? Even that should keep us busy.

In an essay on 'The Language of Novel Reviewing', one of the sixty-three items making up *The State of the Language*, Mary-Kay Wilmers reflects on the kindness of reviewers: 'kind to the old novelist because he is old; kind to the young novelist because he is young; to the English writer because he is English ("all quiet, wry precision about manners and oddities") and not American or German; to others because they are black (or white) or women (or men) or refugees from the Soviet Union.' In which case it is not surprising that reviewers' pens tend to follow well-inked ways. '*Marvellous, delightful, brilliant*: it is hard for a reviewer eager to say good things about a novel to avoid such words, yet they have been used so often in connection with novels which, when compared, say, with *Our Mutual Friend*, are merely mediocre that readers may find some difficulty in giving them credence.' As Miss Wilmers says, these words are important to publishers, who use them in advertisements and on the jackets of succeeding books, and 'a reviewer anxious to promote a novel will be sure to include a few for the publisher to quote'. The effort to avoid clichés can result in tortuous and ambiguous commendations, highly irritating to the publisher looking for a potent quote. For example, 'Through all such knots and breaks of time, a rare aptitude for patience is the unassuming form of Trevor's irreplaceable imagination.'

This point sends us back to Professor Zijderveld in one of his angriest spells, recording the adjectives he found in the publishers' advertisements in one single issue of *The New York Review of Books*, advertisements addressed to 'supposedly *critical* intellectuals on an *academic* level'. They include, some of them occurring many times over: fascinating, marvellous, sensational, electrifying, incomparable, extraordinary, dazzling, explosive, devastating, and (*sic?*) exhilirating. The books advertised, he grumbles, are not just remarkable but 'most remarkable', not just promising but 'exceptionally promising', not just significant but 'most significant', while their authors are described as 'one of the great scholars of our age', 'one of the most important names in twentieth-century philosophy', 'one of the very best living American writers'.

Yes, shocking – but you can hardly expect publishers to call their authors 'one of the scholars of our age' or 'a somewhat leading literary figure' or 'one of the living American writers', or to announce a book as 'illustrated' (as distinct from 'magnificently illustrated') or merely 'promising' or 'rather incomparable' or 'fairly absorbing' or 'mediocre only when compared with *Our Mutual Friend*'. Publishers are always afraid of seeming less than totally confident in a book or an author (doubts move swiftly through the sales force), and hyperbolic language resembles book-jackets – into which go so much time and money, sometimes more than is spent on making the contents easily readable – in that no publisher dares to be the first to call a halt. All this terminology is not meant, as Zijderveld supposes, to (if I may split an infinitive) 'semi-magically enchant the reader' and thus by-pass the mind. Minds are not so stupid as that. Publishers are aware that the reader divides their adjectives by ten – and if they content themselves with saying that a book is 'unassuming' or 'good' or 'entertaining' the reader will deduce that it is half-baked or poor or dull.

The State of the Language, described by the publishers as 'an exceptional gathering of British and American observations on English as the sensitive register of our ideas, feelings, and manners at the beginning of the 1980s', is a good and entertaining book, comprehending such topics as language and ethnic sensibilities,* multilingualism in London schools, liturgical English, Black English, Yiddish syntax and idiom in American English, the language of sisterhood (Angela Carter claims that in England the expression *Ms* has acquired a curious life of its own:

---

*We have all heard about the row in 1959 over the *Concise Oxford Dictionary*'s definition of Pakistan as 'the independent Moslem Dominion in India'. It is less well known that more recently I was instrumental in averting a potentially nastier row by persuading the editors of the same dictionary to change their example of the use of 'not' preceding an emphatic appended pronoun: 'the Chinese will not fight, not they'.

'If *Miss* means respectably unmarried, and *Mrs* respectably married, then *Ms* means nudge, nudge, wink, wink'; if she's right, then by all means let's drop it), Enoch Powell on the language of politics, doctor talk (is it because doctors mumble or because we are deafened by dread that we think they say 'bow and arrow test' when it's really 'bone marrow test'?), the languages of television, prison and homosexuality, malapropisms (Kingsley Amis adduces a staid elderly aunt 'gathering her voluptuous skirts', a question 'illiciting' a reply, and New York City being 'paranoid – with reason – about rising crime'),* and clichés (Christopher Ricks finds Professor Zijderveld's fear of clichés 'inordinate', by the way, but perhaps in this case Zijderveld is paranoid with reason) . . .

I would even go so far as to say that *The State of the Language* is an exceptionally good and most entertaining book, magnificently produced, and crammed with titbits. Among the latter is Marshall McLuhan's story of the boy who, asked by his teacher to use a familiar word in a new way, came up with: 'The boy returned home with a cliché on his face'. When asked to explain himself, he answered: 'The dictionary defines *cliché* as "a worn-out expression".'

Ferocious Alphabets

Words, we might say, are like cats: owned and yet autonomous, both intimate and detached, volatile and dispassionate. No book on words can be wholly boring, nor are we likely to agree completely with anyone else's book on words. The present one opens with five-minute exercises from the Radio 3 series, 'Words', followed by a commentary which seeks to correct, expand, and (by a species of ventriloquism) convert one-way communication into two-way. Denis Donoghue found the original talks a difficult, even a 'doomed' enterprise: there he was pretending to take part in a conversation when really he was musing to himself . . . Leaving aside this sensitive consideration for a moment, I muse on why he found the word 'prime' strange when applied to a pineapple. It carries

*As I am typing, the day after the final of the Wimbledon men's singles championship, *The Times* carries the headline: 'Connors exalts in triumph of the will'.

some sense of the pristine or Platonically archetypal, as in Milton's 'O prime of men', Adam being both the first and (then unfallen, and the only one) the best, or his 'the choice and prime'. The pineapple is Edenic in its beauty of form (though diabolic in some of its effects, removing the flesh from the hands of those who work in canneries). The guest who used the expression was the very pineapple of perfection.

As for singular verbs attached to plural subjects, as in 'The Orlov trial and sentence shows once again . . .' (*The Sunday Times*), the imputed reasoning, that the subjects are so closely related as to be one, is plausible, and yet . . . Accident operates more commonly than intention in this sphere; we can understand and condone, but do not need to defend, let alone vindicate. Linguistic permissiveness easily turns into tyranny: Don't let me catch you talking proper! Between you and I, Shakespeare is full of 'mistakes' . . . But me and you aren't Shakespeare, and our 'mistakes' tend to be mistakes and nothing more.

Speaking of Synge's translation of Irish idioms into English, Donoghue claims that such phrases are charming 'because English audiences are assured that they have nothing to fear from the natives' – adding darkly, 'Since 1968, the charm has largely disappeared.' While I suspect this is a valid comment on *The Playboy of the Western World* (its earliest Irish audiences detected an element of 'laughing with foreign jaws', but were content to focus their fury on the naughty, shaming word 'shift'), it is surely untrue of *Riders to the Sea*, where the native Maurya is in no degree protectively alien to us. The difference must lie as much in matter as in phraseology.

One does not need to be Irish to sympathize with Donoghue's dislike of 'one', the snooty form of 'I' or 'we' or 'you' or 'somebody'. Even in England one feels, does one not, that the usage is best left to Royalty, a lonely leftover from those reserved vocabularies which have always loomed larger in the East. A friend of mine was polishing his Thai by conversation with an elderly princess. 'You would use *that* word only when speaking to a trishaw driver,' she was forever telling him, 'not in addressing *me*.' Her rank called for a higher synonym. Once, having uttered a word for 'dog', he saw her stiffening, and promptly apologized:

'Of course, I would use that form only when speaking to a trishaw driver.' 'No,' she replied: 'Only when speaking to the dog.'*

Donoghue is not free from sheer perversity. He contends that conversation is 'the privileged form of language', that language is 'fulfilled only in speech', since in writing there is no answering voice and full participation is out of the question. In a world of individuals (and what other sort of world do we want?) full participation is always out of the question: something goes unheard, something goes unsaid. Yet after Wordsworth had chatted with some old fellow on the moors, he went home and took up his pen. We all settle for less than all. Plato may once have thought more highly of speech than of writing, but I doubt he does now. While the device enables him to capture Empson's tone ('as if he were moving in upon a conversation already under way') quite neatly, Donoghue's ascription of differing critical styles to the owners' differing sense of their readers or lack of them strikes me as a trifle finely spun. Writers write for themselves, or for that resident reader (someone to converse with?) built up over the years. Style is the little man inside us.

The second half of the book is concerned with such special 'readers' as Harold Bloom, Paul de Man, Derrida, Barthes and Lucette Finas – varyingly fashionable, but analogous to those daring new creations more admired in the shop-window than worn in the course of everyday life. Donoghue boxes, or dances, adroitly with the shadows of his chosen word-wizards, but the performance is rendered elusive in that one (sorry, I) cannot always tell which of them is taking the floor. Now you see it, now you don't – rather like humanism, which (I venture) Donoghue holds to, but which, in the course of some remarks on Bloom, gets itself rather loweringly defined as an absence of willingness 'to see the poet or representative man reduced to a definitive state of destitution'. Ah, but that – that elusiveness or non-insistence – is conversation! 'A definitive statement would transcend the particular desires of conversation' – but do his interlocutors truly respect the convention? The result is not so much to elucidate the act of reading as

*Even so, 'one' comes in handy for a writer on occasions when 'I' sounds both limiting and egotistic and 'we' sounds presumptuous or excessive. 'One' = me and an indefinite number of more or less like minds, one hopes.

to make it seem wellnigh impossible. Since many people find it so already, this seems uncalled-for. More force could have been given to a prime consideration which is invoked somewhat shadowily here: the distinction between 'making trouble for the reader' and 'making the reader face the trouble already there'.

To end with, a short anthology of Denis Donoghue in *propria persona*. 'Meaning is an attribute of the achieved sentence'; 'There are some meanings it's not enough to understand; we're bound to despise them'; 'Principles, once found and defined, are likely to usurp the sensibility the principles are supposed to serve'; 'I detest the current ideology which refers, gloatingly, to the death of the author, the obsolescence of the self, the end of man, and so forth.' Nothing elusive or uninsistent or forked-tongued there. Would he had himself fully occupied his book and not left so much room to ruder and less sensible elbows.

RUST-REMOVERS
Raymond Queneau and G. V. Desani

As the theme for his set of linguistic variations – published in 1947, and in Barbara Wright's English version in 1958 – Raymond Queneau chose a slight, trivial and quite probably actual incident. On a Paris bus, in the rush hour, a young man accuses another passenger of jostling him, flings himself into a vacant seat, and is later seen elsewhere with a friend who is advising him to have an extra button sewn on his overcoat. No violence, no sex, no suffering, no moral, no hidden depths. Nothing much at all – which is the point of course. The simpler the theme, the more distinct and trenchant the variations.

As is often the case with compositions of specific character and intent, the most effective reviewing consists in quoting – though not from all the ninety-nine different ways of relating the incident, some of which are less various and less purposeful than others. The variations fall into sundry general categories (roughly seven, according to Barbara Wright), such as modes of speech, modes of written prose, poetic styles, 'character sketches' conveyed through language habits, exercises in grammatical and rhetorical forms and in jargon.

Metaphorically goes like this: '. . . attracted by a void, the fledgling precipitated itself thereunto', with the young man transformed into a young bird, the empty seat into (perhaps) a nest. Likewise, *The rainbow*, a *façon de parler* in which the colour of everything is meticulously specified: 'I happened to be on the platform of a violet bus. There was a rather ridiculous young man on it – indigo neck . . .'; *Blurb* (*Prière d'insérer'* is the seemlier French expression): 'In this new novel, executed with his accustomed *brio*, the famous novelist X has decided to confine himself to very clear-cut characters who act in an atmosphere which everybody, both adults and children, can understand'; and *Word game*, where given words have to be wedged into the narrative: ' . . . a young man who was rather ridiculous, not because he wasn't carrying a bayonet, but because he looked as if he was carrying one when all the time he wasn't carrying one.' *Hesitation* is both a character sketch and a literary mode: 'I don't really know where it happened . . . in a church, a dustbin, a charnel-house? A bus, perhaps? There were . . . but what were there, though? Eggs, carpets, radishes? Skeletons? Yes, but with their flesh still round them, and alive.' So is *Precision*, and an exercise in police reporting as well: 'In a bus of the S-line, 10 metres long, 3 wide, 6 high, at 3 km. 600 m. from its starting point . . .' *Hellenisms* speaks for itself: 'In a hyperomnibus full of petrolonauts in a chronia of metarush I was a martyr to this microrama . . .' As do also the mode *Noble*: 'I climbed, rapid as a tongue of flame, into a bus, mighty of stature and with cow-like eyes', and the style *Tactile*: 'Buses are soft to the touch especially if you take them between the thighs and caress them with both hands, from the head towards the tail . . .'

Then there are the coy profundities, the false punctilios, of *Negativities*: 'It was neither a standing person, nor a recumbent person, but a would-be-seated person.' *Distinguo* illustrates either a nervous tic – the kind that can afflict ageing writers who have been over-exposed to words, as I have come to see, not to sea – or a dubious sense of humour: 'In an S bus (which is not to be confused with a trespass), I saw (not an eyesore) a chap (not a Bath one) wearing a dark soft hat (and not a hot daft sack) . . .' Here Barbara Wright has improved on Queneau, certainly where decency is concerned: '*je vis (et pas avec mon vit) un personnage (qui ne perd son âge) coiffé d'un feutre mou bleu (et non de foutre blême) . . .*' With apt ingenuity she replaces *Alors* by *You know* ('Then I saw, *you know*, a citizen who, *you* know, caught my eye, sort of'), *Javanais* by *Back slang*, *Loucherbem* (an ornate species of slang involving transposed and added syllables) by a competent piece of *Rhyming slang*, while her *Passive* – 'The bus was being got into by passengers' – is adequate compensation for one of those French tenses not found in English. *For ze Frrensh* ('a beet lattère Ahee saw eem again') is a natural *locum tenens* for *Poor lay Zanglay* ('*ung per plüh tahr jir ler rervee*'), while the substitution of *Consequences* for *Par devant par derrière* provides the translator with an opening for a nice touch of embroidery: 'and the consequence was that a book was written and translated'.

In her entertaining preface Barbara Wright warns of the danger of thinking that these exercises are funny: you might be led to think that they were only funny. We can soon put that right, by adducing Richard Cobb's remark, in the Zaharoff Lecture for 1976, that in addition to its brilliance as parody and as conversation totally recaptured, *Exercices de Style* 'might also be described as an essay on the relative value and interpretation of conflicting or overlapping historical evidence.' That, perhaps, is going it a bit. Queneau himself was more modest in surmising that the book might possibly prove 'a kind of rust-remover to literature' and help to rid it of 'some of its scabs'. Barbara Wright's version constitutes with equal force a form of Guide to Style – or against 'Style' – and demonstrates that, however languages differ one from another, people's ways of using and abusing language are very much the same everywhere. *Exercises in Style* is also, it has to be admitted, a funny book.

All About H. Hatterr

The distinguishing feature of English as spoken in the East by those who speak it a fair amount of the time lies in intonation rather than idiom and is unreproducible in print. Hence what we have most commonly encountered in literature are the pidgin-speaking lumpenproletariat or -peasantry, usually minor figures in the story, sometimes only there for the sake of local low-life colour. The attraction of printed pidgin soon fades.

G. V. Desani is not reproducing so much as inventing or creating, basing himself on 'nature' but improving it quite distinctly. His hero, H. Hatterr, is 'biologically, fifty-fifty of the species', his father 'a European, Christian-by-faith merchant merman', his mother 'an Oriental, a Malay Peninsula-resident lady', non-Christian, presumably of Indian extraction. His ancestry enriches H. Hatterr – just as being Jewish as well as Irish enriches Leopold Bloom – for it makes him heir to all the sages, or to many of them. His range of reference, both verbal and philosophical, is impressively wide, and he can quite feasibly mix babu English with the vernacular of the old British Clubs, while also, as a not uncultivated feller, drawing on diverse languages and literatures from the continong of Europe and You Essay.

His chum, Banerrji, less sophisticated, a simpler exercise in the babu mode, but a man of a truly sweet nature who is forever saving Hatterr's giddy bacon, has the traditional respect for the Bard, whom he quotes frequently and accurately though with an appositeness not always immediately apparent. But no one in this book is being made unkind fun of for the way he speaks – or, come to that, thinks. Or else everyone is. In 1982 Salman Rushdie, himself a smith enormously agile in beating words into rapiers and bludgeons, takes a sterner and more specific view. Desani's triumph, he says, was to take babu English and turn it against itself: 'the instrument of subservience became a weapon of liberation. It was the first great stroke of the decolonizing pen.'

When Hatterr describes his lodgings as 'belle-vue-no-view, cul-de-sack-the-tenant', he is not talking English-as-she-is-spoke, he is speaking Hatterrian; and likewise when he calls England 'that damme paradise', or himself 'a love-brat, a sinfant', or alludes to a 'nymph du pavement woman'. It is Banerrji's mixed and broken idioms that come closer to English as it is or was sometimes spoken somewhere:

You talk such innocent omnibus-wisdom, enough to have my monkey up! You are swapping horses amid-ships. Sometimes, it is better to pay the piper a penny to play and two pennies to leave off!

Elsewhere the humour is phantasmagoric or slapstick: 'We don't have Persian carpets. But we have *real* Persians on the floor! Talking Persian ethics, too!' Or speculative: did Nelson say Kiss me, Hardy! or *Kismet*, Hardy!? Or parodic, as in passages which seem to send up English translations of the utterances of Eastern sages (if not the sages themselves):

'Rest now, *Bombay*! I shall massage thy feet, wisest, to comfort thee. Thou art most fatigued from instructing such dire wisdom to an animal-like intellect such as I.'

'Thy speech, O son,' said the Sage of *Bombay*, lapsing into sleep, 'is most soothing. Mayst thou continue to warble for a century!'

At times we meet such engaging and only seeming non-sequiturs as –
when Banerrji is advising Hatterr to go to England – 'The climate is
non-tropical and the weather extremely bracing. You are a Christian. So
is Lord Nuffield.' And the most violently comic passage of all is a mixed
babu/burrasahib account (it's *all* concerned who need decolonizing) of
a Robbie Burns Night at the Club, where very high-standard men from
Eaten, Westmoreland, Shrewsbury, 'Arrow, Charter's House, Rugby-
Football, the Gun Co. Winchester and 'oh! attend, the *most* mystic of
them all, the *'Ell See See'*, are giving off their native yells,

'blast yer! blast yer!' and calling *'Kon'yak! Kon'yak! boy!'* the spirit in hand, they
toasted, propitiated, and invoked each other, 'Bon sonty, old boy!' 'Bon mud in
yer eye!' 'Salaams, *nulli secundus!*' *Skowl! Shalooteh! Shalooteh! Froze it!* Soon,
they held hands, and *Oldlongsigh!* Till tears flowed, like wine afore!

H. Hatterr receives instruction from seven suspect sages, and disaster
ensues upon practice. But he emerges in good heart: he has learnt
something, and knowledge is fortifying, or fascinating at least. It seems
exceedingly strange at first that the author of so irreverent-seeming a
composition should be a learned Professor of Buddhism and Practitioner of Yoga. In the end it doesn't, for we come to see that, among
other doings, G. V. Desani is expounding in comic guise what in serious
guise he has learnt in India and Japan and taught in America – and in the
process blowing away some of the mist surrounding it:

I say, *accept*!
No dam' use in any case. *Accept*: and say *aye*! Things *are*. They are there. Good
and bad. To hell with judging, it's Take it don't leave it, and every man for
himself!

It has to be admitted that there are *longueurs*, especially in the latter
stretches. T. S. Eliot, who admired the book on its first appearance in
1948, remarked how amazing it was that 'anyone should be able to
sustain a piece of work in this style and tempo at such length.' I think
that at times the linguistic electricity does decline into humid air. But we
ought to be grateful for a book which is so very funny and ingenious and
touching and mischievous and humane – and altogether, in Anthony
Burgess's words, wonderfully heartening.

LIFTING UP ONE'S LIFE
A TRIFLE
On E. B. White

There are times when one finds oneself engaged in championing an author, and even finding it hard to do effectively, while knowing full well how comically gratuitous one's efforts are. This looks like being one of those times.

Dorothy Lobrano Guth remarks in her introduction to E. B. White's collected letters – which constitute a virtual autobiography – that, like his essays, stories, novels and poems, they are 'good company'. This is the handshake of death at a time when the aim of writing is commonly reckoned to be the giving of offence, or worse. 'Good company'! Who would want to keep that? Moreover E. B. White is most widely known as a writer of essays. Essays! As he says in the foreword to his self-selected *Essays*, compared with the novelist and the poet and the playwright, the essayist is a second-class citizen. You do not win the Nobel Prize by writing essays, least of all essays which are not always free of humour. 'The world likes humour, but it treats it patronizingly. It decorates its serious artists with laurel, and its wags with Brussels sprouts.' Nor does it help (even though you were only twenty-nine at the time) to make such admissions as 'I discovered a long time ago that writing of the small things of the day, the trivial matters of the heart, the inconsequential but near things of this living, was the only kind of creative work which I could accomplish with any sincerity or grace.'

It is true that practically anything could set White off. More accurately, he has the sort of mind which snaps up precisely those trifles that can set it off. Writing to Thurber in 1938, he mentions a scrap of conversation he overheard between two men on the street. 'So she had the whole fucking bedroom suite sawed up and put together again.' From that he passes to an advertisement for a record of the sound of a piano being smashed by a man with an axe – 'the sort of thing that you ought to have in your home, for rainy days when the mood is on you.' How much water had to flow over the American dam – the Pilgrims . . . Valley Forge . . . Emerson and transcendentalism . . . Shiloh . . . Verdun – before the disc came along that we have all been waiting for! 'The Instrument of the Immortals, getting it in the teeth from a Keen Kutter . . .' Yet Robert Musil has been heard complaining of the mistrust of higher things demonstrated by a society that talked of the 'genius' of a racehorse!

Some writers seem to hate language the way an axe hates a piano. Not so White, who went on to revise William Strunk Jr's *The Elements of Style*.* Words fascinate him endlessly. As did almost, it must be admitted, chickens. In a *New Yorker* inter-office memo, he deprecates the innocent-seeming transmutation of 'fresh' into 'afresh':

An afresh starter is likely to be a person who wants to get agoing. He doesn't just want to get going, he wants to get *a*going. An afresh starter is also likely to be a person who feels acold when he steps out of the tub. Some of my best friends lie abed and run amuck, but they do *not* start afresh. Never do.

However, if he is obliged to bow to the new situation, then the characters in his forthcoming stories will no longer be typical people: 'they will all be atypical. Some of them, perhaps all of them, will be asexual, even amoral.'

White – who has preserved a seemingly easy balance between the Thurber in him and the Thoreau – ran into trouble with his chickens. There was something wrong with them, they never stopped shaking their heads. Was it worms, fleas, eczema? 'Sometimes I stand there and get thinking that maybe they are shaking their heads over *me*. "Poor old White," they say, shaking their heads.' It was all part of 'the turbulence

---

*In a note in the *Essays* appended to the 1957 piece on Strunk which inspired Macmillan Company to commission a revision from him, White writes: 'Strunk was a fundamentalist; he believed in right and wrong, and so, in the main, do I. Unless someone is willing to entertain notions of superiority, the English language disintegrates, just as a home disintegrates unless someone in the family sets standards of good taste, good conduct, and simple justice.' Not that White is a pedant. Elsewhere he has told of the newspaper editor who changed a man's reported cry on recognizing his wife's body in the morgue – 'My God, it's her!' – to 'My God, it's she!'

of country life'. And things were not so different with words. In a new chapter to *The Elements of Style*, White advised students to be guided by their ear when deciding whether or not to use the conjunction 'that' in a sentence. Take for instance, 'He felt that the girl had not played fair.' White pointed out that, if you omitted the 'that', you had 'He felt the girl . . .' His editor at Macmillan Company judged this particular example likely to create a commotion in the classroom, and he made a substitution, though not without a feeling protest. 'That girl . . . illustrates the embarrassments of prose, and she will be missed if you dismiss her.' He signed the letter, 'Yrs for the iron hand and the felt girl . . .'

Good humour, a quick intelligence, grace, succinctness, lucidity, sureness of aim, excellent manners, yet (the iron fist in the felt glove) an unyielding trueness to himself . . . Such an account may only suggest that E. B. White was a really nice nineteenth-century gentleman (well, he was born in 1899) who thanked people when they did things for him and thanked them in style. Which is true, though inadequate. We are forced back on quotation, since nothing conveys a sense of White's way of writing half so well as his writing. Answering a correspondent's query about using copyright material, he says in his casual and forceful manner: 'I think the law allows you to swipe a little of it, but not much – like taking a single grape as you pass the fruit bowl on the sideboard.' And, asked to supply a puff for a book jacket, he achieves an effective yet disarming brush-off: 'It wouldn't do any good to send me galleys of a book, because I don't comment on books – except to my wife under cover of darkness.'

His children's books brought him many letters from children, and here the brush-off had to be very gently administered, or else their parents or teachers would accuse him of cruelty, and it was of little avail to plead that if he answered all the letters, he would never have time to write anything else. 'I am five feet eight inches tall,' he wrote to one young reader; and to a letter which began, 'I am a confused senior at Newton High School', he replied: 'I am a confused writer at 25 West 43 Street, and one of the reasons for my confusion is that students want me to explain myself.' When a child asked if his wife helped him in his writing, he answered in his usual adult fashion (there was to be no mere whimsicality, not even where kids were concerned) that his wife was indeed helpful (and plainly she was), though 'she is an editor. An editor is a person who knows more about writing than writers do but who has escaped the terrible desire to write.' Softening a little, he went on to admit that 'some of my writings have won prizes but awards of that sort are not very much fun or satisfaction and I would rather have a nice drink of ginger ale, usually. Writing does have its rewards but they do not come in packages.' The tone is much the same when he writes to a children's editor at Harper's:

Actually, books are not safe to read – yesterday I lay down for a half hour after lunch, with a book, and while lying there quietly was stung under the right eye by a tremendous wasp that came along and wanted to put me out of my pain, and almost did.

The greater part of his correspondence over the children's book, *Charlotte's Web*, had to do with getting the illustrations right: Charlotte was to be a true spider, not a woman's face with eight legs attached. (For the delicate precision of White's dealings with animals, see the account of a coon coming down a tree in his essay, 'Coon Tree'.) Later in life White remarked perceptively that he had discovered, quite by accident, that 'reality and fantasy make good bedfellows' and 'there was no need to tamper in any way with the habits and characteristics of spiders, pigs, geese, and rats. No "motivation" is needed if you remain true to life and true to the spirit of fantasy.'

Charlotte's Web, he insisted, was not 'a moral tale', but 'an *appreciative* story', and the distinction, while at times hard to determine, is a crucial one. The huge success of the book proved that children can take a great deal in their stride – considerably more than librarians could, it appeared. Wilbur the pig shows something of his creator's concern for verbal behaviour; he objects to the lamb's remark that 'Pigs mean less than nothing to me' on the grounds that 'Nothing is absolutely the limit of nothingness.' Charlotte sets out to save Wilbur from the slaughter-house by proclaiming his virtues in words woven into her web, a variety of advertising that White could endorse: 'SOME PIG', 'TERRIFIC', 'RADIANT', 'HUMBLE'... She tells Wilbur: 'A spider's life can't help being something of a mess, with all this trapping and eating flies. By helping you, perhaps I was trying to lift up my life a trifle. Heaven knows anyone's life can stand a little of that.' And in conclusion the author sums up: 'Wilbur never forgot Charlotte . . . It is not often that someone comes along who is a true friend and a good writer. Charlotte was both.' We see why he approved of the saying of P. L. Travers, that anyone who writes well for children is probably writing for one child – the child that is him- or herself. In White's case, one who abhorred cheap whimsy and cuteness.

And also the slightest hint of sentimental indulgence. To a Father MacGillivray, who inquired whether some of his writings haunted him, he wrote back with courteous astringency: 'Sure they do. At my age I am haunted by the feeling that everything I write I've written before, only better.' Pretentiousness was another bugbear. In 1958 White declined to be interviewed for the *Writers at Work* series: 'For one thing, they would have to call it "Writers NOT at Work".' And he adduced the Hemingway interview, 'the one that explained that he always wrote standing on the skin of a Lesser Kudu. (I always write sitting on my arse, except when I have piles.)' Granted that parody is essentially parasitic, White's 'Across the Street and Into the Grill' has long struck me as rather more memorable than anything written by Hemingway himself:

This is my last and best and true and only meal, thought Mr Perley as he descended at noon and swung east on the beat-up sidewalk of Forty-Fifth Street. Just ahead of him was the girl from the reception desk. I am a little fleshed up around the crook of the elbow, thought Perley, but I commute good.

'Please keep telling me about your business experiences, but not the rough parts,' the girl says to him in the restaurant as they lie under the table, wrapped in an Indian blanket, and 'she touched his hand where the knuckles were scarred and stained by so many old mimeographings.' But it was Hemingway who got the Nobel Prize.

In matters of public moment White was not so much HUMBLE as adroitly self-protective, a natural non-joiner. When in early 1942 he was co-opted into the production of a pamphlet on the Four Freedoms and entrusted with the writing of the section on freedom of speech, he was most unhappy. 'I couldn't understand anything, and wished I was home,' he wrote to his wife. Archibald MacLeish, Librarian of Congress and in charge of the project, soon took the job away from him, 'almost imperceptibly', and demoted him to rewrite-man for all four freedoms: 'This is a very sobering assignment and only once in a while do I think it is funny.'

But he had his troubles, for he was no evader of responsibilities that made sense to him. In 1947, as 'a member of a party of one', he protested against the loyalty check and the blacklisting of those who refused to answer questions before the House Un-American Activities Committee. 'If I must declare today that I am not a Communist, tomorrow I shall have to testify that I am not a Unitarian. And the day after, that I never belonged to a dahlia club.' The protest appeared in the *New York Herald Tribune*, who in the same issue described members of the party of one – albeit 'valuable elements' in their way – as 'probably the most dangerous single elements in our confused and complicated society'. In his reply to this magisterial rebuke, White said: 'A man who disagreed with a *Tribune* editorial used to be called plucky – now he's called dangerous. By your own definition I already belong among the unemployables.'

This excursion into the realm of civil liberties left him covered 'with a surprising lot of goat feathers'. He found himself being courted by Communist front organizations, and in receipt of so much Red literature at his office at *The New Yorker* that, as he put it, he had to fumigate himself every night before going home. 'It was worse than athlete's foot.'

A month later he was in hot water again, when the *Ellsworth American* (Maine) accused him of unfairness and malice towards his own veterinarian and veterinary medicine in general in his now celebrated piece, 'Death of a Pig', an expert blend of comedy and pathos. White wrote soothingly to his vet – 'After you left I took another drink and consulted only with God. Even He didn't seem able to loosen up that pig' – and remarked to his brother, concerning these recent scrapes, that 'You can't even come out against constipation in America any more.' We are tickled but not surprised to come on a brief letter of 1956 replying to an invitation to join the Committee of the Arts and Sciences for Eisenhower: 'I must decline, for secret reasons.'

In 1963 a professor of English at Cornell University published an article in which he demonstrated that White's collection of columns, *One Man's Meat*, although indisputably a work of literary merit, possessed none of the characteristics of such merit as laid down in a test designed to measure students' appreciation of that important attribute. (White's only comment was that he was delighted.) There's the nub of the rub. White lends himself to self-aggrandizing expatiation as little as does Edward Thomas. He requires no mediator, for he comes complete with sustaining information; his symbols are curiously close to what they symbolize. He is a natural writer – and to be taken seriously, it seems, art needs a strong dose or injection of unnature. That word 'natural' does not imply 'facile' or 'unthinking': White thinks, or whatever it is he is doing, without groaning and sweating and thrashing around – the way a decent traveller ('I got my training in the upper berths of Pullman cars long ago') takes his trousers off.

His 'stance' towards life, his personality as a writer, and the subjects, by no means narrow in compass, to which he is drawn – what these chiefly require of him in the formal or technical sphere is that great negative skill: not getting in the way.* Nothing is more indecorous, in the eyes of many critics, than the form which, though obviously there if only because it clearly isn't absent, cannot be fingered and classified – except possibly those attitudes of mind and heart which colour a man's writing uniquely and yet are unamenable to abstraction and schematic analysis. We would welcome any methodology (excuse the language) that could cope with these features and qualities. White's work leaves the self-regarding subtleties of theoretical criticism hungry, and therefore scornful, but it ought to respond well to that humbler activity, 'practical criticism'. For instance:

The Model T Ford is described as 'hard-working, commonplace, heroic'. Why does the author use these adjectives rather than others?

---

*In his essay on Don Marquis, White notes that archy the cockroach poet was contemptuous of the people who were preoccupied with the 'mere technical details' of his writing. According to archy, 'The question is whether the stuff is literature or not.' To which White adds: 'That question dogged his boss, it dogs us all.'

Expand the following into an essay: 'The Canada jay looks as though he had slept in his clothes.'

'It flows through Orland every day.' Why does White describe this line as a 'fine, lyrical tribute' to the River Narramissic?

'Reading is the work of the alert mind, is demanding, and under ideal conditions produces finally a sort of ecstasy. As in the sexual experience, there are never more than two persons present in the act of reading – the writer, who is the impregnator, and the reader, who is the respondent. This gives the experience of reading a sublimity and power unequalled by any other form of communication.' Discuss these (a) antiquated (b) revolutionary views.

We seem to be back with that dim remark about 'good company' – or at best with the National Book Committee's citation on awarding White their Medal for Literature in 1971: 'We are grateful to E. B. White for . . . the infinite pleasure he has given readers, young and old, over the years.' Pleasure is another of those 'merits' which tend to be immeasurable – especially when infinite.

THAT HAPPY
KINDERGARTEN-STATE

The plums in *Wally's Stories* are the responses of five-year-old American kindergarten pupils to stories read to them, the stories they themselves make up and act, and the subsequent discussions and events. Examples are more potent than precepts. This is how Vivian Gussin Paley, a tactful and unobtrusive mistress of ceremonies, would have it, and how she has contrived it. She makes one want to be a kindergarten pupil oneself, or failing that a kindergarten teacher.

That on balance children of this age are conservative, even conformist, inclined to keep their fantasies within safe bounds, and favouring orderliness and fairness (whether sponsored by God, fairy, teacher or parent), is no new discovery. Sober and limiting though these preferences may sound, the resulting scripts as recorded here remind us of Wordsworth's tribute to the Sonnet: in them children unlock their hearts, give ease to their wounds and cheer themselves up. They spin reassuring explanations of what happens around them, in the fashion of the ancient myth-makers accounting for why winter comes and how spring is reasonably sure to return. Logic was a respected ingredient in those myths, and so it is in these children's stories and debates. A simple example of fantasy stiffened by rationality occurs early in the book, when Wally, a black boy and *primus inter pares* in the classroom, reduces little Fred to tears by knocking down his tower. 'I'm a dinosaur. I'm smashing the city,' Wally justifies himself. Wild fantasy. Fred pulls himself together and tells Wally that he should have asked permission first. Wally replies, in the spirit of the shaggy dog story: 'Dinosaurs don't ask.' Undeniable truth.

Reasonableness in children can look like wit, irony, scepticism, hard-headedness, stoicism and other fruits of long and varied experience. Or like prototypal forms of adult jokes. Does Fred believe that Wally can really change into a mother lion? 'Only if he practises very hard.' More sophisticated, or so it seems, is the conversation about 'checkers'. Eddie, who is losing, wonders why God invented the game in such a way that you can't move backwards. He insists that it *was* God who invented it: 'because a magician would trick you.' (By continually changing the rules, as in his weaker moments Eddie would like to do? Or arranging it so that you could *never* win?) Despite advice, his classmate Warren persists in moving on the wrong spaces – because, Eddie opines, Warren is Chinese. Given an opening for instruction, Mrs Paley expresses doubt that Chinese people play draughts in a different way. Eddie retorts: 'What's the use of being Chinese if you don't do things different?' Again and again imagination and plain logic, fantasy and realism ('good bedfellows', as E. B. White remarked), join forces to achieve effects suspiciously like those of creative genius. Or, to put it perhaps more temperately, like those of the professional philosopher: Don Locke has proposed that the philosopher's questions and even his answers are often much the same as the child's and that (is that last word quite right?) 'philosophy itself can be seen as institutionalized naïvety'.

A phenomenon I found surprising is the large role played in these tales and conversations by God, and the perfectly natural way the children talk of a being generally reckoned to be dead or else peculiarly detached. (Mrs Paley is probably right in telling us very little about their background; Wally and Warren both portrayed fathers in threatening roles, although Wally's father was missing while Warren's was fond and considerate: 'Teachers need to be wary of jumping to conclusions.') Orthodoxly enough, God has created everything. And an amusing piece of back-to-front reasoning serves to account for the diversity of languages in the world: if there were only one language, God wouldn't have felt called on to create China, Japan and so forth. (Little Akemi adds: 'If everyone speak Japan, everyone have to live there. My country too small for the big America.')

Eddie raises the objection that some ideas come from your mother and father. '*After* God puts it into their minds,' Wally asserts; he is something of a theologian, and has been in touch with God: 'He talks very soft.' When teacher asks slyly whether God is a magician, they cry out unanimously against so absurd and even repellent an idea. For them,

Mrs Paley tells us, God is sensible, desires harmony, and represents order and equity. Fairies are associated with pleasant surprises and, like God (though on a lower plane), can be trusted. Magicians cause mischief, are more like people, and must be treated with caution. Witches are reckoned to be fairies who have gone to the bad, though one little girl surmises that after six hundred years (presumably of good behaviour) a witch can turn back into a fairy. It will be seen that this hierarchy of Magical Beings takes care of most eventualities in life.

An elaborate discussion begins with God despatching Jonah into the whale and diverges into the question of how many Christmas trees God gets. 'Infinity,' says Eddie, perhaps not unpreparedly since it was he who raised the point. Are there decorations on the trees? Yes, according to Wally, invisible ones, which God can see because He is invisible too. Eddie comes up with the theory (obviously one is required) that 353 years ago everyone could see God: 'He was young so He could stay down on earth.' Now He is old and floats up in the sky, out of our sight. God hears one's wishes, but the children agree that you shouldn't make too many or God (in this respect like fairies) will grow tired of listening to them. (The sense of 'not grateful' is understood, though the expression is assimilated to 'not great'.) Naturally God features prominently in matters relating to birth and death. He makes babies out of the blood and bones of the dead – rather as vapour rises into the sky and reappears as water. The world, Mrs Paley remarks, is a giant recycling plant 'with heaven as the storage area and God as the distribution manager'.

The teacher's role, as she sees it, is to question gently, to encourage connections in place of non-sequiturs, occasionally to instil some recognition of things-as-they-are in a post-Edenic world or feed in a titbit of information or advice. Not, that is, to wean the children away from imagination, but to moderate and channel the flow. She herself avoids theorizing and its attendant jargon – it would have stuck out like a sore bottom – and so Courtney B. Cazden defines her procedure, in a brief foreword, as 'supporting the children in their imagined worlds and providing firm anchor points to a more stable "reality" as well'. This he opposes to what he terms, in justly inverted commas, 'confrontation pedagogy', a method in which the errors of childish thinking are corrected through exposing inconsistencies and discrediting the belief in magic's efficacy – an approach he considers more comforting to adults than helpful to children.

An even shorter term for this species of pedagogy – 'Teach these boys and girls nothing but Facts. Facts alone are wanted in life' – is Gradgrindery. And yet as a business man Gradgrind would have admired some of the attitudes revealed here. In a sustained exchange on the 'tooth fairy', evidently a big thing in those parts, the children debate the rights and wrongs of passing off a kernel of grain as a tooth (they don't recommend this attempt to cheat: for one thing, it wouldn't work, there'd be no gap in your mouth) and the source of the money the tooth fairy leaves under your pillow (Deana has seen her at the bank, the obvious place: 'she had purple shoes and red hair'). Between them, Wally and Eddie produce a convincing interpretation of the whole transaction: the tooth fairy is not giving you something for nothing but *buying* your milk teeth, in order to pass them on to babies – 'they're baby teeth'. When Wally is asked why, despite all the interest in the topic, there are no printed stories about tooth fairies, he replies that the fairies write in invisible ink so that no one will know where they hide the money – or the teeth. At five Wally seems already well qualified to face the rigours of adult life. Which is perhaps why he is held to be something of a 'problem child' and can often be found in the 'time-out chair', modern and more comfortable equivalent of the corner.

Although they show an attachment to routine, consistency is not a prime virtue in children's imaginings. Sometimes orderliness and pragmatism – or simply flagging invention – lead to inconsistencies; and inconsistencies, as Johnson said, though they cannot all be right, may all be true when imputed to men. At times the children kill their characters off in droves, without twitching a hair. Persisting in his lion fantasy, Wally predicates a little lion who is an orphan and lives alone. Then he changes tack abruptly: the little lion meets his parents while out hunting and so can go and live with them. It could be that the story was proving too sad, particularly after all the talk about Wally himself becoming a lion. When the teacher queries this inexplicable resurrection, Wally's answer is ready: the little lion only *thought* his parents were dead, but in fact 'they really went out shopping and he didn't recognize them because they were wearing different clothes.' If from dead to living is a large leap, calling for explanation, from hunting to shopping is only a small step.

Mrs Paley notes that honesty (or honesty in children) is a quality more prized by grown-ups than by children. After all, honesty isn't always a simple, clear-cut matter. If a child maintains that he hasn't had his turn in some activity, he may mean that his turn was unfairly short or that he has had fewer turns than some of the others or that in some way his turn went wrong. A child may state in the same sentence that he has left things in a mess by accident and also on purpose – possibly in that some accident of excitement or incitement has carried him beyond his original intention. Honestly, one doesn't always mean to do everything that in the event somehow gets done. Any response that shields a child from adult disapproval and perhaps punishment is seen (by the child) as 'a good and honest response'.

While normally tolerant, Mrs Paley takes a stand on certain factual truths, for instance when the children claim to have more brothers or sisters than is actually the case. And one reason for telling the truth, according to Andy, is that (with George Washington and the cherry tree in mind) you may then make president of the United States. It is surely less priggishness than the ever-present urge to make good practical sense of things that causes Wally to defend corporal punishment for the reason that, when it descends on you, 'you know your answer is wrong so you try to think of the right answer.' At this juncture the discussion moves from the sublime to the self-interested. Mrs Paley mentions that in her class they try to behave well even though she never spanks them. 'Maybe you'll give us candy if we're good,' Lisa suggests hopefully. But, Mrs Paley says, she never hands out candy. 'You might change your mind,' Lisa observes.

Fortunately for our *amour propre*, Mrs Paley's pupils (who were beginning to resemble the alarming alien-spawned infants of science fiction) do not dwell permanently on these intellectual heights. They are human. They boast wildly; they talk when they have nothing to say; they contradict for the sake of contradiction; they choose to believe what makes them feel good. Everybody wants to play the soldier in 'The Tinder Box' and nobody wants to play the witch; since there are seventeen of them, the story has to be acted seventeen times, with the teacher as the constant witch. Also, they watch television, which through its addiction to formula indulges their innate conservatism, or abets them in the common tendency to take the easy way out – that is, by rushing around and making loud noises. Thus Captain America kills Green Goblin thirteen times over in a tale less than forty words long; Lassie vanquishes a monster, then twenty monsters, then a hundred and fifty of them . . . Mrs Paley reports that the superhero story was the one classroom genre in which she could not spot the identity of the author, all individuality having been masked, and also that superheroes were never invoked when real problems and occurrences came under serious discussion. Superheroes are not 'magic', which is 'invisible' but 'alive', so much as 'pretend', and evidently their place in the hierarchy of powers is near the bottom.

Mrs Paley doesn't say much about the development of her charges in the course of the kindergarten year. Perhaps she feels it would be unbecoming in her. And perhaps it would have detracted from the charm her book has for the secular reader. (We don't always insist on knowing what happened next.) But she counterpoints her class's fondness for 'The Tinder Box' with the scorn shown by Eddie's nine-year-old brother for the idea that a soldier would spend his newly-gained wealth on such frivolities as candy and toys. Eddie defends the tale by suggesting that some soldiers might *like* candy. (There's no disputing likes: earlier on, the disappearance from the classroom of some seeds was attributed to robbers, and when the teacher said that if she were a robber she would rather take the record-player, Eddie commented, 'Not if you wanted to plant seeds.') Noticing his elder brother's condescending smile, Eddie proposes that, well, the soldier might be thinking of giving the candy 'to some children'.

One effect of Mrs Paley's mild educative intervention manifests itself indirectly when several members of the group protest against 'Hänsel and Gretel' – 'it's too scary' – whereas Eddie clamours to have it read.

Lisa reminds him that 'we have a rule not to make people feel bad', and he accepts this with a docility which one had thought long gone from the world's nurseries: 'Okay, I'll tell my mother to read it to me. She likes it too.' As direct evidence of growing maturity (an ambiguous word in this context), of at least one sad but necessary lesson learnt, the following will suffice: the children have progressed from the belief that foxes eat bunnies because bunnies steal their apples to the knowledge that foxes eat bunnies because they like eating bunnies.

On the subject of photographs helping grown-ups to remember when they were young, Wally uttered one of his wisest sayings: 'You can never take a picture of thinking.' In a book exceptionally modest in manner and unusually substantial in matter and import, Mrs Paley has given a vivid, credible and entertaining picture of how some five-year-olds think. Her findings – and we don't get the impression that she went out of her way to find the exceptional and the striking – are strangely inspiriting, in a way I would be hard pressed to explain.

LAST WORDS
On Anthony Burgess

By the time I had reached the last words of Anthony Burgess's *Earthly Powers* I had accumulated enough notes to make a modest book: a tribute, in part, to the sheer density of the writing, as well as the seriousness of its concerns. It would be unwise to skip during these six hundred and fifty pages. Only in retrospect can you identify for certain what could safely have been skipped as iterative or supererogatory. Since complaints will follow – grave matters incur grave complaint – let me venture at the outset that *Earthly Powers* carries greater intellectual substance, more force and grim humour, more knowledge, than ten average novels put together. It would make a film – 'Sooner or later you get all the books on the movies,' some deplorably innocent youth says: 'Just a matter of waiting' – or rather it would make a dozen films.

Kenneth Marchal Toomey, the narrator, is himself a novelist, born in 1890 and in his mid-eighties when we take leave of him. His lifetime sees momentous events – World War I, the Easter Rising, the aviators Alcock and Brown, Prohibition, Fascism, Nazism, World War II, the death camps, the history of modern literature, the history of cinema, a case of homosexual-style blasphemy (preceding the *Lady Chatterley* case, however), homosexual marriage blessed by autocephalic archbishops (not exactly from outer space, just autonomous), and much else, including in part the life of Toomey's creator. Here is, if not quite God's plenty, plenty of the Devil.

At the age of fourteen Toomey is seduced by George Russell (better known as AE) in a Dublin hotel, on the very day recorded in *Ulysses*. Meeting Joyce in Paris in 1924, Toomey tells him: 'Well, you gave George Russell an eternal and unbreakable alibi for that afternoon. But I know and he knows that he was not in the National Library.' Other celebrities among the great unfictitious dead receive similarly rough (and staggeringly high-handed) treatment; but let us leave that aside for the moment and ask – since Toomey is always with us through these many pages – why his creator has created him homosexual. It would be imprudent, perhaps even inaccurate, to suggest that this affects Toomey's 'representativeness', that it tilts the novel off centre. Beside the point, certainly, in that Toomey is chaste much of the time: for him war drives out sex. Burgess is hardly an author whom one would suspect of straining after new sensations or angles. It could be (I came close to thinking at one stage) that, heterosex being so awful, homosex has to be a little better. But no, Toomey doesn't 'glory in it': far from it, he dislikes his fellows in sex, 'hissing, camping, simpering', and the one man he truly loved – and lost through death, not through betrayal – he loved platonically. Indeed it would involve no serious distortion to say that there is only one good gay here, and lots of bad gays. Possibly homosexuality is an extra twist of the thumbscrew Burgess habitually applies to his central characters: they suffer, therefore they are. Most likely, I think, is that Toomey has to be a Catholic, and a lapsed one, and lapsed for some reason other than mere intellectual doubt or dissent from points of doctrine. God made him homosexual, and in so doing forced him to reject God.

And the Word was God. *Earthly Powers* is theological and linguistic in equal proportions, quite properly. Less properly, it is too heavily both: one can have too much of a good-and-evil thing. Burgess is, of course, an eminent wordsmith, and one of many metals. He knows that the plural of semen (it does sometimes need a plural) is 'semina'. And: ' "Ice in the icebox," I said, pleonastically.' (Yet the working classes might keep their coal in it.) When he gives Toomey's secretary-cum-catamite the name 'Enright', he spells it correctly, for he knows that in transliteration from one language to another it is foolish to introduce silent letters – like a 'w' for instance. (He may even know that the meaning of the name in Gaelic is 'unlawful attack'.) When – twice – Toomey meets an amiable stranger, 'a new planet swam into his, right, Ken it is, Ken'. When someone mentions that he has been sniffing round the town of Gorgonzola, we are nudged into noting the inadvertent aptness of the phrase.

During the Malayan episode, a return to the rich terrain of Burgess's early trilogy, now in a spirit of Maughamery, we are told – alas, jokes involving foreign tongues require explanation – that Mahalingam, the name of a Tamil character, means 'great ah generative organ'. In close proximity (for which state of affairs, among devout Malays, you could get into bad heterosexual trouble) is an account of that peculiar disorder known as *koro*, in which the sufferer believes that his penis is withdrawing into his abdomen and seeks to secure it with a pin or string. I have lived through one such outbreak in Singapore – Western-style doctors attributed it to an exceptionally cool spell of weather – during which the disorder spread to females, who complained of retracting nipples. Women won't be left out these days.

A candidate who lacks basic qualifications, and hence could not present himself in a white toga, is a 'nigrate'. The Maltese censors who finally allow Toomey his copy of Thomas Campion's poems confuse the poet with the martyr Edmund Campion. (A spot of autobiography there, I believe.) 'Richardtionary' is the homosexual euphemism for a useful book of reference: what, indeed, you might call an 'aide de *camp*'. (Less politely, 'shonnary': 'I always leave the dick out.') Burgess hammers in the fact that 'homo' in this connection is Greek and indicates 'same' and not, as some of his characters imagine, Latin and signifying 'man'. And the Rilke joke – ' "The last time I saw him was in a café in Trieste. He cried." "He often cried. But nobody heard him among the angelic orders" ' – palls on the reprise. Far worse, much as one welcomes relief in that area, is the comical-Teutonic: 'Unfortunately have I in the *Hindenburg* not yet flown', *et* at some length *cetera*. The somewhat pop Pope, Gregory XVII, brother-in-law to Toomey, has pop songs sung about him – 'the new Gregorian chants'. Burgess never misses a trick: would he had missed a thousand. God may or may not be mocked, but words aren't to be. Play with them over-much, and they take umbrage, and revenge.

So Burgess is too clever for his own good? That is the sort of accusation made by people who really aren't all that bright themselves. And we had better remember Johnson (though he *was* bright) expressing the view that to Shakespeare a quibble was the fatal Cleopatra, followed at all adventures and sure to engulf him in the mire, for which he lost the world – Shakespeare didn't lose the world. We have come near to objecting to what is most Burgessian in Burgess, what we read him *for*. Undeniably, there is a sickening, suffocating weight to this book. So, one is meant to be sickened and suffocated. At all events, it is egregiously difficult to say precisely where the author has stepped over the line, because it is hard to know where to draw the line. It has to be one's sense of artistic rightness that draws it, not squeamishness, gentility, frivolity or a semi-literate resentment of quibbles and puns. I believe that the author's obsessiveness (yes, writers ought to be obsessed) does fall foul of the dire law of diminishing returns – in respect of squalor and horrors as well as quibbles – and incurs a penalty, though I am not sure how grave the penalty is, how heavily it draws on his capital. Irritation on the reader's part, at the least, followed by lapses of attention; at the most a loss of credence. Oh for an occasional draught of Thomas Mann's coolness!

Toomey's real-life colleagues in the arts get an appallingly bad press. H. G. Wells is 'a satyromaniac', Ford Madox Ford has bad breath and a dirty mind, Norman Douglas is 'filthy' and 'boy-shagging', T. S. Eliot is wrong about the Tarot pack (as pointed out by Nabby Adams in *Time for a Tiger* long ago) and also (in which case, together with many others) about Seneca's act-division: 'there was a lot of the dilettante about Eliot', Bernard van Dieren is a 'dim thing with the grey face in napless velvet', Peter Warlock roars obscenities, Maynard Keynes ('trying to turn himself into a heterosexual with a ballet dancer') leers at Toomey, James Agate ('a well-known sodomite') makes a pass at the dreadful Heinz . . . In its much coarser way, this little world reminds us of the closing stages of Proust's novel, when one by one wellnigh the whole cast show themselves inverts. Toomey might well condemn the fault, the condition that has deprived him of God, but it is the actors of it he detests most vigorously.

The disgust with sex is general and pervasive here. After watching a porn movie in which 'everybody was buggered by or buggered Socrates', Toomey whimpers, 'Sex, sex, sex, Christ, is there to be nothing in this world but bloody sex?' (A common cry of writers, including those who write about it.) True, as someone else has remarked, sex was the very first way of transmitting original sin. Yet it was also the way whereby the novel's few unequivocally admirable characters came into the world – notable among them, Toomey's saintly (and virtually sexless) brother Tom, a professional comedian given to comedy devoid of cruelty, that 'lost empire' (as Toomey calls it) which we all long for in our hearts, and long for the more keenly in the present circumstances.

It is saddening to see Burgess join in the wholesale reduction of old heroes to the ranks, or rank. After this, what kind of treatment can his fictitious persons expect? He has always been hard on them, the harder the more he feels for them, beginning with poor Malayan Victor Crabbe (a Crab-apple cuckolded by a Costard, stung by a crab-like scorpion, then wretchedly drowned), not excluding Shakespeare, and more recently including a whole country. His heroes are Christ-like, but like Christs to whom something lowering is bound to happen, such as falling off the Cross. When one of Toomey's boy-friends, a black, asks if he knows that big word 'humiliation', he replies: 'I practically invented it.' He could also have invented the sayings 'the good die young', 'whom the Lord loveth he chasteneth' and (above all) 'out of good still to find means of evil'.

Visiting Berlin for a film festival in the mid-1930s, sickened by Goebbels and an excess of Sekt, Toomey contrives to vomit on a swastika flag. During the première of a film about Horst Wessel, he pushes a genial short shy man out of the way of Concetta Campanati's pistol – Toomey's sister's mother-in-law, dying of cancer, is anxious to do a last good deed – and finds the man he has saved is Heinrich Himmler. Shortly before the outbreak of war he attempts to smuggle the (invented) Jewish novelist, Jakob Strehler, out of Austria. He fails in this, is caught, and buys his freedom by agreeing to broadcast to Britain. (The young official who conducts the interview apologizes for not liking his work: 'He had had Dr L. C. Knights as a tutor for a year at Cambridge and had been taught a rather rigorous approach to literature.') Back in London, Toomey points out to the court of inquiry that in his remarks he had inserted two acrostics highly offensive to the Nazi leadership – 'cunningly prepared', and all too well concealed.

But now we have to face the horrors, the other horrors. Early in the

1960s Toomey gives his nephew John Campanati, a young anthropologist interested in language structure, the money to go, together with his wife, to research in a new African state. (The money has been earned from writing 'sedative fiction' and film scripts.) By now the reader is likely to guess what will happen, more or less. John and his wife, two of the most likeable people in the book, are killed by terrorists. As if that isn't enough, it turns out later that actually they were murdered to provide the flesh and blood of the Eucharist for an 'African Mass' – *hoc est corpus meum* reconciled with hocus-pocus – a development for which the ecumenical Pope Gregory, uncle of the young anthropologist, brother-in-law of the munificent Toomey, has to be held responsible.

'Too much glamour altogether,' Toomey reflects at one point of the Campanati family. This may be a sign of nervousness on the author's part, yet it must be allowed that considerable enjoyment derives from this blown-up Italo-American version of the Forsyte Saga. Carlo Campanati, burly, gluttonous, forceful, heroic, extremely secular, extremely holy, dominates much of *Earthly Powers*. When (chronologically near its end) the novel begins, he has recently died, as Pope Gregory XVII, and is a candidate (certainly no nigrate) for canonization. Toomey has been asked to testify to Carlo's performance of a miracle, the cure of a child in the last stages of meningitis. ('It happened a long time ago,' he tells the Archbishop of Malta. 'And I don't know whether you, Your Grace, would understand this, but writers of fiction often have difficulty in deciding between what really happened and what they imagine as having happened . . . We lie for a living.') When, towards the close, we hear about a sinister evangelist called God (for Godfrey) Manning (God in Man), my prophetic soul began to get the shakes again. The police close in on the Children of God, Manning's community in California, and the faith healer conducts 1,700 members of his flock into eternity: in Jonestown fashion, except that by an extra turn of the screw the cyanide is administered in the Eucharist. Yes, God Manning was the child saved from meningitis. What is the theology, or the theodicy, of this sequence of events? Man is given free will by a loving God – who otherwise could scarcely *love* him – and hence man can will evil. But a miracle has nothing to do with man or his will, it is the direct intervention of God. And here an all-knowing God has intervened to procure future evil.

Concetta, Carlo's mother or adoptive mother, once remarked that according to Carlo good always won, in the long run: 'Well, that long run's just a little bit too long.' Where this novel is concerned, I think that such is indeed the case. 'What is the point of the dialectic of fiction or drama,' Toomey muses, 'unless the evil is as cogent as the good?' (He has no need to worry about that.) But we can also ask, do good and evil work in as schematic a fashion as a novelist may properly do? And are bad angels quite such sure shots at firing good ones out? At the very end, by a final tact or yielding, one small mercy is shown, shown the reader as well as Toomey and his much-loved sister Hortense. These two battered survivors will pass their remaining days together, waiting for death. For them, it seems, the end of the long run has been reached. 'I have always, all through my literary career, found endings excruciatingly hard. Thank God, or something, the last words were not for my pen . . .'

List of books referred to

Heinrich Heine: A Modern Biography, Jeffrey L. Sammons, Princeton University Press.

The Brothers Mann, Nigel Hamilton, Secker & Warburg/Yale University Press.

Thomas Mann: The Making of an Artist, 1875–1911, Richard Winston, Constable/ Alfred A. Knopf.

The Man Without Qualities, Robert Musil, translated by Eithne Wilkins and Ernst Kaiser, 3 volumes, Secker & Warburg/Alfred A. Knopf.

Bertolt Brecht: Poems 1913–1956, edited by John Willett and Ralph Manheim, Eyre Methuen/Methuen Inc.

Bertolt Brecht in America, James K. Lyon, Princeton University Press.

Man in the Holocene and *Triptych*, Max Frisch, translated by Geoffrey Skelton, Eyre Methuen/Harcourt Brace Jovanovich.

From the Diary of a Snail, The Flounder, The Meeting at Telgte, Headbirths, or The Germans Are Dying Out, Günter Grass, translated by Ralph Manheim, Secker & Warburg/Harcourt Brace Jovanovich.

In the Egg, Günter Grass, translated by Michael Hamburger and Christopher Middleton, Secker & Warburg/Harcourt Brace Jovanovich.

Group Portrait with Lady, The Lost Honour of Katharina Blum, Heinrich Böll, translated by Leila Vennewitz, Secker & Warburg/McGraw-Hill.

The Safety Net, Heinrich Böll, translated by Leila Vennewitz, Secker & Warburg/Alfred A. Knopf.

The Tale of Genji, Murasaki Shikibu, translated by Edward G. Seidensticker, 2 volumes, Secker & Warburg/Alfred A. Knopf.

As I Crossed a Bridge of Dreams, translated by Ivan Morris, Penguin Books/The Dial Press.

The Confessions of Lady Nijō, translated by Karen Brazell, Peter Owen/Doubleday & Co.

Flaubert and an English Governess, Hermia Oliver, Oxford University Press, Oxford and New York.

The Letters of Gustave Flaubert 1830–1857, edited and translated by Francis Steegmuller, Harvard University Press.

The Temptation of Saint Antony, Gustave Flaubert, translated by Kitty Mrosovsky, Secker & Warburg/Cornell University Press.

The Life of Villiers de l'Isle-Adam, A. W. Raitt, Oxford University Press, Oxford and New York.

The Good Soldier Švejk, Jaroslav Hašek, translated by Cecil Parrott, Heinemann.

The Bad Bohemian: A Life of Jaroslav Hašek, Cecil Parrott, Bodley Head.

The Golden Lotus, translated by Clement Egerton, 4 volumes, Routledge & Kegan Paul.

The Yellow Peril: Chinese Americans in American Fiction 1850–1940, William F. Wu, The Shoe String Press.

The Woman Warrior, Maxine Hong Kingston, Allen Lane/Alfred A. Knopf.

China Men, Maxine Hong Kingston, Pan Books/Alfred A. Knopf.

Sexism in Children's Books, edited by the Children's Rights Workshop, Writers and Readers Publishing Co-operative.

Maledicta: The International Journal of Verbal Aggression, Volume 1 Number 2, edited by Reinhold Aman, Maledicta Press.

Bad Mouth: Fugitive Papers on the Dark Side, Robert M. Adams, University of California Press.

Mrs Byrne's Dictionary of Unusual, Obscure, and Preposterous Words, Josefa Heifetz Byrne, Granada Publishing/University Books Inc.

A Dictionary of Catch Phrases: British and American, from the Sixteenth Century to the Present Day, Eric Partridge, Routledge & Kegan Paul/Stein & Day.

On Language, William Safire, Times Books, New York.

On Clichés: The Supersedure of Meaning by Function in Modernity, Anton C. Zijderveld, Routledge & Kegan Paul.

The State of the Language, edited by Leonard Michaels and Christopher Ricks, University of California Press.

Ferocious Alphabets, Denis Donoghue, Faber & Faber.

Exercises in Style, Raymond Queneau, translated by Barbara Wright, John Calder/Riverrun Press.

All About H. Hatterr, G. V. Desani, Bodley Head/Farrar, Straus & Giroux.

Letters of E. B. White, edited by Dorothy Lobrano Guth, Harper & Row.

Essays of E. B. White, Harper & Row.

Wally's Stories, Vivian Gussin Paley, Harvard University Press.

Earthly Powers, Anthony Burgess, Hutchinson/Simon & Schuster.

Index